Readings in

Black American Music

Readings in

Black American Music

Compiled and Edited by

Eileen Southern

ASSOCIATE PROFESSOR OF MUSIC, YORK COLLEGE OF THE
CITY UNIVERSITY OF NEW YORK

W · W · NORTON  & COMPANY · INC ·
⋙ NEW YORK ⋘

FIRST EDITION

Library of Congress Catalog Card No. 70–98892
SBN 393 02165 3 Cloth Edition
SBN 393 09892 3 Paper Edition

1 2 3 4 5 6 7 8 9 0

To my Mother

Contents

Contents   ix

Preface

The purpose of this collection of readings is to make available to persons interested in the history of black American music a representative number of authentic, contemporary documents illustrating that history from the seventeenth century to the present time. While the book may be used as an independent anthology, it was originally intended to serve as a companion work to the present author's *The Music of Black Americans: A History* (New York, 1971). The main criterion used in selecting the readings was their relevance to the history of music, and, although the readings follow in chronological order, they are grouped under topics that derive from the history. To my knowledge, this collection represents the first publication of a documentary history of black American music that not only covers the full three and a half centuries of the black man's sojourn in the United States but his African heritage as well.

Inevitably, there were choices to be made among sources that represented similar points of view or that illustrated the same subjects. Generally, I have given preference to the statements of black music makers, to the accounts of eyewitnesses to musical events, and to the writings of persons deeply involved with the music of black folk in one way or another. In some instances, however, it seemed important to include the comments of men who, although not musicians themselves, had profound insight into the power and significance of the black man's music. Thus, Frederick Douglass and W. E. B. DuBois are represented along with composers, performers, local historians, song collectors, and music critics. As always happens with anthologies, a large number of valuable documents had to be rejected despite their suitability according to these criteria. The projected size of this volume precluded the possibility of including *all* relevant materials, no matter how excellent. Finally, it became a matter of selecting, sometimes arbitrarily, those documents that seemed to me to be *most* significant and *most* illuminating. I must assume full responsibility, therefore, for errors of judgment in this respect.

The biographical notes that precede each document indicate the circumstances under which it was produced. Wherever possible, the complete text of a selection is given, but in some instances I have eliminated passages that bear no relationship to the subject at hand. All such cuts are indicated by the conventional ellipses. In the interest of authenticity, spelling and punctuation have been corrected or modernized only where this seemed necessary for purposes of clarification. Editorial insertions are indicated by brackets. For the most part, music examples that appeared in the original sources have been retained.

I am grateful for the permissions granted by various authors, publishers, and curators of special library collections to use their materials. My deep appreciation goes to David Hamilton, music editor at W. W. Norton & Company, and to Claire Brook, also of Norton, for counsel and valuable suggestions. Finally, I acknowledge my special indebtedness to my husband, who has helped in many different ways and has given unflagging encouragement.

EILEEN SOUTHERN

Readings in
Black American Music

I. The African Heritage

1. RICHARD JOBSON

➤➤➤ There is extant a considerable body of literature about West Africa during the slave-trade period—not only books written by European travelers and traders, but also letters, journals, memoirs, ledgers, minute books, and various other kinds of official records. Such materials are immensely valuable to the historian, since until recent times black Africa relied chiefly upon oral tradition to preserve its history. Several of the sources provide surprisingly rich details about musical practices in Africa. From such records we are able to obtain some understanding of the African heritage brought to the New World by enslaved Africans.

In 1618 King James I of England created the Company of Adventurers of London Trading into Parts of Africa. The charter of the company was granted to Sir Robert Rich (later earl of Warwick) and thirty other patentees, giving them control over trade on the West African coast south of the Barbary. The company first sent out George Thompson, a merchant, to explore the Gambia River region and to report back on its commercial potential. When Thompson failed to return, Richard Jobson, an English captain, was sent out on the same mission in 1620. Jobson's explorations of 1620–21 were successful, and upon his return, he published an account of his journey. Since he was an unusually perceptive man, Jobson's lively descriptions of African life are very useful. His book, *The Golden Trade or a Discovery of the River Gambra and the Golden Trade of the Aethiopians*, contains one of the earliest reports on West African music. ➤➤➤

From *The Golden Trade* [1623] †

There is without doubt, no people on the earth more naturally affected to the sound of musicke than these people; which the principall persons do hold as an ornament of their state, so as when wee come to see them their musicke will seldome be wanting; wherein

---

† Text: The original edition (London, 1623), pp. 105–07. Courtesy of the Rare Book Division, the New York Public Library, Astor, Lenox, and Tilden Foundations.

they have a perfect resemblance to the Irish Rimer, sitting in the same manner as they doe upon the ground, somewhat remote from the company; and as they use [the] singing of Songs unto their musicke, the ground and effect whereof is the rehearsall of the ancient stock of the King, exhalting his antientry, and recounting over all the worthy and famous acts by him or them [that] hath been achieved: singing likewise *extempore* upon any occasion is offered, whereby the principall may be pleased; wherein diverse times they will not forget in our presence to sing in the praise of us white men, for which he will expect from us some manner of gratification. Also, if at any time the Kings or principall persons come unto us trading in the River, they will have their musicke playing before them, and will follow in order after their manner, presenting a shew of state.

They have little varieties of instruments; that which is most common in use, is made of a great gourd, and a necke thereunto fastened, resembling in some sort, our Bandora; but they have no manner of fret, and the strings they are such as the place yeeldes or their invention can attaine to make, being very unapt to yeeld a sweete and musicall sound, notwithstanding with pinnes they winde and bring to agree in tunable notes, having not above six strings upon their greatest instrument. In consortship with this they have many times another who playes upon a little drumme which he holds under his left arme, and with a crooked stick in his right hand, and his naked fingers on the left he strikes the drumme, and with his mouth gaping open, makes a rude noyse, resembling much the manner and countenance of those kinde of distressed people which amongst us are called changelings.

I do the rather recite this that it may please you to marke, what opinion the people have of the men of this profession, and how they dispose of them after they are dead: but first I would acquaint you of their most principall instrument, which is called Ballards [and is] made to stand a foot above the ground, hollow under, and hath uppon the top some seventeen woodden keyes standing like the organ, upon which hee that playes, sitting upon the ground just against the middle of the instrument, strikes with a sticke in either hand, about a foote long, at the end whereof is made fast a round ball, covered withe some soft stuffe, to avoyd the clattering noyse the bare stickes would make; upon either arme hee hath great rings of Iron: out of which are wrought pretty hansomly smaller Irons to stand out, who hold upon them smaller rings and juggling toyes which as hee stirreth his armes, makes a kinde of musicall sound agreeing to their barbarous content: the sound that proceeds from this instrument is worth the observing for we can heare it a good English mile, the making of this instrument being one of the most ingenious things amongst them: for to every one of these keyes there belongs a small Iron the bignesse of a quill, and is a foote long, the breadth of the instrument, upon which hangs two gourdes under the hollow, like bottles, who receives the sound, and returnes it againe with that extraordinary loudness; there are not many of these, as we can perceive, because they are not common, but when they doe come to any place, the resort unto them is to be admired; for both day and night, more especially all the night the people continue dancing, until he that playes be quite tyred out; the most desirous of dancing are the women, who dance without men, and but one alone, with crooked knees and bended bodies they foot it nimbly, while the standers-by seeme to grace the dancer, by clapping their hands together after the manner of keeping time; and when the men dance they doe it with their swords naked in their hands, with which they use some action, and both men and women when they have ended their first dance, do give somewhat unto the player: whereby they are held and esteemed amongst them to be rich.

2. MUNGO PARK

⇶ In 1788 in London, a group of Englishmen under the leadership of Sir Joseph Banks founded the African Association, with the stated goal of encouraging the exploration of the interior of black Africa (at that time unknown to Europeans) for commercial and humanitarian reasons. The Scottish surgeon Mungo Park (1771–1805) accepted a commission from the association in 1795 to explore the region of the middle and upper reaches of the Niger River, the land of the Mandingos and the Malinkes.* Accompanied only by a servant, two donkeys, and a horse, Park became the first European to explore this region. He kept a journal of his travels, which was published as *Travels in the Interior Districts of Africa, Performed Under the Direction and Patronage of the African Association in the Years of 1795, 1796, and 1797, by Mungo Park, Surgeon* (New York, 1800).

Park left an excellent description of the country, its inhabitants, and their way of life. More important, he recorded the text of an African song, the first time in history that such a song had been translated into English. Park heard the song when he spent a night in a village on the banks of the Niger River, opposite Ségou (now in Mali), the prosperous capital city of the Bambara States. ⇷

From *Travels in the Interior Districts of Africa* [1800] †

. . . When we arrived at this ferry, we found a great number waiting for a passage; they looked at me with silent wonder, and I distinguished, with concern, many Moors among them. There were three different places of embarkation, and the ferrymen were very diligent and expeditious, but from the crowd of people, I could not

---

* Park's explorations in Africa are traced on a map in Paul Marc Henry, *Africa Aeterna* (Lausanne, 1965), p. 331.

† Text: The original edition (New York, 1800), pp. 200–02, 275–76, 319–21. Courtesy of the Rare Book Division, the New York Public Library, Astor, Lenox, and Tilden Foundations.

immediately obtain a passage, and sat down upon the bank of the river, to wait for a more favourable opportunity. The view of this extensive city [i.e. Ségou]; the numerous canoes upon the river; the crowded population, and the cultivated state of the surrounding country, formed altogether a prospect of civilization and magnificence, which I little expected to find in the bosom of Africa.

I waited more than two hours without having an opportunity of crossing the river; during which time the people who had crossed, carried information to Mansong the king, that a white man was waiting for a passage, and was coming to see him. He immediately sent over one of his chief men, who informed me that the king could not possibly see me, until he knew what had brought me into his country, and that I must not presume to cross the river without the king's permission. He therefore advised me to lodge at a distant village, to which he pointed, for the night; and said, that in the morning he would give me further instructions how to conduct myself. This was very discouraging. However, as there was no remedy, I set off for the village; where I found, to my great mortification, that no person would admit me into his house. I was regarded with astonishment and fear, and was obliged to sit all day without victuals in the shade of a tree; and the night threatened to be very uncomfortable, for the wind rose, and there was great appearance of a heavy rain; and the wild beasts are so very numerous in the neighbourhood, that I should have been under the necessity of climbing up the tree, and resting amongst the branches: About sunset however, as I was preparing to pass the night in this manner, and had turned my horse loose that he might graze at liberty, a woman, returning from the labours of the field, stopped to observe me, and perceiving that I was weary and dejected, inquired into my situation, which I briefly explained to her; whereupon, with looks of great compassion, she took up my saddle and bridle, and told me to follow her. Having conducted me into her hut, she lighted up a lamp, spread a mat on the floor, and told me I might remain there for the night. Finding that I was very hungry, she said she would procure me something to eat. She accordingly went out, and returned in a short time with a very fine fish, which, having caused to be half broiled upon some embers, she gave me for supper. The rites of hospitality being thus performed towards a stranger in distress, my worthy benefactress, pointing to the mat, and telling me I might sleep there without apprehension, called to the female part of her family, who had stood gazing on me all the while in fixed astonishment, to resume their task of spinning cotton, in which they continued to employ themselves great part of the night. They lightened their labour by songs, one of which was composed extempore, for I was myself the subject of it. It was sung by one of the young women, the rest joining in a sort of chorus: The air was sweet and plaintive, and the words, literally translated, were these. "The winds roared, and the rains fell:—The poor white man, faint and weary, came and sat under our tree: He has no mother to bring him milk; no wife to grind his corn. *Chorus.* Let us pity the white man; no mother has he, &c. &c." . . .

Among the free men [in the slave-coffle procession] were six Jillikea (singing men) whose musical talents were frequently exerted, either to divert our fatigue, or obtain us a welcome from strangers. . . . We marched towards the town in a sort of procession, nearly as follows. In front, five or six singing men, all of them belonging to the coffle; these were followed by the other free people; then came the slaves. . . . In this manner we proceeded, until we came within a hundred yards of the gate; when the singing men began a loud song, well calculated to flatter the vanity of the inhabitants, by extolling their known hospitality to strangers. . . . the people gathered round us to hear our *dentegi* (history). This was related publicly by two of the singing men; they enumerated every little circumstance which had happened to the coffle beginning with the events of the present day, and relating everything in a backwards series, until they reached Kamalia. . . .

When a person of consequence dies, the relations and neighbours meet together, and manifest their sorrow by loud and dismal howlings. A bullock or goat is killed for such persons as come to assist at the funeral, which generally takes place in the evening of the same day on which the party died. The Negroes have no appropriate burial places, and frequently dig the grave in the floor of the deceased's hut, or in the shade of a favourite tree. The body is dressed in white cotton, and wrapped up in a mat: It is carried to the grave in the dusk of the evening by the relations. If the grave is without the walls of the town, a number of prickly bushes are laid upon it, to prevent the wolves from digging up the body; but I never observed that any stone was placed over the grave as a monument or memorial.

Hitherto I have considered the Negroes chiefly in a moral light, and confined myself to the most prominent features in their mental character: Their domestic amusements, occupations, and diet, their arts and manufactures, with some other subordinate objects, are now to be noticed.

Of their music and dances, some account has incidentally been given in different parts of my journal. On the first of these heads, I have now to add a list of their musical instruments, the principal of which are,—the *koonting*, a sort of guitar with three strings;—the *korro,* a large harp with eighteen strings;—the *simbing,* a small harp with seven strings;—the *balafou,* an instrument composed of twenty pieces of hard wood of different lengths, with the shells of gourds hung underneath to increase the sound;—the *tangtang,* a drum open at the lower end;—and lastly, the *tabalu,* a large drum, commonly used to spread an alarm through the country. Besides these, they make use of small flutes, bow-strings, elephants' teeth, and bells; and at all their dances and concerts, *clapping of hands* appears to constitute a necessary part of the chorus.

With the love of music is naturally connected a taste for poetry, and fortunately for the poets of Africa, they are in a great measure exempted from that neglect and indigence, which in more polished countries commonly attend the votaries of the Muses. They consist of two classes; the most numerous are the *singing men,* called *Jillikea,* mentioned in a former part of my narrative; one or more of these may be found in every town; they sing extempore songs in honour of their chief men, or any other persons who are willing to give "solid pudding for empty praise." But a nobler part of their office is, to recite the historical events of their country; hence, in war, they accompany the soldiers to the field, in order, by reciting the great actions of their ancestors, to awaken in them a spirit of glorious emulation. The other class are devotees of the Mahomedan faith, who travel about the country, singing devout hymns, and performing religious ceremonies, to conciliate the favour of the Almighty, either in averting calamity, or in insuring success to any enterprize. Both descriptions of these itinerant bards are much employed and respected by the people, and very liberal contributions are made for them.

3. Thomas Edward Bowdich

⇛ In 1817 the African Committee of London sent a mission to Africa to explore the dominions of the king of Ashanti and to arrange with him for commerce. Thomas Edward Bowdich (1791–1824) was a member of this four-man mission. Bowdich apparently was an amateur musician and an artist of considerable talent. When he returned to London he published an account of his experiences in Africa, *Mission from Cape Coast Castle to Ashantee*, which includes a number of African songs that he had written down from the playing of an African musician, and several drawings, one of which depicts the scene of a mammoth African festival, "The First Day of the Yam Customs." In this unique drawing are seen the "long" flutes, string instruments, horns, and drums of many sizes described by Bowdich in his book.* ⇚

From *Mission from Cape Coast Castle to Ashantee* [1819]†

We entered Coomassie [Kumasi] at two o'clock, passing under a fetish, or sacrifice of a dead sheep, wrapped up in red silk, and suspended between two lofty poles. Upwards of 5000 people, the greater part warriors, met us with awful bursts of martial music, discordant only in its mixture; for horns, drums, rattles, and gong-gongs were all exerted with a zeal bordering on phrenzy, to subdue us by the first impression. The smoke which encircled us from the incessant discharges of musquetry, confined our glimpses to the foreground and we were halted whilst the captains performed their Pyrrhic dance, in the centre of a circle formed by their warriors; where a confusion of flags, English, Dutch, and Danish, were waved and flourished in all directions; the bearers plunging and springing from side to side, with

---

* Reproductions of the drawing may be found in the New York, 1966 reprint of the book, and in Eileen Southern, *The Music of Black Americans: A History* (New York, 1971), plates IV & V.
† Text: The original edition (London, 1819), pp. 31–40, 358–69, 449–52.

a passion of enthusiasm only equalled by the captains. . . . This exhibition continued about half an hour, when we were allowed to proceed, encircled by the warriors, whose numbers, with the crowds of people, made our movement as gradual as if it had taken place in Cheapside; the several streets branching off to the right, presented long vistas crammed with people, and those on the left hand being on an acclivity, innumerable rows of heads rose one above another: the large open porches of the houses, like the fronts of stages in small theatres, were filled with the better sort of females and children, all impatient to behold white men for the first time; their exclamations were drowned in the firing and music, but their gestures were in character with the scene. When we reached the palace, about half a mile from the place where we entered, we were again halted, and an open file was made, through which the bearers were passed, to deposit the presents and baggage in the house assigned to us. Here we were gratified by observing several of the caboceers [chiefs] pass by with their trains, the novel splendour of which astonished us. The bands, principally composed of horns and flutes, trained to play in concert, seemed to soothe our hearing into its natural tone again by their wild melodies; whilst the immense umbrellas, made to sink and rise from the jerkings of the bearers, and the large fans waving around, refreshed us with small currents of air, under a burning sun, clouds of dust, and a density of atmosphere almost suffocating. We were then squeezed, at the same funeral pace, up a long street to an open-fronted house, where we were desired by a royal messenger to wait a further invitation from the king. . . . We were soon released by permission to proceed to the king, and passed through a very broad street, about a quarter of a mile long, to the market place.

Our observations *en passant* had taught us to conceive a spectacle far exceeding our original expectations; but they had not prepared us for the extent and display of the scene which here burst upon us: an area of nearly a mile in circumference was crowded with magnificence and novelty. The king, his tributaries, and captains, were resplendent in the distance, surrounded by attendants of every description, fronted by a mass of warriors which seemed to make our approach impervious. The sun was reflected, with a glare scarcely more supportable than the heat, from the massy gold ornaments, which glistened in every direction. More than a hundred bands burst at once on our arrival, with the peculiar airs of their several chiefs; the horns flourished their defiances, with the beating of innumerable drums and metal instruments, and then yielded for a while to the soft breathings of their long flutes, which were truly harmonious; and a pleasing instrument, like a bagpipe without the drone, was happily blended. At least a hundred large umbrellas, or canopies, which could shelter thirty persons, were sprung up and down by the bearers with brilliant effect, being made of scarlet, yellow, and the most shewy cloths and silks. . . . Innumerable small umbrellas, of various coloured stripes, were crowded in the intervals, whilst several large trees heightened the glare, by contrasting the sober colouring of nature. . . .

The king's messengers, with gold breast plates, made way for us, and we commenced our round, preceded by the canes and the English flag. We stopped to take the hand of every caboceer, which, as their household suites occupied several spaces in advance, delayed us long enough to distinguish some of the ornaments in the general blaze of splendour and ostentation.

The caboceers, as did their superior captains and attendants, wore Ashantee cloths, of extravagant price from the costly foreign silks which had been unravelled to weave them in all the varieties of colour, as well as pattern; they were of an incredible size and weight, and thrown over the shoulder exactly like the Roman toga; a small silk fillet generally encircled their temples, and massy gold necklaces, intricately wrought; suspended Moorish charms, dearly purchased, and enclosed in small square cases of gold, silver, and curious embroidery. Some wore necklaces reaching to the navel entirely of aggry beads; a band of gold and beads encircled the knee, from which several strings of the same depended; small circles of gold like guineas, rings, and casts of animals, were strung round their ancles; their sandals were of green, red, and delicate white leather; manillas, and rude lumps of rock gold, hung from their left wrists, which were so heavily laden as to be supported on the head of one of their handsomest boys. Gold and silver pipes, and canes dazzled the eye in every direction. . . . The large drums [were] supported on the head of one man, and beaten by two others. . . . The kettle drums resting on the ground, were scraped with wet fingers, and covered with leopard skin. The wrists of the drummers were hung with bells and curiously shaped pieces of iron, which gingled loudly as they were beating. The smaller drums were suspended from the neck by scarves of red cloth; the horns (the teeth of young elephants) were ornamented at the mouth-piece with gold. . . .

The prolonged flourishes of the horns, a deafening tumult of drums, and the fuller concert of the intervals, announced that we were approaching the king: we were already passing the principal officers of his household; the chamberlain, the gold horn blower, the captain of the messengers, the captain for royal executions, the captain of the market, the keeper of the royal burial ground, and the master of the bands, sat surrounded by a retinue and splendor which bespoke the dignity and importance of their offices. . . . [The king] was seated in a low chair, richly ornamented with gold; he wore a pair of gold castanets on his finger and thumb, which he clapped to enforce silence. The belts of the guards behind his chair, were cased in gold, and covered with small jaw bones of the same metal; the elephants tails, waving like a small cloud before him, were spangled with gold, and large plumes of feathers were flourished amid them. His eunuch presided over these attendants, wearing only one massy piece of gold about his neck: the royal stool, entirely cased in gold, was displayed under a splendid umbrella, with drums, sankos, horns, and various musical instruments, cased in gold, about the thickness of cartridge paper. . . .

We pursued our course through this blazing circle, which afforded to the last a variety exceeding description and memory; so many splendid novelties diverting the fatigue, heat, and pressure we were labouring under; we were almost exhausted, however, by the time we reached the end; when, instead of being conducted to our residence, we were desired to seat ourselves under a tree at some distance, to receive the compliments of the whole in our turn.

The swell of their bands gradually strengthened on our ears, the peals of the warlike instruments bursting upon the short, but sweet responses of the flutes; the gaudy canopies seemed to dance in the distant view, and floated broadly as they were springing up and down in the foreground; flags and banners waved in the interval, and the chiefs were eminent in their crimson hammocks, amidst crowds of musquetry. They dismounted as they arrived within thirty yards of us; their principal captains preceded them with the gold-handled swords, a body of soldiers followed with their arms reversed, then their bands and gold canes, pipes, and elephant tails. . . . The king's messengers who were posted near us, with their long hair hanging in twists like a thrum mop, used little ceremony in hurrying by this transient procession; yet it was nearly 8 o'clock before the king approached. . . .

From the following song, I imagined the Fantees (for the Accra's are said to possess none but fetish hymns in their own language) to have some idea of rhyme, considering the inversion of the first line as forced, and expressly accommodated to the metre,

> Abirrikirri croom ogah odum,
> Ocoontinkïi bonoo fum,
> Cooroompun,
> Coom agwun,

but I have not met with any other instance.

The Ashantees generally use much and vehement gesture, and

speak in recitative: their action is exuberant, but graceful; and from
the infancy of the language,[1] nouns and verbs are constantly repeated,
for force, and distinction, as *one, one,* for, *one by one,* or, *each; one
tokoo one tokoo,* for, *one tokoo a-piece.* They frequently are obliged
to vary the tone, in pronouncing a word which has more than one
meaning, as the Chinese do. They have no expression short of "you
are a liar," and the king was surprised, when I told him we made a
great difference between a mistake and a lie; he said the truth was
not spoken in either case, and, therefore, it was the same thing; they
did not consider the motive but only the fact.

   Like the American languages, those of this part of Africa, are full
of figures, hyperbolical and picturesque. One of the kings of the interior, whose territories the Ashantees had long talked of invading,
sent forty pots of palm oil to Coomassie, with the message, that, "he
feared they could not find their way, so he sent the oil to light them."
The Accras instead of good night, say "*wooäu d'tcherrimong,*" [i.e.]
"sleep till the lighting of the world": one of their imprecations against
their enemies, is, "may their hiding place be our flute," that is, "our
plaything:" when they speak of a man imposing on them, they say, "he
turned the backs of our heads into our mouths." Having occasion,
whilst at Coomassie, to protest against the conduct of an individual,
the king replied, through Adoosee, "The horse comes from the bush,
and is a fool, but the man who rides him knows sense, and by and by
makes him do what he wishes; you, by yourself, made the horse, who
was a fool, do better the other day, therefore, three of you ought to
teach a man, who is not born a fool, and does not come from the
bush, to do what you know to be right by and by, though I see he
does wrong now." Other instances will appear in their songs. . . .

   The wild music of these people is scarcely to be brought within
the regular rules of harmony, yet their airs have a sweetness and animation beyond any barbarous compositions I ever heard. Few of their
instruments possess much power, but the combination of several frequently produces a surprising effect. The flute is made of a long
hollow reed, and has not more than three holes; the tone is low at all
times, and when they play in concert they graduate them with such
nicety as to produce the common chords. Several instances of thirds
occur, especially in one of the annexed airs, played as a funeral dirge;
nor is this extraordinary considering it is the most natural interval;

   1. "In the infancy of language, while words were yet scanty, the most natural way,
whereby a writer or speaker might give an additional force to his discourse, was to *repeat*
such terms as he wished to render *emphatic.* The more ancient any language is, the
more numerous appear the traces of such repetitions; and next to the Hebrew, they
form a remarkable feature in the Greek tongue. Thus $\mu\alpha\omega$ $\mu\alpha\omega$, "I desire desire," blended
into one word, become $\mu\iota\mu\alpha\omega$, and mean, "I greatly desire." $\beta\alpha\omega$ $\beta\alpha\omega$, "I walk walk,"
$\beta\iota\beta\alpha\omega$, "I stride," &c. &c. &c." . . .

the addition of fifths, at the same time, is rare. The natives declare they can converse by means of their flutes, and an old resident at Accra has assured me he has heard these dialogues, and that every sentence was explained to him.

On the Sanko . . . they display the variety of their musical talents, and the Ashantees are allowed to surpass all others. It consists of a narrow box, the open top of which is covered with alligator, or antelope skin; a bridge is raised on this, over which eight strings are conducted to the end of a long stick, fastened to the fore part of the box, and thickly notched, and they raise or depress the strings into these notches as occasion requires. The upper string assimilates with the tenor C of the piano, and the lower with the octave above: sometimes they are tuned in Diatonic succession, but too frequently the intermediate strings are drawn up at random, producing flats and sharps in every Chromatic variety, though they are not skilful enough to take advantage of it. I frequently urged this by trying to convince them they were not playing the same tune I had heard the day before, but the answer was invariably, "I pull the same string, it must be the same tune." The strings are made from the runners of a tree called Enta, abounding in the forests. All airs on this instrument are played very quick, and it is barely possible to make even an experienced player lessen the time, which quick as it is, is kept in a surprising manner, especially as every tune is loaded with ornament. They have a method of stopping the strings with the finger, so as to produce a very soft and pleasing effect, like the Meyer touch of the harp.[2]

The horns form their loudest sounds, and are made of elephant's tusks, they are generally very large, and, being graduated like the flutes, their flourishes have a martial and grand effect. It has been mentioned in the Military Customs of the Ashantees, that peculiar sentences are immediately recognized by the soldiers, and people, in the distinct flourishes of the horns of the various chiefs: the words of some of these sentences are almost expressible by the notes of the horns; the following, uttered by the horns of a captain named Gettoä, occurs to me as an instance

"O Saï tïntïntoo, ma yūāyïä pa pa."

"O Sai great king! I laud thee everywhere, or exceedingly." The Bentwa . . . is a stick bent in the form of a bow, and across it, is fastened a very thin piece of split cane, which is held between the lips at one end, and struck with a small stick; whilst at the other it

2. A reference to the harp-playing technique of Philippe-Jacques Meyer (1737–1819), one of the earliest authorities on the harp. Mayer's historically important manual, *Essai sur la vraie manière de jouer de la harpe avec une méthode pour l'accorder*, was published in 1763. [*Editor*]

is occasionally stopped, or rather buffed, by a thick one; on this they play only lively airs, and it owes its various sounds to the lips.

The Mosees, Mallowas, Bournous, and natives from the more remote parts of the interior, play on a rude violin: the body is a calabash, the top is covered with deer skin, and two large holes are cut in it for the sound to escape; the strings, or rather string, is composed of cow's hair, and broad like that of the bow with which they play, which resembles the bow of a violin. Their grimace equals that of an Italian Buffo [opera singer]; they generally accompany themselves with the voice, and increase the humour by a strong nasal sound.

The Oompoochwa is a box, one end of which is left open; two flat bridges are fastened across the top, and five pieces of thin curved stick, scraped very smooth, are attached to them, and (their ends being raised) are struck with some force by the thumb. I can compare it to nothing but the Staccado nearly deprived of its tone.

The Ashantees have an instrument like a Bagpipe, but the drone is scarcely to be heard.

The rest of the instruments can hardly be called musical, and consist of drums, castanets, gong-gongs, flat sticks, rattles, and even old brass pans.

The Drums . . . are hollow'd trunks of trees, frequently carved with much nicety, mostly open at one end, and of many sizes: those with heads of common skin (that is of any other than Leopard skin) are beaten with sticks in the form of a crotchet rest [i.e. ❧]; the largest are borne on the head of a man, and struck by one or more followers; the smaller are slung round the neck, or stand on the ground; in the latter case they are mostly played with the inside of the fingers, at which the natives are very expert: amongst these drums are some with heads of leopard skin, (looking like vellum,) only sounded by two fingers, which are scraped along, as the middle finger is on the tamborine, but producing a much louder noise. The gong-gongs are made of hollow pieces of iron, and struck with the same metal. The Castanets are also of iron. The Rattles are hollow gourds, the stalks being left as handles, and contain shells or pebbles, and are frequently covered with a network of beads; the grimaces with which these are played make them much more entertaining to sight than hearing.

I was fortunate enough to find a rare instance of a native able to play the radical notes of each tune; he is the best player in the country, and I was enabled to collect the airs now offered: with some of the oldest date I have also selected a few of the latest compositions. Their graces are so numerous, some extempore, some transmitted from father to son, that the constant repetition only can distinguish the commencement of the air: sometimes between each beginning they introduce a few chords, sometimes they leave out a bar, some-times they only return to the middle, so entirely is it left to the fancy of the performer. The observation made on the time of the Sanko may be extended to almost every other instrument, but it is always perfect, and the children will move their heads and limbs, whilst on their mother's backs, in exact unison with the tune which is playing: the contrasts of piano and forte are very well managed.

The singing is almost all recitative, and this is the only part of music in which the women partake; they join in the chorusses, and at the funeral of a female sing the dirge itself; but the frenzy of the moment renders it such a mixture of yells and screeches, that it bids defiance to all notation. The songs of the Canoe men are peculiar to themselves, and very much resemble the chants used in cathedrals. but as they are all made for the moment, I have not been able to retain any of them.

[NOTES ON THE MELODIES] [3]

To have attempted anything like arrangement, beyond what the annexed airs naturally possess, would have altered them, and de-stroyed the intention of making them known in their original char-acter. I have not even dared to insert a flat or a sharp.

No. 1 is the oldest air in the whole collection, and common both to Ashantees and Warsaws; I could trace it through four generations, but the answer made to my enquiries will give the best idea of its antiquity; "it was made when the country was made." The key appears to be E minor.

The old and simple air No. 2, is almost spoiled from the quick method of playing it, but when slow it has a melancholy rarely found in African music, and it is one of the very few in which the words are adapted to the tune. I think it is decidedly in the key of C major. The noun *aganka*, an orphan, is from the verb *agan*, to leave. Oboïbee is a bird that sings only at night, for which I know no other name than the Ashantee. The Warsaw air, No. 3, also in C major, was com-posed in consequence of a contest between the two principal cabo-ceers of that country, Intiffa and Attobra; one extremely thin and the other very fat; Attobra ran away, and is derided by Intiffa in the fol-lowing satirical words:

Asoom cōŏčoŏrŏŏcōō ŏninny ăgwanny

Asoom is a dolphin, which, as a beardless creature, is an epithet of the strongest contempt. The literal translation is,

3. For music, see pp. 18–23. [*Editor*]

The big dolphin runs away from the small man.

No. 5, which I should conjecture to begin in E minor, and to end in D minor, was occasioned by an English vessel bringing the report of a battle, in which the French were defeated and their town burned. The words are allegorical.

Abirrikirri croom ogah odum;
French   town   fire   put in;
Ocoontinkii   bonoo fum;
Great fighting man, wolf   take you away;
Cooroompun coom agwun.
Cooroompun kills   all goats.

Abirrikirri applies indiscriminately to all nations beyond the sea, as Dunko does to all nations far in the interior. Cooroompun is a very large insect of the genus mantis (soothsayer) frequently met with here, and the natives believe that it kills the sheep and goats by fascination, standing with its eyes fixed on those of the object, and swinging its head and body from side to side without moving its feet, until the animal falls in fits and dies.[4] Agwun is a noun of multitude, comprehending all the goat kind.

A long tale accompanies No. 6. An Ashantee having been surprised in an intrigue with another man's wife, becomes the slave of the King, and is obliged to follow the army in a campaign against the celebrated Attah, the Akim caboceer mentioned in the history. The Ashantee army having retired, this man either deserted or could not join his division, and after concealing himself some time in the forest, was taken by a party of Attah's, whom he addresses in the following words:

Eqqwee odin ahi,
Panther bush here (belongs to)
Minăwoo! Minăwoo!
I die!   I die!
Me'din adoo croom,
Bush now my croom,
Minăwoo! Minăwoo!
I die!   I die!
Babisseäche Minăwoo! Minăwoo!
For woman's sake I die! I die!
Attah m'incomie!   Attah m'incomie!
Attah don't kill me! Attah don't kill me!

4. The power of fascination by the eyes, is believed and dreaded in those parts of Africa as mortal, whether exercised by the fetish priests against men, or by the cooroompun against animals. The idea prevailed in Pliny's time, but it was ascribed to the voice. . . . A cooroompum will be found amongst the specimens for the British Museum.

The man's life, it was added, was preserved when he urged that he understood how to make sandals. The key appears to be E minor.

No. 7, in G major, seems to convey the moral, that riches prompt mankind to wickedness, the word *"makes"* is understood.

No. 9, became a common song in March last in praise of the present Governor in Chief; who, in consequence of the famine occasioned by the preceding invasion from the Ashantees, daily distributed corn to the starving multitude: the words are even more incoherent and figurative than the others, therefore I have not written them, but the meaning to be gathered is, "Poor woman and poor child got no gold to buy kanky; good white man gives you corn." It will be observed that the air much resembles No. 11, wherefore I suspect it is an alteration, and not a composition; although the key seems to be G major, and it is impossible to attach any key to the latter.

The dirge, No. 12, certainly in the key of C major, has been mentioned before, but here I must add, that in venturing the intervening and concluding bass chord, I merely attempt to describe the castanets, gong-gongs, drums, &c. bursting in after the soft and mellow tones of the flutes; as if the ear was not to retain a vibration of the sweeter melody.

No. 13, in D minor, is played by only two flutes, and is one of the softest airs I have met with.

No. 14, is an Accra fetish hymn, sung by one man and one woman, or more, at Christmas:

> Afĭnaïē pweë,
> *The year's ends have met,*
> Gnōr woorra
> *Somebody's child*
> Mŏrbee.
> *Take blessing.*

"Somebody's child," means the child of a person of consequence, reminding us of Hidalgos, "the son of somebody," so applied in Spanish. Its regularity is surprising, and its transition from G major to C major is very harmonious.

No. 15, in G major, is a specimen of the Kerrapee or Kerrapay music, which I have made a point of preserving, as it appeared to me superior even to Ashantee. A young man acknowledges a crime he had attempted to conceal:

> Kennĕövay nooblou adomevai,
> *Oh pity!   the palaver is spoiled,*
> Noodooloo   adomevai,
> *It is found, it is spoiled;*

Ĕnnŏblou;
Think for me;
Dootŏh mĕ pŏ mĕ blōh,
Elders, settle it for me,
Adăn vō,
I am at a loss,
Ïëe!
Oh!

The following is a translation of a long Ashantee song, with little
or no air. The men sit together in a line on one side, with their
sankos and other instruments; and the women in a line opposite to
them. Individuals rise and advance, singing in turn.[5]

1st Woman.	My husband likes me too much,
	He is good to me,
	But I cannot like him,
	So I must listen to my lover.
1st Man.	My wife does not please me,
	I tire of her now;
	So I will please myself with another,
	Who is very handsome.
2nd Woman.	My lover tempts me with sweet words,
	But my husband always does me good,
	So I must like him well,
	And I must be true to him.
2nd Man.	Girl you pass my wife handsome,
	But I cannot call you wife;
	A wife pleases her husband only,
	But when I leave you, you go to others.

No. 1 The Oldest Ashantee and Warsaw Air

5. I never heard this sung without its recalling Horace's beautiful little dialogue ode,
(9. lib. 3) "Donec gratus eram tibi."

No. 2 A very old Ashantee Air

Sanko

Aganka oshoom noofa Oboibee oshoom noofa Aganka oshoom noofa wekirree wekirree

oimiyow wekirree   wekirree wekirree oimiyow

No. 3 Warsaw Air

Sanko

* The rhythm of measure 3 is reproduced exactly as notated in the source.

No. 4 Ashantee Air

Sanko

No. 5 Fantee Air

No. 6 An Ashantee Air

Sanko

No. 7 An Ashantee Air

Sanko

O – noom-pah yah-pah   o – noom-pah yah-pah   o – noom-pah yah-pah
(Makes) Per – son   do bad   –   –   –

sic – ca sic – ca   o – noom-pah yah-pah   o – noom-pah yah-pah
gold   gold (makes) per – son   do bad   –   –

o – noom-pah yah-pah   A – kim   sic – ca   o – noom-pah yah-pah.
–   –   –   A – kim   gold (makes) per – son   do bad.

*The rhythm of measure 4 is reproduced exactly as notated in the source.

No. 8 Modern Fantee Air

Sanko

No. 9 Modern Fantee Air

Sanko

No. 10 Ashantee Air

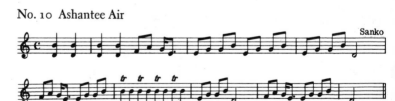

Sanko

No. 11 Ashantee Air

No. 12 A Fantee Dirge

No. 13 An Ashantee Air

No. 14 An Accra Fetish Hymn

A - fi - naie - pwa - ëe   gnorwoorra a fi - naie - pwa - ëe

gnorwoorra   gnorwoorra

gnorwoorra a-fi - naie - pwa - ëe   gnor-woor-ra mor-bee gnor-woor-ra

gnorwoorra gnor-woor-ra mor-bee gnor-woor-ra

No. 15 A Kerrapee Song

No. 16 Fantee Air

No. 17 Fantee Air

No. 18 Ashantee Air

No. 19 Mallowa Air

No. 20 Mosee Air

. . . The music of Empoöngwa [i.e. Gaboon [6]] is, generally, very
inferior to that I have before noticed. The enchambee, their only
peculiar instrument, resembles the mandolino, but has only five
strings, made from the root of the palm tree; the neck consists of
five pieces of bamboo, to which the strings are fastened, and, slipping
up and down, are easily, but not securely tuned; it is played with
both hands; the tones are sweet, but have little power or variety.
Long stories are recited to the enchambee in the moon-light evenings,
in a sort of recitative; a favourite one is an account of the arts by
which the Sun gained the ascendancy over the Moon, who were first
made of coeval power by their common father.

No. 1, (which, I imagine, commences in F major, and ends in G
major) is an Empoöngwa air played on the enchambee. I do not know
if the inversion of words is common in their conversation as well as
in their songs. A native envies a neighbour, named Engaëlla, who has
ivory to barter with a vessel.

> Amorill injanja   Engaëlla; impoongee m'adgillinjanja.
> *A brass pan he has got Engaëlla; ivory,   I have got none.*

Here again we find *me* answers to the personal pronoun *I*.

No. 2, in G major, is a song in which the men sing the air alone,
and the women join in the chorus. It is an old one, and the subject
the first appearance of a white man. One verse will be quite enough
to satisfy others and exculpate myself. At least half a dozen followed it.

> Ma bengwoo   ma bengwa   baïa.
> *A fine strange thing, A fine strange thing, my mother.*
> Deboonga sai   camberwoona nayennee.
> *Like the leaf of the fat tree,[7] true I say,   so it is.*
> Sangwa moochoo,   baïa.
> *I make you look to-day, my mother.*
> Baï   yamgwan boonoo.
> *My mother fears   this fetish man.*

---

6. For music, see pp. 25–26. [*Editor*]
7. The vegetable butter.

My patience during a series of dull Empoöngwa songs, was rec-
ompensed by the introduction of a performer, as loathsome as his
music was atonishing. It was a white negro from the interior country
of Imbeekee; his features betrayed his race, his hair was woolly, and of
a sandy colour, with thick eyebrows of the same; his eyes small,
bright, and of a dark grey; the light seemed to hurt them, and their
constant quivering and rolling gave his countenance an air of insan-
ity, which was confirmed by the actions of his head, and limbs, and
the distortions of his mouth. His stature was middling, and his limbs
very small; his skin was dreadfully diseased, and where it was free
from sores bore the appearance of being thrown on, it hung about
him so loose and so shrivelled; his voice was hollow, and his laugh
loud, interspersed with African howls. His harp was formed of wood,
except that part emitting the sound, which was covered with goat
skin, perforated at the bottom. The bow to which the eight strings
were fixed, was considerably curved, and there was no upright; the
figure head, which was well carved, was placed at the top of the body,
the strings were twisted round long pegs, which easily turned when
they wanted tuning, and, being made of the fibrous roots of palm
wine tree, were very tough and not apt to slip. The tone was full,
harmonious, and deep. He sat on a low stool, and supporting his harp
on his knee and shoulder, proceeded to tune it with great nicety; his
hands seemed to wander amongst the strings until he gradually
formed a running accompaniment (but with little variety) to his
extraordinary vociferations. At times, one deep and hollow note burst
forth and died away; the sounds of the harp became broken; presently
he looked up, pursuing all the actions of a maniac, taking one hand
from the strings, to wave it up and down, stretching forth one leg
and drawing it up again as if convulsed, lowering the harp on to the
other foot, and tossing it up and down. Whilst the one hand continued playing, he rung forth a peal which vibrated on the ear long
after it had ceased; he was silent; the running accompaniment served
again as a prelude to a loud recitative, uttered with the greatest
volubility, and ending with one word, with which he ascended and
descended, far beyond the extent of his harp, with the most beautiful
precision. Sometimes he became more collected, and a mournful air
succeeded the recitative, though without the least connection, and he
would again burst out with the whole force of his powerful voice in
the notes of the Hallelujah of Handel. To meet with this chorus in
the wilds of Africa, and from such a being, had an effect I can
scarcely describe, and I was lost in astonishment at the coincidence.
There could not be a stronger proof of the nature of Handel, or the
powers of the negro.

I naturally enquired if this man was in his senses, and the reply was that he was always rational but when he played, when he invariably used the same gestures, and evinced the same incoherency. The accompanying notes were caught whilst he was singing; to do more than set them down in their respective lengths was impossible, and every notation must be far inadequate.

As regards the words, there was such a rhapsody of recitative, of mournful, impetuous, and exhilarated air, wandering through the life of man, throughout the animal and vegetable kingdom for its subjects, without period, without connection, so transient, abrupt, and allegorical, that the Governor of the town could translate a line but occasionally, and I was too much possessed by the music, and the alternate rapture and phrenzy of the performer, to minute the half which he communicated. I can only submit the fragments of a melancholy and a descriptive part.

Burst of a man led to execution,

> Yawa yawa wo wo oh
> Yawa waï yawa
> *What have I done? what have I done?*

Bewailing the loss of his mother,

> Yawa gooba shangawelladi yaisa
> Wo na boo, &c.
> *My mother dies; who'll cry for me now*
> *When I die? &c.*
> Pahmbolee gwoongee yayoo, &c.
> *Which path shall I seek my love?*
> *Hark! I know now,*
> *I hear her snap the dry sticks,*
> *To speak, to call to me.*

Jiggledy jiggledy, jiggledy, too too tee too, often invaded or broke off a mournful strain; it was said to be an imitation of the note of a bird, described as the wood-pecker.

No. 1 Empoöngwa song

No. 2 Empoöngwa song

No. 3 Notes Sung by the White Negro from Imbeekee

*Long rapid recitative.

II. Black Singers and Instrumentalists of Early America

4. SAMUEL DAVIES AND OTHERS

»»» References to the psalm singing of slaves are contained in a number of letters and reports of clergymen who worked as missionaries among the slaves in the eighteenth century. The Presbyterian minister Samuel Davies (1723–61) did missionary work in Virginia before he became president in 1759 of Nassau Hall (later Princeton University) in New Jersey. Some of the letters sent by Davies and other clergymen to sympathetic "benefactors" in London requesting psalm books and Bibles for members of their parishes, both black and white, were published in book form: *Letters from the Rev. Samuel Davies, and Others; Shewing the State of Religion in Virginia, S.C., etc. Particularly Among the Negroes* (London, 1761). Further excerpts from the letters of Samuel Davies are contained in Benjamin Fawcett, *A Compassionate Address* (London, 1755), and Charles Colcock Jones, *Religious Instruction of the Negroes* (Savannah, Ga., 1842). Among other missionaries who discussed the singing of slaves in their letters or reports were members of the Society for the Propagation of the Gospel in Foreign Parts (the established Church of England) and the Associates of Doctor Bray.*

Despite the publicity given to the slaves' singing of psalms, relatively few slaves were actually allowed to attend religious services. As late as 1841, only about 5 per cent of the slaves in the South were members of the church, according to the Reverend Charles Jones. «««

From *Letters from the Rev. Samuel Davies and Others*†

» 1. From a letter written by Samuel Davies is 1755 to "a friend and member of the Society in London for promoting Christianity" [quoted by Charles Colcock Jones] «

The books were all very acceptable, but none more so than the Psalms and Hymns, which enable them [i.e. the slaves] to gratify their pe-

---

* See further in Edgar Pennington, "Thomas Brays' Associates Work among Negroes" in the *American Antiquarian Society. Proceedings,* New Series, 48 (1938), pp. 311–403.

† Text: The original edition (London, 1761), pp. 12–17, 27 (except for items 1 and 2). Courtesy of the Rare Book Division, the New York Public Library, Astor, Lenox, and Tilden Foundations. Item 1, Charles Colcock Jones, *Religious Instruction of the*

culiar taste for psalmody. Sundry of them have lodged all night in my kitchen, and sometimes when I have awaked about two or three-o'clock in the morning, a torrent of sacred harmony has poured into my chamber and carried my mind away to heaven. In this seraphic exercise some of them spend almost the whole night. I wish, Sir, you and other benefactors could hear some of these sacred concerts. I am persuaded it would surprise and please you more than an Oratorio or a St. Cecilia's day. . . .

» 2. From a letter written by Samuel Davies in 1755 [quoted by Benjamin Fawcett] «

The Books I principally want for them are the Watts's Psalms and Hymns. . . . they cannot be supplied with any other Way than by a Collection, as they are not among the Books which your Society give away. I am the rather importunate for a good Number of these, as I cannot but observe that the Negroes, above all the Human Species that I ever knew, have an Ear for Musick, and a kind of extatic Delight in *Psalmody*; and there are no Books they learn so soon or take so much pleasure in, as those used in that heavenly Part of divine Worship.

Some Gentlemen in *London* were pleased to make me a private Present of these Books for their Use, and from the Reception they met with, and their Eagerness for more, I can easily foresee, how acceptable and useful a larger Number would be among them. Indeed, Nothing would be a greater Inducement to their Industry to learn to read, than the Hope of such a Present; which they would consider both as a Help, and a Reward for their Diligence. . . .

» 3. From *A Letter from the Rev. Mr. Davies in Virginia, to Mr. J. F. Dated August 26, 1758* «

Dear Sir,

Heaven and earth seem to conspire to afflict me and my fellow-labourers in this *remote* corner of the world, in promoting Christianity among the *Out-casts* of mankind. The large collection of Books sent from the SOCIETY and other Benefactors have been distributed in various parts of the country by my own hands. . . .

The Spelling-books have been a new excitement to the Negroes to learn to read; and many of them are making good progress in it.—I can hardly express the pleasure it affords me to turn to that part of the Gallery where they sit, and see so many of them with their Psalm or Hymn Books, turning to the part then sung, and assisting their

---

fellows who are beginners, to find the place; and then all breaking out in a torrent of sacred harmony, enough to bear away the whole congregation to heaven. . . .

» 4. From *A Letter from the Rev. Mr. Hutson at South Carolina, to Mr. J. F. Dated July 11, 1758* «

This is accompanied with the warmest gratitude for the late parcel of Books received from the SOCIETY, to distribute among the poor with us. These may now inform you, that I have disposed of them in the best manner I could; and that they were received with abundant thanksgivings to their benefactors; praising GOD that he hath put it into the hearts of Christians to be thus useful. Particularly the poor Negroes, many of whom seem to be under serious impressions; and a number of them I trust are savingly converted. I must confess that the vital part of Religion among us at this time, seems to be chiefly among them.—I was extremely glad of the Books for their sakes, especially the Bibles, Dr. Watts' Psalms and Hymns, and the Compassionate Address. But, O! with what thankfulness were they received by them; and I doubt not but that honourable SOCIETY has had many of their prayers put up to God for them.

I understand that several of them meet once a week and spend some time in singing, praying, and reading the Bible, or some of those good books. What a mercy is it that the Lord is stretching forth his hand toward *Ethiopia!* . . .

» 5. From *A Letter from the Rev. Mr. Todd at Hanover, Virginia, to Mr. B. F. Dated November 18, 1758* «

Dear Sir,

I beg leave to inform you that I have with unspeakable pleasure and satisfaction distributed the greatest part of the books I had the happiness to receive from that charitable SOCIETY, which I am persuaded is approved of GOD, and is inexpressibly dear to multitudes in this guilty and distant land. The blessing of many ready to perish I doubt not will rest upon the good benefactors.

With uncommon eagerness, multitudes of Negroes and white people flocked to my house to get books, upon the first notice of my having them to dispose of; they received them with the utmost thankfulness, and with serious promises religiously to improve them. —The poor Slaves are now commonly engaged in learning to read; some of them can read the Bible, others can only spell; and some are just learning their letters.—But there is a general alteration among them for the better. The sacred hours of the *Sabbath*, that used to be spent in frolicking, dancing, and other profane courses, are now employed in attending upon public ordinances, in learning to read at home, or in praying together, and singing the praises of God and the Lamb. . . .

» 6. From *A Letter from the Rev. Mr. Wright of Cumberland County, Virginia, to Messrs. J. and B. F. Dated January 6, 1761* «

My landlord tells me, when he waited on the colonel at his county-seat two or three days, they heard the Slaves at worship in their lodge, singing Psalms and Hymns in the evening, and again in the morning, long before break of day. They are excellent singers, and long to get some of Dr. Watts' Psalms and Hymns, which I encouraged them to hope for. . . .

5. SLAVE ADVERTISEMENTS

⋙ Colonial newspapers provide much valuable information about contemporary society, and perhaps no section of the newspapers reveals more about the role of the slave in that society than the slave-advertisement column. The advertisements generally fall into three categories: those offering slaves for sale; those offering slaves "for hire" by the day, week, month, or even year; and those giving notice of runaway slaves. If a slave possessed special skills, the advertisement emphasized this, for a skilled craftsman or a musician commanded a better price than a field hand. As for noting the skills of runaway slaves, slaveowners obviously thought that the more detailed their descriptions, the easier it would be to recover their slaves. Slave advertisements reveal which instruments were most commonly played by slaves (violins, flutes, and French horns); how well the slaves had developed their musical skills; and, occasionally, how the slaves learned to play instruments (see No. 3 below). ⋘

Eighteenth-Century Newspapers: Slave Advertisements †

If any Gentlemen living in the Country are disposed to send their children to Charlestown they may be boarded with George Logan who also intends to open his school to teach to dance, next Monday being the 19th instant. He will likewise go into the country if he meets with Encouragement. Any white person that can play on the violin, or a Negro may be employ'd by the said Logan living in Union Street.   [*South Carolina Gazette*, September 17, 1737]

RUN AWAY the 3rd Instant December from Combahee Ferry, a middle-sized Negro Fellow named Sam; had on when he went away a Negro Cloth Jacket died with red oak bark with Mohair Buttons, and a new Hat, can play upon the violin, and pretends he was born free in Virginia. Whoever apprehends the said Fellow shall have

---

† Original sources are cited below each advertisement. Two useful tools for locating such material in colonial newspapers are Lester Cappon and Stella Duff, *The Virginia Gazette. Index, 1736–1780* (Williamsburg, 1950), and Hennig Cohen, *The South Carolina Gazette. 1732–1775* (Columbia, S.C., 1953).

twenty pounds reward on Delivery either to the Work House in
Charleston or to me at Combahee Ferry.   Alexander Moon
[*South Carolina Gazette*, December 26, 1741]

Whereas Cambridge, *a Negro Man belonging to* James Oliver *of
Boston doth absent himself sometimes from his Master: SAID
NEGRO PLAYS WELL UPON A FLUTE, AND NOT SO WELL
ON A VIOLIN. This is to desire all Masters and Heads of Families
not to suffer said Negro to come into their Houses to teach their
Prentices or Servants to play, nor on any other Accounts. All Masters
of Vessels are also forbid to have anything to do with him on any
Account, as they may answer it in the Law. N. B. Said Negro is to be
sold: Enquire of said* Oliver.   [*Boston Evening Post*, October 24, 1743]

RUN AWAY from the Pelham Privateer—Thomas Ebsery, born
in Jamaica, a tall slim Fellow hard of Hearing; he beats a Drum
very well and is well known amongst the Negroes in Charles Town
having been here before with Captain Abrasher. Whoever apprehends
the said Negro shall have 5 lb. Reward by applying to Reid and
Kennan.   [*South Carolina Gazette*, April 15, 1745]

RAN-away from Capt. Joseph Hale of Newbury, a Negro Man
named *Cato*, the 6th Instant, about 22 Years of Age, short and
small, SPEAKS GOOD ENGLISH AND CAN READ AND WRITE,
understands farming Work carry'd with him a striped homespun
Jacket and Breeches, and Trousers, and an outer Coat and Jacket
of home-made Cloth, two Pair of Shoes, sometimes wears a black
Wigg, has a smooth Face, a sly Look, TOOK WITH A VIOLIN,
AND CAN PLAY WELL THEREON. Had with him three Linnen
Shirts, home-made pretty fine yarn Stockings. Whoever shall bring
said Negro to his Master or secure him so that he may have him
again shall have *five Pounds* Reward and all necessary Charges paid
by me.   Joseph Hale, Newbury, July 8th, 1745
[*Boston Gazette or Weekly Journal*, July 9, 1745]

RUN AWAY from the Subscriber's Plantation, in the Isle of Wright,
on the 17th Day of November last, a likely young Negroe Man,
named Tom; he is a middle-sized Fellow, Country-born, and plays
very well on the Violin; he had on when he went away a lightish-
colored Kercey Waistcoat and Trousers. Whoever will take up the

said Runaway and convey him to me, shall have Four Pistoles Reward. Robert Whitfield

[*Virginia Gazette*, December 5, 1745]

Ran away from his Master *Eleazer Tyng, Esq. at* Dunstable, *on the 26th May past, a Negro Man Serrant Call'd* Robbin, *almost of the complexion of an Indian, short thick square shoulder'd Fellow, a very short neck, and thick legs, about 28 Years old, talks good English, can read and write, and plays on the Fiddle; he was born at* Dunstable *and it is thought he has been entic'd to enlist into the service, or to go to* Philadelphia: *Had on when he went away, a strip'd cotton and Linnen blue and white Jacket, red Breeches with Brass Buttons, blue Yarn Stockings, a fine Shirt, and took another of a meaner Sort, a red Cap, a Beaver Hat with a mourning Weed in it, and sometimes wears a Wig. Whoever will apprehend said Negro and secure him, so that his Master may have him again, or bring him to the Ware-House of Messiers* Alford *and* Tyng, *in* Boston, *shall have a reward of* Ten Pounds, old Tenor, *and all reasonable Charges.*

N. B. And all Masters of Vessels or others are hereby cautioned against harbouring, concealing or carrying off said Servant, on Penalty of the Law.

[*New York Gazette Revived in the Weekly Post-Boy*, July 18, 1748]

RUN AWAY from the subscriber in Hanover about the middle of December last a likely Negro man named Damon, about 5 feet 9 or 10 inches high, has a scar on his forehead and cheek, is a brisk lively fellow, speaks good English, was born in the West Indies, beats the drum tolerably well, which he is very fond of, and loves liquor; had on when he went away Negro cotton clothes, and an old hat bound round with linen.

Sara Gist

Whoever takes up the said Negro and contrives him to me, shall have 3 lb. reward.

[*Virginia Gazette*, April 17, 1766]

RUN AWAY from the subscriber on Monday, the 20th of this instant, a mulatto slave named David Gratenread; he is an arch fellow, very well known by most people, plays the fiddle extremely well, has a wide mouth, a little piece bit out of one of his ears, has a large bump upon one of his shins, about 37 years of age, 5 ft 6 or 7 inches high, and may perhaps change his name and pretend to pass as a free man; he carried with him a new brown cloth waistcoat lappelled, lined with white taminy, and yellow gilt buttons, a new pair of buckskin breeches, gold-laced hat, a fine Holland shirt, brown cut wig, and several old clothes that I cannot remember, except an old lappelled kersey waistcoat. I believe he carried his fiddle with him. . . . Whoever apprehends the said runaway, and brings him to me, or commits him to any goal, so that I get him again, shall have five pounds reward if taken in this colony, if out thereof ten pounds.

Richard King

[*Virginia Gazette*, May 14, 1767]

RUN AWAY from the subscriber in Amelia, in the year 1766, a black Virginia born Negro fellow named Sambo, about 6 ft high, about 32 years old. He makes fiddles, and can play upon the fiddle, and work at the carpenter's trade.

[*Virginia Gazette*, August 18, 1768]

Ranaway on the Monday the 7th of June, a likely mulatto man named Francis, of a middle stature; he is about 25 years old, has a small scar on one of his cheeks, and some time ago received a fall from a horse, which has caused the skin about one of his eyes to be somewhat darker than the rest of his face. He can write a pretty good hand: plays on the fife extremely well, and is an incomparable good house servant. He had when he left home, 6 good linen shirts, a fine new brown broad cloth coat, a green shaggy jacket, breeches of several kinds, with shoe-boots and shoes. I do suppose that he intends to ship himself for Europe or elsewhere. I therefore forewarn all masters and captains of vessels as well as all other persons, from having any thing to say to the servant above described, and will give a reward of Five Guineas to any Person or Persons who will either deliver him to me in Halifax town, North Carolina, or secure him in any jail so that I get him again.

June 24, 1790   Halcot B. Pride

[*Norfolk and Portsmouth Chronicle*, July 10, 1790]

RUN AWAY—a Negro Man named Robert, 23 years old, about five feet, ten inches high; speaks good English, is a fiddler and took his fiddle with him. He also took with him a considerable quantity of clothing, among which is a blue coat, snuff colored velvet breeches, velvet white jacket, etc—had also considerable money.

Godfred Wolner

[*Poughkeepsie Journal*, November 24, 1791]

RUN AWAY—a Negro man, named Zack, about 20 years of age, 5 feet 7 or 8 inches high, slender built, sprightly walk, has lost the sight of his left eye, born in Connecticut, speaks good English, plays on the fife and German flute; had a fife with him; had on a coat, waistcoat and overalls of light-colored homemade bearskin, round hat, and shoes; carried with him a new green broadcloth coat striped cotton waistcoat, fustian overalls, namkeen do. [ditto], white cotton stockings, thread do., several shirts and other clothing.

Samuel Barber

[*Poughkeepsie Journal*, January 6, 1796]

Five Dollars Reward

Absented himself from the subscriber about the 10th of April, a likely young NEGRO FELLOW named CAROLINA) he has always been accustomed to wait in the house; he was seen in the city about ten days ago, dressed in a sailor jacket and trowsers. CAROLINA plays remarkably well on the violin.

The above reward will be paid to any person delivering him to the Master of the Work-House or at No 11 East Bay.

All Masters of vessels and others are hereby cautioned against carrying said Negro out of the State, as they will, on conviction, be prosecuted to the utmost rigor of the law.

June 13 Robert Smith

[*City Gazette and Daily Advertiser*, July 30, 1799]

Ran Away

On the 25th ultimo, from the subscriber, living near Culpepper Court-house, A *Negro Man* named Jack, about 30 years old, 5 feet 10 or 11 inches high, very muscular, full faced, wide nostrils, large eyes, a down look, speaks slowly and wore his hair cued; had on when he eloped, a white shirt, grey broadcloth coat, mixed cassimere waistcoat and breeches, a brown hat, faced underneath with green, and a pair of boots. He formerly belonged to Mr. *Augustin Baughan*, of Fredericksburg, now of Baltimore, and I am told was seen making for Alexandria, with the intention of taking the stage thither: he is artful and can both read and write and is a good fiddler; it is therefore probable that he may attempt a forgery and pass as a free man. . . . Masters of Vessels and stage drivers are forewarned carrying him out of the State, under penalty of the law. Carter Beverley

[*Virginia Herald* (Fredericksburg), January 21, 1800]

6. GEORGE CHAMPLAIN MASON

≫ It may well be that when Newport Gardner (1746–1826) opened up a music studio in 1791 in Newport, Rhode Island, he became the first black singing-school master in the nation. More than one contemporary writer reported on the remarkable slave who developed a regional reputation among New Englanders as a musician and a religious leader. George Champlain Mason (1820–94), local historian of Newport, devoted a chapter to Gardner in *Reminiscences of Newport* (Newport, R.I., 1884). Obviously, Mason had no personal contact with Gardner, but gathered his information from contemporary sources and from old-timers who had known the black leader; for example, John Ferguson points out, in his book *Memoir of the Life and Character of Rev. Samuel Hopkins, D.D.* (Boston, 1830), that Gardner "became so well acquainted with the science and art of music, that he composed a large number of tunes, some of which have been highly approved by musical amateurs, and was for a long time the teacher of a very numerously-attended singing school in Newport." A collection of music published at Boston in 1803, *A Number of Original Airs, Duettos and Trios*, includes a song, *Crooked Shanks*, attributed to Gardner. His *Promise* anthem was published in 1826 in Boston. ≪

From *Reminiscences of Newport* [1884] †

NEWPORT GARDNER

Of Newport's early years we know nothing. It has always been understood that he was brought here directly from the coast of Africa when about fourteen years of age, and that he was entrusted to the captain of the vessel, who, having pledged himself to see that the boy was properly instructed, sold him into slavery. He was still a savage and unable to speak other than the language of his tribe when he became the property of Caleb Gardner, a prominent

† Text: The original edition (Newport, 1884), pp. 154–59. Gardner's African name was Occramer Marycoo.

merchant in Newport; but, quick to learn and docile in his ways, he soon acquired a recognized place in the house of his master. But while learning English, he never relinquished his hold on his native tongue, which he could speak fluently when he had attained to his eightieth year; at which time he declared that when light dawned on his intellect, he felt that the day might come when he should return to his native country to convert many there who were still in darkness It has been said that he taught himself to read after receiving a few lessons in the elements of written language, and having mastered the rudiments of music, he became very proficient, and ultimately a skilful leader. Mrs. Gardner took great interest in him, and helped to further his wishes. There was a singing-master named [Andrew] Law who occasionally came to Newport to give lessons, and it was Newport's ambition to join one of his classes. Through the indulgence of Mrs. Gardner this wish was gratified, and soon the pupil showed himself to be more than the equal of his teacher. He read and wrote music with ease, and his voice was remarkably strong and clear. Sacred music alone claimed his attention. He never essayed to master any instrument, but as a leader of the little band of singers that gathered around him, he started the tune with a pitch pipe. Soon he was able to teach men and women who had had better schooling, and had enjoyed more advantages in musical training. A strict disciplinarian and of staid demeanor, no one even thought of taking liberties with him. One of his pupils recently said of him: "He carried a cane with an ivory head. I have often seen him rap some of his pupils over the head with it when they broke the rules of the school." But I judge from the remarks of others that he seldom had occasion to enforce authority in this way, for all were ready to be guided by him. He was very companionable, and nothing pleased him more than to have one say, "Come, Uncle Newport, let us try Coronation," or some other of the tunes that were then most popular. With his family he lived in Pope Street, but he had a room in the Bella "Bouse" house (probably a corruption of Bours, often so pronounced, the name of a Newport family of the last century), on High Street, and but a short distance from the residence of Dr. Hopkins, who lived on Division Street. There, "in an upper chamber," he gathered his pupils and gave instruction,—and here I must digress for a moment.

In 1770 Dr. Hopkins was settled over the Congregational Church in Newport. Here he was brought into closer relations with colored people than ever before—with men and women and children fresh from the wilds of Africa, and among them he discovered many who not only made good, faithful servants, but were also consistent Christians. The bond between the master and slave was strong, and the latter felt and believed that he was a part of the household. The interest of his owner was his interest, and, aside from other considerations, it was the interest of the owner to see that those who served him were properly cared for. The boys and girls had some schooling, at least during a portion of the year, and when a man's allotted work was done, whether in the field or in the shop, the remainder of the day or week was his own, to employ as he pleased. As a class they were religiously inclined, and loved to come together to sing and pray. Dr. Hopkins found them ready and apt scholars. As early as 1776 he published a work on emancipation. On this, as on other subjects that gained his attention, he had clear and settled views. It was a part of his plan that the Africans in America, when properly qualified to teach others, should return to their own country. And it was a strange state of things that, while Dr. Hopkins was thus discoursing, the presiding elder in another place of worship was giving thanks in prayer on the Sunday morning after the arrival of every slaver from the coast of Africa, "that another cargo of benighted beings had been brought to a land where they might have the benefit of a gospel dispensation!"

Newport attended the Congregational church, and had come to man's estate when Dr. Hopkins took charge of the society. All that he heard was new to him, and he early became an attentive listener. The seed fell on good ground, and soon he was an earnest worker. His fine voice and attentive manner at once attracted the attention of the Doctor, who, finding of what material he was made, learned to place great confidence in him, and in mapping out a plan for colonizing Africa, assigned him an important position. In a letter on this missionary enterprise, he writes:

"Bristol Yamma is the first black on my list for a missionary; Salmar Nubia, alias Jack Mason, has been thought of for another by Dr. Stiles and me. He is sufficiently zealous to go. Newport Gardner is, in my view, next to Bristol, and in some things excels him. He is a discerning, judicious, steady, good man, and feels greatly interested in promoting a Christian settlement in Africa, and promoting Christianity there. . . . Newport's master offers to free him, his wife, and all his children but one, on condition he will live with him two years from the first of this month, and receive three dollars per month during that time. This offer is beyond our expectation, and we hope he will give up the consideration last mentioned."

This was as late as 1791. The same year, while Newport was looking for the ways and means to return to Africa, he with nine others in bondage bought a lottery ticket—a thing then common enough with all classes—which was so fortunate as to draw two thousand dollars. This helped him on, but it did not suffice to buy the freedom of all the family, and it is related that while praying for their liberation, he was overheard by his master, who sent for him and placed in his hands a paper manumitting him, his wife, and children. Newport, in speaking of this, said, "the all-wise Disposer had signally answered his request before he had finished his supplication." He was now free to go, but the project lagged for want of proper support, and it was not till many years after the death of the Doctor that it was carried into effect. Newport meanwhile found that his pastor was becoming infirm, and it was to him alike a duty and a privilege to aid him with his arm in his walk to and from the church. In those walks they were always in earnest conversation, and we know from the character of the men what subject was ever uppermost in their thoughts.

With the death of Dr. Hopkins, Newport's zeal did not abate. There was work at home, and at the front of it he was always to be found. Opposite the house where the doctor lived on Division Street there was an old building, roomy enough, but low, and poorly adapted for public gatherings. It was called "the salt box" for some reason it is hardly worth while to inquire about. Through the exertions of Newport, this building was purchased, renovated, and fitted up as a place of worship; and here he gathered many of his race and organized the Colored Union Church and Society in Newport. Newport was a leading spirit, and his memory is there kept green. The society, now known as the Union Congregational Church, is in a prosperous condition, and on the site of the old "salt box" there is a commodious and comely church edifice, presided over by the Rev. Mahlon Van Horne, a graduate from Princeton. How it would have gladdened Newport's heart could he have foreseen all this, and have known that the seed he planted would so grow and expand in the fulness of time.

Newport was now advanced in years, and his wish to return to his native land was still ungratified. He had won the confidence and merited the respect of every one, and about the year 1823 he was ordained a deacon in the Congregational Church in Newport. During all these years of struggle, means had been gathered little by little to pave the way, and at last a sum sufficiently large to take the colonists to Africa had been raised. Then Newport and Salmar gathered their little band and prepared to go. Newport was eighty years of age and Salmar seventy. Newport's wife was dead, but his son, a good bass singer, was of the party. They all assembled in Boston, sixteen in number, and organized a church previous to their departure. Newport and Salmar were chosen deacons, and were ordained by the Rev. Samuel Greene. Newport had years before composed an anthem. The words were taken from the Bible, but the music was his own composition. His friends in Boston procured a copy of it, which they placed in the hands of the choir to practice, and at the conclusion of the ceremony it was sung. For this Newport was wholly unprepared, and it moved him to tears. One week from that day, the last of December, 1825, the brotherhood set sail from Boston in the brig "Vine," for Liberia. Ferguson, in his memoir, says:

"One aged black was among the number, who seemed to be filled with almost youthful enthusiasm for the cause. 'I go!' he exclaimed, 'to set an example to the youth of my race; I go to encourage the young. They can never be elevated here; I have tried it for sixty years—it is vain.' "

The brig arrived at her place of destination Feb. 6, 1826; but ere six months had fled, Newport and Salmar had passed away—not dying of the coast fever, but of a rapid decline. Soon they were joined by Newport's son, who died of the same disease.

III. Slave Holidays and Festivals

7. JAMES EIGHTS

⇶ Colonial life offered few recreational activities, so white and black colonists alike looked forward to holidays, when the strenuous demands of everyday life could be temporarily set aside. No holiday was more popular with black folk in the Middle Colonies than Pinkster, a holiday of Dutch origin. The term Pinkster as used in reference to Pentecost or Whitsunday (in the Anglican Church) occurs as early as 1667 in the title of a sermon by Adrian Fischer: "Story of the Descent of the Holy Ghost on the Apostles on 'Pinckster Dagh.'"* The celebration began on the Monday following Pentecost, which takes place fifty days after Easter, and continued for a period of three to six days, depending upon local custom. New York historians in the nineteenth century seem to have been fascinated by the traditional slave celebrations of Pinkster, and several descriptions of the event are extant.

One such description, written by a certain Dr. James Eights, is included in Joel Munsell (1808–80), *Collections on the History of Albany* (Albany, 1867). Munsell does not indicate the original date of this material, nor does he give any information about the writer, other than the fact that his title was "Dr." Based upon the available evidence, we may surmise that the event as described by Eights took place before the Revolutionary War. ⇷

Pinkster Festivities in Albany [1867] †

[This great festival of the negroes when slavery existed in the state, and when every family of wealth or distinction possessed one or more slaves, took place usually in May, and continued an entire week. It began on the Monday following the Whitsunday or Pentecost of the Catholic and Episcopal churches, and was the carnival of the African race, in which they indulged in unrestrained merriment and revelry. The excesses which attended these occasions were so great that in 1811 the common council was forced to prohibit the erection of booths

* See further in Alice Morse Earle, *Colonial Days in Old New York* (New York, 1896), p. 195.
† Text: The original edition (Albany, 1867), II, 323–27.

and stalls, the parades, dances, gaming and drunkenness, with which they were attended, under penalty of fine or imprisonment; and being thereby deprived of their principal incitements and attractions, the anniversary soon fell into disuse, and is therefore unknown to the present generation. The following account of the Pinkster jubilee is taken from the *Cultivator*, for which it was written by Dr. James Eights, as the recollections of what he witnessed in his youth, when the custom was at its zenith. Pinkster hill, the scene of these celebrations, was the site of the Capitol, before the hand of man was stretched forth to pull down that eminence. Afterwards it was held at various places, but on the death of King Charles, it was observed with less enthusiasm, and finally sank into such a low nuisance as to fall under the ban of the authorities.] [1]

Bright and beautifully broke the morning that ushered in the first great day of the Pinkster jubilee. The air was filled with melody, and the purple hued martins, from their well provided shelter against the walls, or from the far-projecting eaves of many antiquated mansions, were chattering with noisy garrulity, as if in thankfulness for having been brought safely through the night to witness the light of this new-born day. The lilacs in the garden around were everywhere redolent with sweet smelling odors, while the pink blossomed azaleas from the neighboring plains fairly saturated the bright morning air with their ever-delicious fragrance. But, within doors, all was bustling commotion, nor did the overjoyous little ones, with their merry, gleesome mirth-ringing music to the ear, contribute greatly to quell these conflicting tumults within, and bring peace and order to this bewildering scene; but at every turn, where'er you went, you would be sure to encounter some one or more of these juvenile prattlers, frisking about with various garments on their arms and sometimes strewing them in wild dismay, all over the chamber floor, calling lustily for aid to adjust them in their befitting position; nor could a frown or even a scolding tongue for a moment quiet them in their noisy vociferations and frolicsome glee.

Quiet in some degree was at length restored to the household. The younger members of the family—both white and colored—had peacefully submitted to the process of cleansing, and were now tastefully adorned in all their varied finery, with numberless small coins merrily jingling in their ample pockets, seemingly keeping time to their sprightly movements, as well as to the silvery music of their mirthful voices. To witness this scene of innocent delight was a pleasing sight to all, and caused the bright eye of the mother to sparkle with pride, and her affectionate heart to expand within her bosom.

1. Headnote by Joel Munsell. [*Editor*]

Under the careful guidance of a trusty slave, forth we were ushered into the densely thronged streets, and never shall we forget the scene of gayety and merriment that there prevailed—joyous groups of children, all under the protecting care of some favorite old dame or damsel, gayly decorated with ribbons and flowers of every description, blithely wending their way along the different avenues that led to the far-famed Pinkster hill—and long before we reached the appointed place of rejoicing, were our ears greeted with the murmuring sound of many voices, harmoniously intermingled with the occasional shouts of boisterous mirth, and when we arrived on the field we found the green sward already darkened by the gathering multitude, consisting chiefly of individuals of almost every description of feature, form and color, from the sable sons of Africa, neatly attired and scrupulously clean in all their holiday habiliments, to the half clad and blanketed children of the forest, accompanied by their squaws, these latter being heavily burdened with all their different wares, such as baskets, moccasins, birch-bark, nick-nacks, and many other things much too numerous for us even here to mention, and boys and girls of every age and condition were everywhere seen gliding to and fro amid this motley group.

The Pinkster grounds, where we now found ourselves comfortably provided for in a friendly booth or tent, securely protected from the pressure of the swaying multitude without, gave us a most convenient opportunity to inspect the place, and witness at our leisure the entire proceedings of this tumultuous mass of human beings, as they passed in disorderly review before our eyes. The grounds were quaintly laid out in the form of an oblong square, and closely hemmed in with the rude buildings on every side save one, and this was left free, so as to give entrance and freely to admit the crowd. Beyond this square, and in the rear of all the tents, were to be found the spaces appropriated to the various exhibitions, such as of wild animals, rope dancing, circus-riding and the playing ground of all simple gaming sports. Here might be seen for a moderate pittance, the royal tiger of Bengal, and the lordly lion from Africa, with a monkey perched over the entrance door, profusely provided for by the youth and children of the white population; and much did these little ones enjoy themselves in witnessing the wonderful agility with which this diminutive satire on man caught the numerous cakes and other good things thrown within his reach; and then there was Mademoiselle Some-one, with a hard, unpronounceable name, to perform amazing wonders on the slack rope; and in the next enclosure was Monsieur Gutta Percha, to ride the famous horse Selim, and throw a somerset through a blazing hoop, attended by the great

Rickett, the celebrated clown of the day, to display his stock of buffoonery on horseback, and break his neck, if necessary, to afford the amplest satisfaction to the assembled auditors.

Thus passed the first day of the festival, merry enough, no doubt, but, [it] being considered vastly ungenteel for the colored nobility to make their appearance on the commencing day, we must defer our more minute details of the ceremonies until the approaching morrow.

The morning sun rose again as beautifully over the smiling landscape as on the preceding day, and cast a cheerful glow of animation over everything around; the excited youngsters, too, were all awake at the early chirping of the birds, and with their silver-toned voices gave a lively chorus to the surrounding scene. After the preliminary preparation, as on the previous day, each was again attired in an appropriate manner to revisit the festal meeting at the usual hour. Early again the crowd were assembled, fully prepared to enter with pleasurable feelings into all the exciting events, as they from time to time should transpire; but far more circumspect were they, and orderly in their demeanor, as all the more respectable members of their community were there to witness any discreditable act, and ever afterward be sure to reward the transgressors with their most severe indignation and contempt.

The master of ceremonies, on this occasion—the Beau Brummel of the day—was Adam Blake, then body servant to the old patroon, and a young man in all the grace and elegance of manner, which so eminently characterized his progress through life until his dying day; to him was unanimously entrusted the arduous duty of reducing to some kind of order this vast mass of incongruent material, which his superior ability soon enabled him to accomplish with complete success.

The hour of ten having now arrived, and the assembled multitude being considered most complete, a deputation was then selected to wait upon their venerable sovereign king, "Charley of the Pinkster hill," with the intelligence that his respectful subjects were congregated, and were anxiously desirous to pay all proper homage to his majesty their king. Charles originally came from Africa, having, in his infant days, been brought from Angola, in the Guinea gulf; and soon after his arrival became the purchased slave of one of the most ancient and respectable merchant princes of the olden time, then residing on the opposite bank of the Hudson. He was tall, thin and athletic; and although the frost of nearly seventy winters had settled on his brow, its chilling influence had not yet extended to his bosom, and he still retained all the vigor and agility of his younger years. Such were his manly attributes at this present time.

Loud rang the sound of many voices from the neighboring street, shoutingly proclaiming the arrival of the master of the revels, and soon the opening crowd admitted him within their presence, and never, if our memory serve us, shall we forget the mingled sensations of awe and grandeur that were impressed on our youthful minds, when first we beheld his stately form and dignified aspect, slowly moving before us and approaching the centre of the ring. His costume on this memorable occasion was graphic and unique to the greatest degree, being that worn by a British brigadier of the olden time. Ample broadcloth scarlet coat, with wide flaps almost reaching to his heels, and gayly ornamented everywhere with broad tracings of bright golden lace; his small clothes were of yellow buckskin, fresh and new, with stockings blue, and burnished silver buckles to his well-blacked shoe; when we add to these the tri-cornered cocked hat trimmed also with lace of gold, and which so gracefully set upon his noble, globular pate, we nearly complete the rude sketch of the Pinkster king.

The greetings were at length over, and the hour of twelve having arrived, peace and tranquility had once more been partially restored to the multitude; his majesty, the king, was in the midst of his assembled friends and subjects, and the accomplished master of the ceremonies, with his efficient aids were busily employed in making the necessary arrangements to commence the festivities with zeal and earnestness; partners were then selected and led out upon the green, and the dancing was about to commence.

The dance had its peculiarities, as well as everything else connected with this august celebration. It consisted chiefly of couples joining in the performances at varying times, and continuing it with their utmost energy until extreme fatigue or weariness compelled them to retire and give space to a less exhausted set; and in this successive manner was the excitement kept up with unabated vigor, until the shades of night began to fall slowly over the land, and at length deepen into the silent gloom of midnight.

The music made use of on this occasion, was likewise singular in the extreme. The principal instrument selected to furnish this important portion of the ceremony was a symmetrically formed wooden article usually denominated an *eel-pot*, with a cleanly dressed sheep skin drawn tightly over its wide and open e..tremity—no doubt obtained expressly for the occasion from the celebrated *Fish slip*, at the foot of the Maiden's lane. Astride this rude utensil sat Jackey Quackenboss, then in his prime of life and well known energy, beating lustily with his naked hands upon its loudly sounding head, successively repeating the ever wild, though euphonic cry of *Hi-a-bomba,*

bomba, bomba, in full harmony with the thumping sounds. These vocal sounds were readily taken up and as oft repeated by the female portion of the spectators not otherwise engaged in the exercises of the scene, accompanied by the beating of time with their ungloved hands, in strict accordance with the eel-pot melody.

Merrily now the dance moved on, and briskly twirled the lads and lasses over the well trampled green sward; loud and more quickly swelled the sounds of music to the ear, as the excited movements increased in energy and action; rapid and furious became their motions, as the manifold stimulating potions, they from time to time imbibed, vibrated along their brains, and gave a strengthening influence to all their nerves and muscular powers; copiously flowed the perspiration, in frequent streams, from brow to heel, and still the dance went on with all its accustomed energy and might; but the eye at length, becoming weary in gazing on this wild and intricate maze, would oftimes turn and seek relief by searching for the king, amid the dingy mass; and there, enclosed within their midst, was his stately form beheld, moving along with all the simple grace and elastic action of his youthful days, now with a partner here, and then with another there, and sometimes displaying some of his many amusing antics, to the delight and wonderment of the surrounding crowd, and which, as frequently, kept the faces of this joyous multitude broadly expanded in boisterous mirth and jollity. And thus the scene continued until the shades of night and morning almost mingled together, when the wearied revelers slowly retired to their resting places, and quickly sought their nightly repose.

Morning again returned with all its renovating influence, when most of the sable throng were seen loitering along the streets toward the accustomed field of sports; and the bright day moved merrily onward to its close, with all the happy enjoyments of that which had preceded it; and long ere the night had again arrived, the upper class of revelers had left the ground to seek entertainment elsewhere, or spend the evening in tea-party gossip, among their numerous friends and visitors. And thus terminated the third day of the Pinkster festival.

On the succeeding fourth and fifth days, the grounds were left to the free enjoyment of the humbler classes, and well did they improve the time in joyous merriment until near the close of the latter, when, instigated by the more potent draughts they swallowed, speedily brought on wrangling discord, quickly succeeded by rounds of fighting, bruised eyes, and blood noses unnumerated, big Jack Van Patten, the city bully, being unanimously declared the champion of the lists, having successfully overthrown all his numerous opponents.

The last day of the week, and also of the Pinkster revels, was chiefly occupied in removing the unpurchased materials from the field, and also in the distribution of the remaining vestiges of the broken meats and pastries to the poorer classes of individuals who still lingered about the now almost abandoned ground of rejoicing. Some few liquoring establishments still continued their traffic, being amply patronized by the more rude and belligerent number that yet remained, as if loth to leave the endearing spot as long as a stimulating drop could there be procured.

The following sabbath was literally considered by them as really a day of rest, and mid-day's sun was at its height e'er many awoke from their refreshing slumbers, and the succeeding day found the numerous visitors joyfully journeying toward their respective homes. Our ancient city was at length again left to its usual quietude, and all things within its confines soon became properly restored to its accustomed routine of duty and order. And thus ended the Pinkster holidays, with all its rolicking festivities.

8. Isaac W. Stuart

⇛ Slaves of New England established early in the eighteenth century the tradition of electing their own rulers in elaborate ceremonies paralleling those of the white populace. In some places these "officials" were called governors; in New Hampshire, they were called kings. It was said that many claimed descent from genuine kings of Africa. Music was an important element, of course, in "'Lection Day" proceedings. At no place was the celebration more animated than in Hartford, Connecticut. Isaac W. Stuart (1809–61), writing under the pen name of Scaeva, described a typical holiday in one of a series of articles he published first in the *Hartford Daily Courant* and later in book form as *Hartford in the Olden Time: Its First Thirty Years* (Hartford, 1853). Since Hartford was founded in 1636, the events described would have taken place during the second half of the seventeenth century. ⇚

From *Hartford in the Olden Time* [1853] †

BLACK GOVERNORS IN CONNECTICUT

Not a veritable, constitutional black Governor for the whites, Reader—no—but a chief executive black officer, among the blacks, for themselves! We alluded to the circumstances in our Article Third on Hartford, but finding it little understood, we cheerfully comply with a request from several sources to explain it.

For many years previous to the American Revolution, throughout this event, and long after—down nearly to 1820, and perhaps a little later—it was the custom of the negroes of Connecticut, in imitation of the whites, to elect a Governor for themselves. This they generally effected on some day, usually the Saturday next succeeding the Election Day of the whites, and they called it *their* "Lection Day." At this time they were generally assembled in unusual numbers, with their masters, in one of the capitals of the State. They of course made their elec-

† Text: The original edition (Hartford, 1853), pp. 37–39.

tion to a large extent, deputatively, as all could not be present, but uniformly yielded to it their assent—and their confidence was at times so unlimited, that without any choice by themselves, they readily permitted their existing Governor to assign his office over to another one of his color—as will be seen in a case we shall soon quote.

The person they selected for the office in the question, was usually one of much note among themselves, of imposing presence, strength, firmness and volubility, who was quick to decide, ready to command, and able to flog. If he was inclined to be a little arbitrary, belonged to a master of distinction, and was ready to pay freely for diversions— these were circumstances in his favor. Still it was necessary he should be an honest negro, and be, or appear to be, "wise above his fellows." When elected, he had his aids, his parade, and appointed military officers, sheriffs, and justices of the peace. The precise sphere of his power we cannot ascertain. Probably it embraced "matters and things in general" among the blacks, morals, manners, and ceremonies. He settled all grave disputes in the last resort, questioned conduct, and imposed penalties and punishments sometimes for vice or misconduct. He was respected as "Gubernor," say many old gentlemen to us, by the negroes throughout the State, and obeyed almost implicitly.

His parade days were marked by much that was showy, and by some things that were ludicrous. A troop of blacks, sometimes an hundred in number, marching sometimes two and two on foot, sometimes mounted in true military style and dress on horseback, escorted him through the streets, with drums beating, colors flying, and fifes, fiddles, clarionets, and every "sonorous metal" that could be found, "uttering martial sound." After marching to their content, they would retire to some large room which they would engage for the purpose, for refreshments and deliberation. This was all done with the greatest regard to ceremony. His ebony excellency would pass through the files of his procession, supported by his aids, with an air of consummate dignity, to his quarters, and there receive the congratulations of his friends, and dispense the favor of his salutations, his opinions and his appointments. . . .

9. Benjamin Henry B. Latrobe

➤➤➤ In the exotic city of New Orleans, long before the Louisiana Territory was annexed to the United States in 1803, slaves established the custom of dancing in the Place Congo (now Beauregard Square) on Sunday afternoons, and continued it through the first half of the nineteenth century. Of the several contemporary descriptions of the dancing, that of the architect-engineer Benjamin Henry Boneval Latrobe (1764–1820) is richest in musical details. Latrobe, born in England, emigrated to the United States in 1793. His activity as one of the most distinguished architects of the nineteenth century included building the first cathedral in the United States (in Baltimore) and designing the south wing of the Capitol building. After the Capitol was destroyed during the War of 1812, Latrobe supervised its reconstruction.

Like many learned men of the time, Latrobe kept a journal, which he filled with scientific observations, pen sketches, and creative writing, as well as everyday notes. In 1876 his son, John Hazelhurst Boneval Latrobe, edited the journal and added an introduction, but the work was not published until 1905. ◀◀◀

From *Journal of Latrobe* [1905] †

This long dissertation has been suggested by my accidentally stumbling upon an assembly of negroes, which, I am told, every Sunday afternoon meets on the Common in the rear of the city. My object was to take a walk on the bank of the Canal Carondelet as far as the Bayou St. John. In going up St. Peter's Street and approaching the Common, I heard a most extraordinary noise, which I supposed to proceed from some horse-mill—the horses tramping on a wooden floor. I found, however, on emerging from the house to the Common that it proceeded from a crowd of five or six hundred persons, assembled in an open space or public square. I went to the spot and crowded near enough to see the performance. All those who were engaged in the business seemed to be blacks. I did not observe a

† Text: The original edition (New York, 1905), pp. 179–81.

dozen yellow faces. They were formed into circular groups, in the midst of four of which that I examined (but there were more of them) was a ring, the largest not ten feet in diameter. In the first were two women dancing. They held each a coarse handkerchief, extended by the corners, in their hands, and set to each other in a miserably dull and slow figure, hardly moving their feet or bodies. The music consisted of two drums and a stringed instrument. An old man sat astride of a cylindrical drum, about a foot in diameter, and beat it with incredible quickness with the edge of his hand and fingers. The other drum was an open-staved thing held between the knees and beaten in the same manner. They made an incredible noise. The most curious instrument, however, was a stringed instrument, which no doubt was imported from Africa. On the top of the finger board was the rude figure of a man in a sitting posture, and two pegs behind him to which the strings were fastened. The body was a calabash. It was played upon by a very little old man, apparently eighty or ninety years old. The women squalled out a burden to the playing, at intervals, consisting of two notes, as the negroes working in our cities respond to the song of their leader. Most of the circles contained the same sort of dances. One was larger, in which a ring of a dozen women walked, by way of dancing, round the music in the center. But the instruments were of different construction. One which from the color of the wood seemed new, consisted of a block cut into something of the form of a cricket bat, with a long and deep mortise down the center. This thing made a considerable noise, being beaten lustily on the side by a short stick. In the same orchestra was a square drum, looking like a stool, which made an abominable, loud noise; also a calabash with a round hole in it, the hold studded with brass nails, which was beaten by a woman with two short sticks. A man sung an uncouth song to the dancing, which I suppose was in some African language, for it was not French, and the women screamed a detestable burden on one single note. The allowed amusements of Sunday have, it seems, perpetuated here those of Africa among its former inhabitants. . . .

IV. Religious Music in the Nineteenth Century

10. RICHARD ALLEN

➤➤➤ In 1787, because of racial discrimination, a group of dissident black Methodists withdrew from historic Old St. George's Methodist Episcopal Church in Philadelphia and formed the African Free Society. From this organization came two independent Negro congregations: the St. Thomas African Episcopal Church, led by Absalom Jones, and the Bethel African Methodist Episcopal Church, led by Richard Allen (1760–1831). Bethel was dedicated on July 29, 1794. Eventually the church severed all connections with the established Methodist Church and set up branches in other cities, thus becoming the first independent Negro religious denomination in the United States. In 1816 the A. M. E. Church held its first General Conference and elected Allen its first bishop.

One of Allen's initial acts as the minister of Bethel was to compile a collection of hymns for the exclusive use of his congregation. Two editions appeared in 1801, the first entitled *A Collection of Spiritual Songs and Hymns Selected from Various Authors by Richard Allen, African Minister* (printed by John Ormrod), and the second, *A Collection of Hymns and Spiritual Songs from Various Authors, by Richard Allen, Minister of the African Methodist Episcopal Church* (printed by T. L. Plowman). To the fifty-four hymns of the first edition, ten more were added in the second.

Richard Allen's hymnal is of historic significance for several reasons. It was the first hymnbook compiled by a black man for use by a black congregation. As a "folk-selected" anthology, it indicates which hymns were popular among black Methodists at the beginning of the nineteenth century. Many of these hymns served as source material for the spirituals of the slaves—the so-called Negro spirituals. To phrases, couplets, and stanzas culled from favorite hymns, the slaves added other verses and refrains to compose the texts of their spirituals. Finally, according to all evidence, Allen's hymnal is apparently the earliest source in history that includes hymns to which choruses or refrains are attached. ◄◄◄

From A Collection of Hymns and Spiritual Songs
[1801] †

TABLE OF CONTENTS

† Text: The second, enlarged printing, Philadelphia, 1801. (To consult microprint copies in public libraries, see the Shaw-Shoemaker *Early American Imprints,* Series No. 2 [1801–20], Nos. 38 and 39.) None of the hymns is provided with an author or an indication of the music to which it should be sung. My author identifications, which are bracketed in this Table of Contents, were obtained through concordances.

No. I

1. The voice of Free Grace cries, escape to the mountain,
   For Adam's lost race Christ hath open'd a fountain,
   For sin and transgression, and every pollution,
   His blood it flows freely in plenteous redemption.
   Refrain:
   Hallelujah to the Lamb who purchas'd our pardon,
   We'll praise him again when we pass over Jordan.

2. That fountain so clear, in which all may find pardon,
   From Jesus's side flows plenteous redemption,
   Though your sins were increas'd as high as a mountain,
   His blood it flows freely in streams of salvation.

   Hallelujah to the Lamb, etc.

3. Oh! Jesus ride on, thy kingdom is glorious,
   O'er sin, death and Hell, thow wilt make us victorious:
   Thy name shall be prais'd in the great congregation,
   And saints shall delight in ascribing salvation.

   Hallelujah to the Lamb, etc.

4. When on Zion we stand, having gain'd the blest shore,
   With our harps in our hands we'll praise him evermore;
   We'll range the blest fields on the bank of the river,
   And sing Hallelujah for ever and ever.

   Hallelujah to the Lamb, etc.

No. X

1. Behold the awful trumpet sounds,
     The sleeping dead to raise,
   And calls the nations underground:
     O how the saints will praise!

2. Behold the Saviour how he comes
     Descending from his throne
   To burst asunder all our tombs
     And lead his children home.

3. But who can bear that dreadful day,
     To see the world in flames:
   The burning mountains melt away,
     While rocks run down in streams.

4. The falling stars their orbits leave,
     The sun in darkness hide:
   The elements asunder cleave,
     The moon turn'd into blood!

5. Behold the universal world
     In consternation stand,
   The wicked into Hell are turn'd
     The Saints at God's right hand.

6. O then the music will begin
     Their Saviour God to praise,
   They are all freed from every sin
     And thus they'll spend their days!

No. XI

1. What poor despised company
   Of travellers are these,
   That's walking yonder narrow way,
   Along that rugged maze?

2. Why they are of a royal line,
   They're children of a King;
   Heirs of immortal crown divine,
   And loud for joy they sing.

3. Why do they then appear so mean,
   And why so much despis'd,
   Because of their rich robes unseen
   The world is not appriz'd.

4. Why some of them seem poor distress'd
   And lacking daily bread;
   Heirs of immortal wealth possess'd
   With hidden Manna fed.

5. Why do they shun that pleasant path,
   Which worldings love so well?
   Because it is the road to death,
   The open way to hell.

6. Why do they walk that narrow road
   Along that rugged maze?
   Because this way their leader trod,
   They love and keep his ways.

7. Why is there then no other road
   To Salem's happy ground?
   Christ is the only way to God,
   No other can be found.

No. XXVI

1. When I can read my title clear
   To mansions in the skies,
   I'll bid farewell to ev'ry fear,
   And wipe my weeping eyes.

2. Should earth against my soul engage,
   And hellist darts be hurl'd,
   Then I can smile at Satan's rage
   And face a frowning world.

3. Let care, like a wild deluge come,
    And storms of sorrow fall;
  May I but safely reach my home,
    My God, my heav'n, my all:

4. There shall I bathe my weary soul,
    In seas of heav'nly rest,
  And not a wave of trouble roll
    Across my peaceful breast.

No. XXVII

1. There is a land of pure delight,
    Where saints immortal reign.
  Infinite day excludes the night,
    And pleasures banish pain.

2. There everlasting Spring abides.
    And never-with'ring flow'rs:
  Death, like a narrow sea divides
    This heav'nly land from ours.

3. Sweet fields beyond the swelling flood,
    Stand dress'd in living green;
  So, to the Jews, old Canaan stood,
    While Jordan roll'd between.

4. But tim'rous mortals start and shrink,
    To cross this narrow sea,
  And linger, shiv'ring on the brink,
    And fear to launch away.

5. Oh! could we make our doubts remove
    Those gloomy doubts that rise
  And see the Canaan that we love,
    With unbeclouded eyes!

6. Could we but climb where Moses stood,
    And view the landscape o'er,
  Not Jordan's stream, nor death's cold flood,
    Should fright us from the shore.

No. XLV

1. Now the Saviour stands a pleading
    At the sinner's bolted heart
  Now in heaven is interceding,
    Undertaking sinners part.

Chorus
Sinners can you hate that Saviour,
　　Can you thrust him from your arms;
Here he died for your behaviour,
　　Now he calls you to his charms.

2. Now he pleads his sweat and bloodshed,
　　Shews his wounded hands and feet
Father save them tho' they're blood red,
　　Raise them to an heavenly seat.

Sinners, etc., etc.

3. Sinners hear your God and Saviour,
　　Hear his gracious voice today;
Turn from all your base behaviour,
　　Now return, repent, and pray.

Sinners, etc., etc.

4. Open now your hearts before him,
　　Bid your Saviour welcome in;
Now receive, and love, adore him,
　　Take a full discharge from sin.

Sinners, etc., etc.

5. Now he's waiting to be gracious,
　　Now he stands and looks on thee:
See what kindness, love, and pity,
　　Shines around, on you and me.

Sinners, etc., etc.

6. Come! for all things now are ready
　　Yet there's room for many more.
O ye blind, ye lame, and needy,
　　Come to grace's boundless shore.

Sinners, etc., etc.

No. L

1. From regions of Love, lo! an angel descended,
　　And told the strange news, how the babe was attended!
　　"Go shepherds, and visit this wonderful stranger,
　　"See yonder bright star—there's your God in a manger!"

> Hallelujah to the Lamb
> Who has purchas'd our pardon,
> We will praise him again
> When we pass over Jordan.

2. Glad tidings I bring unto you and each nation,
   Glad tidings of joy, now behold your salvation:
   Then sudden a multitude raise their glad voices,
   And shout the Redeemer, while Heaven rejoices.

> Hallelujah, etc.

3. Now glory to God in the highest is given,
   Now glory to God, is re-echo'd thro' Heaven:
   Around the whole earth let us tell the glad story,
   And sing of his love, his salvation, and glory.

> Hallelujah, etc.

4. Enraptur'd I burn with delight and desire,
   Such love, so divine, sets my soul all on fire:
   Around the bright throne now hosannas are ringing,
   O, when shall I join them, and ever be singing?

> Hallelujah, etc.

5. Triumphantly ride they in chariot victorious,
   And conquer with love, O Jesu, all-glorious:
   Thy banners unfurl, let the nations surrender,
   And own thee their Saviour, their God, and defender.

> Hallelujah . . .

No. LVI

1. Hail the gospel jubilee,
   Jesus comes to set us free,
   Who for us shed his precious blood
   To raise our fallen souls to God,
   And since the work of suffering's death,
   We'll glory give to God alone.
   > Free salvation be our boast
   > Ever mindful what it cost,
   > Ever grateful for the prize,
   > Let our praises reach the skies.

Chorus
Firm united let us be,
In the bonds of charity:
As a band of brothers join'd,
Loving God and all mankind.

2. Rise ye heralds of the Lord,
Take the breast-plate, shield and sword,
Against the hosts of hell proclaim
A war in Christ's all conquering name,
Nor fear to gain the victory
When for this glorious liberty,
You on Jesus Christ depend
He'll the suffering cause defend,
Place, O place in him your trust
He's almighty, wise, and just.

Chorus
Firm united brethren stand,
Firm an undivided band.
Brethren dear in Jesus join'd
Fill'd with all his constant mind.

3. Sound the gospel trumpet sound
Through the earth's remotest bound;
Let Jesus' name, with loud applause,
Ring thro' the world his righteous laws
He gives, and rules in mercy mild.
Believe, and be ye reconciled
To a God of truth and love,
Sending blessings from above
Now is the accepted time,
Listen every joyful chime.

Chorus
Hail the Gospel jubilee,
Jesus comes to set us free.
He is come no more to bleed
Free we then shall be indeed.

4. Now the sovereign of the sky
Comes, the troops of hell multiply.
He is the rock of ages sure,
And all who to the end endure:
A glorious crown of righteousness
Shall wear in realms of endless bliss.

There with blood-wash'd throngs above,
Wondering at redeeming love,
Evermore will shout and sing,
Heaven's palace loud shall ring.

Chorus
Firm united let us go,
On in Jesus' steps below,
As a band of brothers join,
And eternal glory find.

11. John F. Watson

→≫ The earliest references to the original religious songs of blacks—as distinguished from the standard Protestant hymns that they sang—occur in writings of men who lived or visited in Philadelphia at the beginning of the nineteenth century. Later, these songs would be called "Negro spirituals," but during the first decades of the nineteenth century there was no label for these religious songs, which were strikingly similar in poetic form, musical structure, and mood to the songs sung by slaves at their frolics and jubilees. Churchmen were shocked by the songs and made strenuous efforts to discourage the blacks from singing them. They were even more outraged over a religious dance practiced by the blacks, the music for which consisted of such songs accompanied by clapping and striking of the thighs and legs. Later in the century, the dance would be called a "shout" and the striking of the body, "pattin'" or "pattin' juba."

Among the several books published during the period, a work by John F. Watson, *Methodist Error or Friendly Christian Advice to Those Methodists Who Indulge in Extravagant Religious Emotions and Bodily Exercises* (Trenton, 1819), contains one of the most vivid descriptions of early Negro spirituals and the shout. Watson's reference to the "illiterate *blacks* of the [Methodist] society" obviously point to the followers of Richard Allen, the dominant black Methodists in the Philadelphia Conference at the time. In their own churches, freed from the supervision of white clergymen, these black Methodists developed their own distinctive body of religious songs in response to their own special needs. ≪←

From *Methodist Error* [1819] †

We have too, a growing evil, in the practice of singing in our places of public and society worship, *merry* airs, adapted from old *songs*, to hymns of our composing: often miserable as poetry, and

† Text: The original edition (Trenton, 1819), pp. 28–31. Courtesy of the Huntington Library, San Marino, California.

senseless as matter,[1] and most frequently composed and first sung by the illiterate *blacks* of the society. Thus instead of inculcating sober christianity in them who have least wisdom to govern themselves; lifting them into spiritual pride and to an undue estimation of their usefulness: overlooking too the counsel of Mr. Wesley, who has solemnly expressed his opinion in his book of hymns, as already amply sufficient for all our purposes of rational devotion: not at all regarding his condemnation of this very practice, for which among other things he actually expelled three ministers (Maxwell, Bell and Owen . . .) for singing "*poor, bald, flat, disjointed hymns:* and like the people in Wales, singing the same verse over and over again with all their might 30 or 40 times, "to the utter discredit of all sober christianity;" neglecting too, the counsel of Dr. Clarke in this matter, "never to sing hymns of your own composing in public, (these are also the very words of injunction of our own Discipline . . .) unless you be a first rate poet, such as can only occur in every ten or twenty *millions* of men; for it argues incurable vanity." Such singing as has been described, has we know, been ordinarily sung in most of our prayer and camp meetings: sometimes two or three at a time in succession. In the meantime, one and another of musical feelings, and consonant animal spirits, has been heard stepping the merry strains with all the precision of an avowed *dancer.* Here ought to be considered too, a most exceptionable error, which has the tolerance at least of the rulers of our camp meetings. In the *blacks'* quarter, the coloured people get together, and sing for hours together, short scraps of disjointed affirmations, pledges, or prayers, lengthened out with long repetition *choruses.* These are all sung in the merry chorus-manner of the southern harvest field, or husking-frolic method, of the slave blacks; and also very greatly like the Indian dances. With every word so sung, they have a sinking of one or other leg of the body alternately; producing an audible sound of the feet at every step, and as manifest as the steps of actual negro dancing in Virginia, &c. If some, in the meantime sit, they strike the sounds alternately on each thigh. What in the name of religion, can countenance or tolerate such gross perversions of true religion! but the evil is only occasionally condemned, and the example has already visibly affected the religious manners of

1. "Touch but one string, 'twill make heaven ring," is of this character. What string is that which can effect this! Who can give any sense to it? Take another case: "Go shouting all your days," in connexion with "glory, glory, glory," in which go shouting is repeated six times in succession. Is there one particle of sense in its connexion with the general matter of the hymn? and are they not mere idle expletives, filled in to eke out the tunes? They are just exactly parallel to "go *screaming, jumping,* (or any other participle) *all your days! O splendour, splendour.*" Do those who are delighted with such things, consider what delights them? Some times too, they are from such impure sources, as I am actually ashamed to name in this place.

some whites. From this cause, I have known in some camp meetings, from 50 to 60 people crowd into one tent, after the public devotions had closed, and there continue the whole night, singing tune after tune, (though with occasional episodes of prayer) scarce one of which were in our hymn books.[2] Some of these from their nature, (having very long repetition choruses and short scraps of matter) are actually composed as sung, and are indeed almost endless.

2. It is worthy of remark, that not one of our appointed hymns under the article "rejoicing and praise," nor among the "new hymns," have any hymns of this character, therefore they who want them most, have to forsake that standard.

12. Daniel Alexander Payne

→→→ Born of free Negro parents in Charleston, South Carolina, Daniel Alexander Payne (1811–93) received a fairly good education according to the standards of the time. In 1829 he opened a school for free black children, but was forced to close it in 1834 when South Carolina passed a law prohibiting the education of *all* blacks, whether free or enslaved. Payne left for the North and was persuaded by friends in New York to study for the ministry. His long career in the African Methodist Episcopal Church, which he joined in 1841, included service as minister, church historian, college president (Wilberforce University), and bishop. Payne's observations on musical practices in the churches of his denomination, as set down in *Recollections of Seventy Years* (Nashville, 1888), are lively and penetrating. It seems fair to assume that such practices were common to most independent black churches of the nineteenth century. ←←←

From *Recollections of Seventy Years* [1888] †

In the department of Church music, both instrumental and vocal, the most remarkable improvements and progress have taken place within the last forty years. The first introduction of choral singing into the A. M. E. Church took place in Bethel, Philadelphia, Pa., between 1841 and 1842. It gave great offense to the older members, especially those who had professed personal sanctification. Said they: "You have brought the devil into the Church, and therefore we will go out." So, suiting the action to the word, many went out of Bethel, and never returned. These well-meaning people must be pitied rather than censured. They acted according to their convictions—according to the light which they had taken into their intellects. But that light was darkness; hence their convictions were false, erroneous, destructive.

Here we pause to remark that an individual man or woman must never follow conviction in regard to moral, religious, civil, or political questions until they are first tested by the unerring word of God. If a

† Text: The original edition (Nashville, 1888), pp. 233–38, 253–55.

conviction infringes upon the written word of God, or in any manner conflicts with that word, the conviction is not to be followed. It is our duty to abandon it. Moreover, I will add that light on a doubtful conviction is not to be sought for in the conscience, but in the Bible. The conscience, like the conviction, may be blind, erroneous, misled, or perverted; therefore it is not always a safe guide. The only safe guide for a man or woman, young or old, rich or poor, learned or unlearned, priest or people is the Bible, the whole Bible, nothing but the Bible.

Had these self-called sanctified ones been Bible-readers—Bereans instead of mere African Methodists—they never would have called choral singing the "devil;" they never would have forsaken that Church in the bosom of which they had been reared, convicted, converted, and sanctified—if sanctified at all. So great was the excitement and irritation produced by the introduction of the choir into Bethel Church that I, then a local preacher and school-master, was requested by the leader of the choir and other prominent members in it to preach a special sermon on sacred music. This I did as best I could. In my researches I used a small monograph on music written by Mr. Wesley, but drew my information chiefly from the word of God. The immediate effect of that discourse was to check the excitement, soothe the irritation, and set the most intelligent to reading as they had never done before.

Similar excitements and irritations, resulting in withdrawals and small splits, followed the introduction of choral singing in the majority of our Churches—not in the cities only, but in the large towns and villages also. Rev. Elisha Weaver, stationed in Chicago, was impeached in 1857 by his Board for introducing vocal and instrumental music into his Church, and at the Annual Conference of that year an animated discussion followed, relative to a resolution declaring instrumental music detrimental to the spiritual interests of the Church. But now it is the aim of every Church in the Connection to have a good choir.

The moral and religious effects of choral singing have been good, especially when the whole or a majority of the choir were earnest Christians. I have witnessed spiritual effects produced by Bethel choir in Philadelphia, and by Bethel choir in Baltimore, equal to the most unctuous sermons from the lips of the most eloquent and earnest preachers, so that Christians did rejoice as though they were listening to the heavenly choir which the shepherds heard on the plains of Bethlehem announcing the advent of the Saviour.

Instrumental music was introduced into our denomination in the year 1848–9. It commenced at Bethel, in Baltimore, under the following circumstances: We had erected the present grand house of

God in 1848, at a cost of about fifteen thousand five hundred dollars. We had paid, at its completion and dedication, five thousand of it, and had eight years in which to pay the remainder, which was divided into eight equal notes. Immediately after the dedication dissensions arose among its officers. While the new church was in progress, as I have stated elsewhere, Ebenezer Chapel was sold to its Church-members for the nominal sum of ten dollars, which fact, and the signing of transfer documents, produced so much antagonism among the trustees of Bethel as to render the raising of the first note uncertain; so it was deemed prudent and wise to resort to extraordinary measures in order to raise the sum needed. This was a concert of sacred music under the management of Dr. James Fleet, of Georgetown, D. C., whose musical taste was exquisite. The lyrics were composed by myself in order that I might be certain that nothing incongruous in sentiment to the sanctuary should go into it. The novelty of the measure was a powerful attraction. It filled Bethel to overflowing, produced a fine effect, and gave us three hundred dollars net. The next sacred concert held in Bethel was for a similar purpose, and consisted of seven stringed instruments, the conductor being Mr. William Appo, then the most learned musician of the race. As in the former concert, so in this, all the music was sacred. After this the members of Bethel Church were convinced that instrumental music could be as fully consecrated to the service of the living God under the New Testament dispensation as it was under Old Testament, when King David wrote the following rapturous Psalm:

> Praise ye the Lord.
> Praise God in his sanctuary: praise him in the
>   firmament of his power.
> Praise him for his mighty acts:
> Praise him according to his excellent greatness.
> Praise him with the sound of the trumpet:
> Praise him with the psaltery and harp.
> Praise him with the timbrel and dance: [1]
> Praise him with stringed instruments and organs.
> Praise him upon the loud cymbals:
> Praise him upon the high-sounding cymbals.
> Let every thing that hath breath praise the Lord.
> Praise ye the Lord.[2]

By reading and studying the one hundred and forty-eighth Psalm some of the reasons will be seen why David wrote and doubtless set to music the one hundred and fiftieth Psalm. In this one hundred

1. Not our vulgar dance, but an instrument by that name. Dr. Clarke called it the "pipe."
2. This arrangement is according to the French version by Louis Segond, D.D., of Geneva, Switzerland.

and forty-eighth Psalm the inspired poet calls upon all creation to praise the Lord—all animate and inanimate, all the works of God in the heaven of heavens, all the works of God in the earth and ocean. If he is right and pious in this psalm, who will dare to say that he is not right and pious in the one hundred and fiftieth Psalm? If it be right to call upon all the works of God to praise him, why not call upon all the works of men to praise him? Man is a product of God's wisdom and power; therefore he should be called upon to praise God with his mouth. The instruments are the product of man's genius and skill. Why not use the sounds of these instruments to praise the Creator?

A choir, with instruments as an accompaniment, can be made a powerful and efficient auxiliary to the pulpit. Two things are essential to the saving power and efficiency of choral music—a scientific training and an earnest Christianity. Two things are necessary to make choral singing always profitable to a Church—that the congregation shall always join in singing with the choir, and that they shall always sing with the spirit and the understanding.

In a musical direction what progress has been made within the last forty years! There is not a Church of ours in any of the great cities of the republic that can afford to buy an instrument which is without one; and there are but few towns or villages where our Connection exists that are without an instrument to accompany the choir. What is true of the Church is also true of the homestead. Every pastor and bishop who loves music and can afford to buy an instrument has one of some kind to make his household joyous and happy. . . .

In May it was my privilege to visit the Sunday-school of Old Bethel, in Philadelphia, and at a meeting of the Sunday-school teachers I conducted responsive reading of the First and Second Psalms of David. I showed them how England had become great by habitually making her people read the Scriptures on Sunday in the great congregations; and how the colored race, who had been oppressed for centuries through ignorance and superstition, might become intelligent, Christian, and powerful through the enlightening and sanctifying influences of the word of God. I also stated that thereafter, by my orders, every pastor occupying the pulpit of Bethel should make responsive readings of the Holy Scriptures a part of the public worship. Bethel Church about this time had set about furnishing the music-room at our university [i.e. Wilberforce], which they completed by June.

I have mentioned the "Praying and Singing Bands" elsewhere. The strange delusion that many ignorant but well-meaning people labor under leads me to speak particularly of them. About this time I attended a "bush meeting," where I went to please the pastor whose circuit I was visiting. After the sermon they formed a ring, and with coats off sung, clapped their hands and stamped their feet in a most ridiculous and heathenish way. I requested the pastor to go and stop their dancing. At his request they stopped their dancing and clapping of hands, but remained singing and rocking their bodies to and fro. This they did for about fifteen minutes. I then went, and taking their leader by the arm requested him to desist and to sit down and sing in a rational manner. I told him also that it was a heathenish way to worship and disgraceful to themselves, the race, and the Christian name. In that instance they broke up their ring; but would not sit down, and walked sullenly away. After the sermon in the afternoon, having another opportunity of speaking alone to this young leader of the singing and clapping ring, he said: "Sinners won't get converted unless there is a ring." Said I: "You might sing till you fell down dead, and you would fail to convert a single sinner, because nothing but the Spirit of God and the word of God can convert sinners." He replied: "The Spirit of God works upon people in different ways. At camp-meeting there must be a ring here, a ring there, a ring over yonder, or sinners will not get converted." This was his idea, and it is also that of many others. These "Bands" I have had to encounter in many places, and, as I have stated in regard to my early labors in Baltimore, I have been strongly censured because of my efforts to change the mode of worship or modify the extravagances indulged in by the people. In some cases all that I could do was to teach and preach the right, fit, and proper way of serving God. To the most thoughtful and intelligent I usually succeeded in making the "Band" disgusting; but by the ignorant masses, as in the case mentioned, it was regarded as the essence of religion. So much so was this the case that, like this man, they believe no conversion could occur without their agency, nor outside of their own ring could any be a genuine one. Among some of the songs of these "Rings," or "Fist and Heel Worshipers," as they have been called, I find a note of two in my journal, which were used in the instance mentioned. As will be seen, they consisted chiefly of what are known as "corn-field ditties:"

> "Ashes to ashes, dust to dust;
> If God won't have us, the devil must.

> "I was way over there where the coffin fell;
> I heard that sinner as he screamed in hell."

To indulge in such songs from eight to ten and half-past ten at night was the chief employment of these "Bands." Prayer was only a secondary thing, and this was rude and extravagant to the last degree. The man who had the most powerful pair of lungs was the one who made the best prayer, and he could be heard a square off. He who could sing loudest and longest led the "Band," having his loins girded and a handkerchief in hand with which he kept time, while his feet resounded on the floor like the drum-sticks of a bass drum. In some places it was the custom to begin these dances after every night service and keep it up till midnight, sometimes singing and dancing alternately—a short prayer and a long dance. Some one has even called it the "Voudoo Dance." I have remonstrated with a number of pastors for permitting these practices, which vary somewhat in different localities, but have been invariably met with the response that he could not succeed in restraining them, and an attempt to compel them to cease would simply drive them away from our Church.

V. Music on the Plantation

13. JAMES HUNGERFORD

≫ Little is known about James Hungerford except that he was born in 1811, probably in Baltimore, Maryland. At the time that he visited the plantation of his cousin in the summer of 1832, he was a law student. He seems also to have been an amateur musician, for in his book *The Old Plantation and What I Gathered There in an Autumn Month* [of 1832] (New York, 1859) he recorded the music and texts of two slave songs. Hungerford's book is thus apparently the earliest extant source of slave songs. Predictably, his writing is tinged with the unconscious racism of the slaveholder, but the book is useful for its excellent descriptions of the various kinds of slave music heard on plantations—the songs, slave dance music, and fiddling for dances of the slaveholders. ≪

From *The Old Plantation* [1859] †

In the summer of 1832 the Asiatic Cholera raged fearfully in Baltimore. . . . At that time I was in my twenty-first year, and was, I think, as light-hearted a being as ever breathed. Singularly enough, I had no dread of the pestilence; and being engaged in the study of the law, to which I was enthusiastically attached, it was with some reluctance that I heard my father announce his intention of closing our city house and removing his family to our country-place in one of the southern counties of Maryland. For my own part, I accepted the invitation of a male cousin of mine, some years older than myself, to pass a month or two at his father's plantation in the same county. . . .

A negro girl met us at the door. Her dress was neat, and her whole appearance was tidy; yet she looked exceedingly strange. Her complexion was essential black ultimated; her features were very regular for one of her race, her teeth white, her form symmetrical; but her eyes, remarkably bright, with a wild, unsettled glance, gave to her whole countenance a weird, or rather elfish expression.

† Text: The original edition (New York, 1859), pp. 99–101, 183–85, 190–99, 251–53.

"Marse Lucy un Miss Clarence," was the singular address given to us by this girl, "dinner's ready on de table for you."

Whereupon she carried herself in a whirling dance-like motion around us to take the same message to Cousin Walter, who still sat under the shade.

"Who is that queer being?" I asked of Cousin Lucy.

"Her name is Clotilda. Your fellow-passenger, Mr. Worthington, says that under 'expanding circumstances' she might have been a genius; in her present condition she is only eccentric. She can make you rhymes all day long, and is a great help to the corn-bank singers, furnishing them with any number of jingling lines for the corn-husking season, and with tunes for them too; for she can make melodies as well as rhymes."

"I should like to hear her rhyme, and sing her own original airs also."

"Oh, she does not rhyme for the asking, but only when in the wood, and then whether asked or not. As to her singing, she has such an unearthly, screeching voice, that those who can not prevent her music run away from it. She is only listened to by the negroes willingly when she is teaching them a new tune."

"She is quite an original; I should like to know more of her."

"You will have opportunities enough before your visit is over."

At this moment Cousin Walter joined us, and we went in to dinner. . . .

We left Crystal Cave about an hour and a half before sunset. Until we got out of the cave the motion of the boat was smooth and steady; but when we dashed out upon the creek she rose and fell with swell and subsidence of the water. The ladies—all of whom had frequently been upon the water—bore this quietly enough, and were lively and talkative; but when we came out upon the larger and rougher waves of the river they became silent and began to look serious.

"This is getting dull," said the major, after the silence had lasted some minutes. "Come Charley, give us a song to enliven us a little."

In obedience to this order, Charley struck up a song; the other oarsmen answered in chorus, all timing the strokes of their oars to the measure. The song was not by any means enlivening, however, either in words or tune. . . .

Sold Off to Georgy

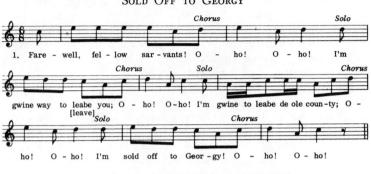

1. Fare - well, fel - low sar - vants! O - ho! O - ho! I'm gwine way to leabe you; O - ho! O-ho! I'm gwine to leabe de ole coun-ty; O - ho! O - ho! I'm sold off to Geor-gy! O - ho! O - ho!

2. Farewell, ole plantation, (Oho! Oho!)
   Farewell, de ole quarter, (Oho! Oho!)
   Un daddy, un mammy, (Oho! Oho!)
   Un marster, un missus! (Oho! Oho!)

3. My dear wife un one chile, (Oho! Oho!)
   My poor heart is breaking; (Oho! Oho!)
   No more shall I see you, (Oho! Oho!)
   Oh! no more foreber! (Oho! Oho!)

The reader will observe that the lines of the song do not rhyme; and it may be remarked that the negro songs—that is, such as they can compose themselves—are mostly without rhymes. When they do attempt to rhyme they frequently take more than the poetic license, being satisfied—when they can not do better—if the vowel-sounds at the ends of the lines agree.

The tone of voice in which this boat-song was sung was inexpressibly plaintive, and, bearing such a melancholy tune, and such affecting words, produced a very pathetic effect. I saw tears in the eyes of the young ladies, and could scarcely restrain my own. We heard but the three verses given (such songs are sometimes stretched out to many verses); for at the end of the third verse the major interrupted the song.

"Confound such *lively* music," he exclaimed; "it is making the girls cry, I do believe. And with such slow measure to sing to, we shall scarcely get into Weatherby's Creek tonight."

"De boat-songs is always dat way, marster," said Charley—"dat is mo' er less."

"Well, try to find something better than that," said the major; "I am sure that it is impossible for any thing to be more low-spirited in words, or tune, or manner of singing."

"Yas, marster," was Charley's answer. And the negroes sang another boat-song, but not so very sad as their first.

"Charley is right," said Miss Bettie, with a laugh; "the boat-songs are 'all that way, more or less.' I think that we had better have silence than such low-spirited music. Do you not think so, uncle?"

"Entirely," said the major. "The pathetic is well enough when there is need of stirring up our feelings of humanity, but I can see no use in creating mere low spirits."

"I like the music," said Lizzie; "it is sometimes pleasant—if I may speak such a seeming paradox—to be made sad without any personal cause for being so. Such a state of feeling may be called 'the luxury of woe.' " . . .

We had some time before rounded Point Quiet, the long point to the south of the Flats, and had nearly gained the channels leading into Weatherby's Creek. Our boat was now speeding at a swift rate along a lee shore; and the water, shielded from the wind by the high cliffs of the river, lay tranquil around us.

"How clear the water is," remarked Miss Susan, looking over the side of the boat; "I can see the fishes moving among the sea-grass on the bottom."

"Our river is famous for the purity of the water," said the major, with some enthusiasm of manner, "and has been said by those who are competent to give an opinion, to be one of the most beautiful streams in the world."

"I have been told," observed Lizzie, "that its present title is a literal interpretation of the name given to it by the Indians."

"So they say," answered the old gentleman; "and the red men were sensible in that at any rate. But let us have some music; I always like to hear singing when on the water. Lizzie, will you sing us the Canadian Boat Song? Bettie and Susan do not sing, they say."

"I will, with pleasure," replied Lizzie, "if Clarence will assist me with his voice."

So we sang, keeping time to the action of the oars.

"Charley looks as if he would sing us another song," said Miss Bettie. "What is that lively little song, Charley, which I heard you and some of the hands sing the other day, when you were hanging tobacco at the barn? I am sure that you can row to that."

"Sure unnuff, young misstis," answered Charley; "I had forgot dat. But dat's a corn song; un we'll hab ter sing it slow ter row to."

"Try it, at any rate," said the major.

"Sartinly, sah, ef de marsters un mistisses wants it."

Charley was evidently somewhat vexed at the disparaging remarks made by the petitioners on his previous performance. Nevertheless, there came a quiet smile to his face as he began the following song:

Roun' De Corn, Sally

Chorus *Solo*

1. Hoo-ray, hoo-ray, ho! Roun' de corn, Sal - ly! Hoo-ray for all de lub-ly la-dies!
[lovely]

Chorus *Solo* *Chorus*

Roun' de corn, Sal - ly! Hoo-ray, hoo-ray, ho! Roun' de corn, Sal - ly!

Solo *Chorus* *Fine*

Hoo - ray for all de lub - ly la - dies! Roun' de corn, Sal - ly!

Solo *Chorus*

Dis lub's er thing dat's sure to hab you, Roun' de corn, Sal - ly!

Solo *Chorus*

He hole you tight, when once he grab you, Roun' de corn, Sal - ly!

Solo *Chorus*

Un ole un ug - ly, young un prit - ty, Roun' de corn, Sal - ly!

Solo *Chorus* *D. C.*

You need - en try when once he git you, Roun' de corn, Sal - ly!

2. Dere's Mr. Travers lub Miss Jinny;
   He thinks she is us good us any.
   He comes from church wid her er Sunday,
   Un don't go back ter town till Monday.
       Hooray, hooray, ho! etc.

3. Dere's Mr. Lucas lub Miss T'reser,
   Un ebery thing he does ter please her;
   Dey say dat 'way out in Ohio,
   She's got er plenty uv de rhino.
       Hooray, hooray, ho! etc.

4. Dere's Marster Charley lub Miss Bettie;
   I tell you what—he thinks her pretty;
   Un den dey mean ter lib so lordly,
   All at de Monner House at Audley.
       Hooray, hooray, ho! etc.

5. Dere's Marster Wat, he lub Miss Susan;
   He thinks she is de pick un choosin';
   Un when dey gains de married station,
   He'll take her to de ole plantation.
   Hooray, hooray, ho! etc.

6. Dere's Marster Clarence lub Miss Lizzy;
   Dressing nice, it keeps him busy;
   Un where she goes den he gallants her,
   Er riding on his sorrel prancer.
   Hooray, hooray, ho! etc.

This song caused much amusement at the expense of each one of us who in turn became the subject of satire. The hit at Lizzie and me was the hardest, as we were both present, and was, therefore, I suppose, introduced at the end. Several laughing efforts were made by the ladies to interrupt the singing, when the words began to have reference to those who were present; but the old major insisted on "having it out," as he expressed himself. The decided "effect" produced by his song completely re-established Charley's good-humor. The old major, being the only white person present who was spared, of course enjoyed the occasion immensely; his laughter rang loud and far through the clear air, and was echoed back from the banks of the creek.

"Those are not the words, Charley," said Miss Bettie, "that you sang to that tune the other day."

"No, miss," was the answer. "Marse Weatherby's little Sam was ober at Sin Joseph's tud-day, un larnt um ter me. He said Clotildy made um un larnt um ter him dis morning."

"But why did she make that verse," I asked, "about my 'gallanting' Miss Lizzie, as she calls it? I never rode out with Miss Lizzie till this morning."

"Sam said," answered Charley, "dat he asked Clotildy ubbout dat, un she said you was er gwine ter do it."

"I say, young Audley," said the major, "you forget that the poet has a right to foreshadow coming events. I have a dim recollection of having read somewhere that there was a time at least

> " 'When the name
> Of poet and of prophet was the same.' " . . .

. . . Aunt Mary invited uncle and me to her sitting-room to take part in a consultation with the ladies about the arrangements for the morrow. Our conclave was soon interrupted by the appearance of Clotilda.

"Missus," she said, "de young niggers is er dancin' ober at Aun' Jinny's quarter; may I go ummong um?"

"You may, presently," said aunt; "I have something for you to do first which will occupy you but a little while."

"Cousin Clarence," said Lucy, when Clotilda had gone upon aunt's commission, "if you will go to Aunt Jinny's, I think you will have an opportunity of hearing Clotilda make some juber rhymes. I am almost certain that she made her request of ma in the presence of you and Miss Lizzie, because she wishes to have you both among her audience."

"Mary," observed uncle, "suppose we adjourn our consultation while the young people go to see the fun. Perhaps you would like to go, too?"

"No," answered aunt. "I think that you and I had better stay at home. Our presence might act as a restraint upon the merriment."

So Lizzie and Lucy and I hastened off to Aunt Jinny's quarter, which was one of those before spoken of as being in the edge of the wood to the north of "the house"—as the negroes name, *par excellence,* their master's dwelling—and which stood not far from Aunt Kate's, which it almost exactly resembled. The full moon shone so brightly from an unclouded sky that her lustre seemed

"Like daylight sick and turned a little paler."

Upon benches placed against the outside wall of the hut upon each side of the door sat several of the older negroes of both sexes from the neighboring quarters. Ike was singing the *words* of a jig in a monotonous tone of voice, beating time meanwhile with his hands alternately against each other and against his body. To this music about a dozen or so negro boys and girls were dancing on the hard-beaten ground before

"The old cabin door."

Their idea of excellence in dancing seemed to be that it consisted in a rapid motion of the feet; and some of the dancers absolutely moved their feet so swiftly as to cause them to be indistinct in the moonlight; yet even in this rapid action the blows of the feet kept time and tune with the music, and gave it emphasis. The scene was one of hearty glee; all seemed to be enjoying themselves vastly.

Our arrival momentarily checked the dancing, everybody had to say "Good ebenin' young missuses! Good ebenin' young marster!" But the jig was immediately renewed. Shortly afterward we saw Clotilda speeding toward the hut across the moonlit field.

"Dere comes dat crazy Till," said Uncle Jim, "runnin' same as

ef er ghost wus arter her. Gwine ter hab de Juber now sure's you
born. Ike, you mout as well gib in."

As soon as she joined the throng, Clotilda, without a moment's
pause, whirled herself among and through the crowd of dancers, till,
having gained the opposite side to that at which she had entered,
she turned and faced them, and began to recite the following verses
in a shrill sing-song voice, keeping time to the measure, as Ike had
done, by beating her hands sometimes against her sides, and patting
the ground with her feet. An interval of some seconds between the
verses afforded time for the dancers to follow the direction given in
each; but the beating of the hands and feet continued without inter-
mission. It should be understood that, in making the imitations mentioned below, the dancer has to take care that the motions of his feet
keep time to the measure.

JUBER DANCE

> Laudy! how it make me laugh
> Ter see de niggers all so saf';
> See um dance de foolish jig,
> Un neber min' de juber rig.
>   Juber!

(Negroes dancing every one after his or her own fashion, but keeping
time to the beat.)

> Juber lef' un Juber right;
> Juber dance wid all yo' might;
> Juber here un Juber dere,
> Juber, Juber ebery where.
>   Juber!

(The dancers get into confusion in their frantic efforts to follow the
directions. *Clotilda* rebukingly,

> "Git out, you silly breed!
> Can't you dance de Juber reed?")

> Once ole Uncle Will
> Gwine ullong de side de hill,

> Stump his toe uggin er weed,
> Un spill all his punkin seed.
>   Juber!

(Ludicrous imitations of Uncle Will stumbling and trying to recover
himself, and to prevent his pumpkin seed from falling at the same
time. *Uncle Will*, with great disgust, "Imperdin piece!")

> Dere's ole Uncle Jack
> Hab er pain in his back;

> Ebery time he try ter skip
> Den he hab ter get er limp.
> > Juber!

(Active skips suddenly changed to a variety of awkward limps expressive of great pain in the back. *Uncle Jack*, angrily, "De outrageous hussy!")

> Guess I knows er nigger gal—
> Dere she is, her name is Sal—
> Un she hab to min' de baby,
> Show us how she rock de cradle.
> > Juber!

(A variety of swaying motions, intended to represent cradle-rocking in a ridiculous view. *Sall*, a daughter of Aunt Kate, and nurse of a baby sister, indignantly, "I alwus said Clotildy wus crazy!")

> Ebery body know Aunt Jinny,
> Nothing ken be said uggin her;
> When she fever nigger take,
> My! how dat ole lady shake.
> > Juber!

(All the dancers are suddenly seized with a terrible shaking ague. *Aunt Jinny*, with much feeling, "Neber min', you onfeelin' cretur, maybe you git it yo'se'f next time.")

> Uncle Meshach, Uncle Jim,

(Most of the dancers hesitate and look alarmed.)

> Once I seed 'em saw er lim',
> Fur ter men' de garden palin's,
> Un ter make de pos' un railin's.
> > Juber!

(Possum and Crowley make an amusing imitation of two old men working at a cross-cut saw; the rest dance a jig step. Uncle Meshac looks savage, but says nothing. *Uncle Jim*, ferociously, "Neber min', I pay you yit!" *Clotilda*, offended at not being obeyed by all,

> "Ain't you shame, you lazy niggers?
> Wonner if dem's de Juber riggers?")

> Marser Clarry, 'pon er time,
> Want ter hear Clotildy rhyme;
> One good turn disserb unnudder,
> Lemme see him dance de Juber.
> > Juber!

(Laughable imitations of one not acquainted with the Juba, trying to dance it. "Marser Clarry" seeming to be as much amused at the fun as any one else, the "colored" individuals who have been burlesqued, look pleasant again.)

> Try de Juber reed uggin;
> Try yo' bes', un try to win.

> Juber forrud, Juber back;
> Juber dis way, Juber dat;
> Juber in, un Juber out;
> Juber, Juber, all ubbout.
>   Juber!

(*Finale*, uproar and confusion. Some of the dancers run out from among the rest in alarm; the most of them, trying to follow the instructions of the Juber beater, get entangled with each other, are "tripped up" in the confusion and fall, in various positions, in a struggling heap. Unrestrained laughter by every one.)

"Now," said Clotilda, "you kin dance your jigs un reels, un whateber you likes; but de Juber fus'."

"Clotilda," asked Lizzie, "why did you not give Uncle Porringer a verse? His being sometimes fiddler, sometimes preacher, gave you a good chance at him."

" 'Cause we's bof house servants, Miss; un Uncle Porringer has power in de house. Dat's de reason Crowley un Possum didden min' Uncle Jim. Den I want Uncle Porringer ter play on de fiddle for us. Uncle Porringer," she continued, crossing over to the bench where he sat, "wone-you gib us er fiddle tune? Do please, dat's er good Uncle Porringer."

The fiddle was soon brought from Uncle Porringer's quarter, which was near, and the young Negroes arranged themselves for a dance, a lively and rattling jig tune was struck up. . . .

. . . When we left Aunt Jinny's quarter, the young negroes were dancing with unflagging zeal, and seemed determined to keep the frolic up as long as Uncle Porringer's patience lasted. As the old fellow was fond of "hard" cider, a bucketful of which had been sent over from "the house" shortly after our arrival, the prospect was that his patience would last as long as the drink, more than half of which was yet unused. Most of the old folks left when we did. . . .

[DANCING AMONG THE SLAVEHOLDERS]

The sounds made by Uncle Porringer and another fiddler—an elderly negro man belonging to Major Sullivan—while tuning their violins, reminded us that the time was at hand for the cotillons to be forming; and each of us hastened off to seek his partner. Cousin Lucy was not far; I found her in company with Mrs. Dalton, Mrs. Wilton, Miss Susan Sullivan, and Miss Teresa King. Mr. Travers and Mr. Lucas were with them, and one or two other gentlemen. Cousin Walter soon joined us.

The scene around us at this moment was very stirring. Gentlemen were hurrying about among the groups seeking their partners, mostly no doubt already engaged, for the first cotillon. The boys—who immediately on leaving the dinner-table had straggled away in parties along the shores, or through the adjoining woods—were seen returning in all directions. The young girls, too, who were straying through all parts of the grove, were hastening toward the green plot of ground between the table and the creek-shore, which was intended for the dancers. The negroes, male and female, who were engaged in waiting upon their masters and mistresses, hung around as near to the dancing-ground as a proper respect for the white superiors would allow. Lively chat and gay laughter on all sides mingled with the noise of hurrying feet and the tuning of violin-strings.

"The Siege of Plattsburg"—played with such spirit that, as I heard a black critic near me observe, " 'twas jes' de same us ef de fiddles wus er speakin' "—soon gave note that Uncle Porringer and his companion were ready for us. Cousin Walter gave his hand to Miss Susan, Mr. Lucas attached himself to Miss King, Mr. Travers made his bow to Miss Jane; and we formed a cotillon on the spot. A number of others were formed around us, but taking such space that the breeze from the water was felt everywhere.

In the background, separated from the place occupied by the white company by the table, those of the negro servants not employed in attending upon their masters and mistresses also arranged themselves for dancing, and frequent bursts of laughter gave token that they were enjoying themselves greatly. . . .

The second cotillon was soon formed, which I was engaged to dance with Lizzie. The first tune played was "The Girl I left behind me." . . .

I afterward danced with Miss Jane and Miss Maria Wilton, Miss Bettie and Miss Susan Sullivan (Cousin Walter almost monopolized this young lady), and with Miss King and others. . . .

So sped the afternoon in mirth, music, and dancing. Young and old alike took part in the exercise.

14. FREDERICK DOUGLASS

➤➤➤ Born a slave in Maryland, Frederick Douglass (1817–95) escaped from
bondage at the age of twenty-one. Thereafter, he dedicated his life to the
abolition of slavery, and developed into one of the most outstanding orators
of the movement. His travels as a lecturer for the Anti-Slavery Society carried
him all over the North and through parts of England as well. Douglass's love
of music is reflected in his autobiographies, of which the first, *The Narrative
of the Life of Frederick Douglass: An American Slave* (Boston, 1845), was
written while he was yet a fugitive slave. Friends raised money to buy his
freedom in 1845, and two years later Douglass began the publication of a
newspaper, first called the *North Star* and later *Frederick Douglass's Paper*.
His other autobiographical works include *My Bondage and My Freedom* (New
York, 1853) and *Life and Times of Frederick Douglass* (Hartford, 1887).
Douglass, himself an amateur violinist, was immensely proud of the musical
attainments of his grandson, Joseph Douglass, the first Negro concert violinist
to tour the nation. His explanation of the meaning of the slave songs could
have come only from one who had personally experienced the degradation of
slavery. ◀◀◀

From *My Bondage and My Freedom* [1855] †

. . . The business-like aspect of Col. Lloyd's plantation . . . was
much increased on the two days at the end of each month, when the
slaves from the different farms came to get their monthly allowance
of meal and meat. These were gala days for the slaves, and there was
much rivalry among them as to *who* should be elected to go up to
the great house farm for the allowance, and, indeed, to attend to
any business at this, (for them,) the capital. The beauty and grandeur
of the place, its numerous slave population, and the fact that Harry,
Peter and Jake—the sailors of the sloop—almost always kept, pri-
vately, little trinkets which they bought at Baltimore, to sell, made it
a privilege to come to the great house farm. Being selected, too, for

† Text: The Boston 1855 edition, pp. 96–101, 193–94, 217, 278–79.

this office, was deemed a high honor. It was taken as a proof of confidence and favor; but, probably, the chief motive of the competitors for the place, was, a desire to break the dull monotony of the field, and to get beyond the overseer's eye and lash. Once on the road with an ox team, and seated on the tongue of his cart, with no overseer to look after him, the slave was comparatively free; and, if thoughtful, he had time to think. Slaves are generally expected to sing as well as to work. A silent slave is not liked by masters or overseers. *"Make a noise," "make a noise,"* and *"bear a hand,"* are the words usually addressed to the slaves when there is silence amongst them. This may account for the almost constant singing heard in the southern states. There was, generally, more or less singing among the teamsters, as it was one means of letting the overseer know where they were, and that they were moving on with the work. But, on allowance day, those who visited the great house farm were peculiarly excited and noisy. While on their way, they would make the dense old woods, for miles around, reverberate with their wild notes. These were not always merry because they were wild. On the contrary, they were mostly of a plaintive cast, and told a tale of grief and sorrow. In the most boisterous outbursts of rapturous sentiment, there was ever a tinge of deep melancholy. I have never heard any songs like those anywhere since I left slavery, except when in Ireland. There I heard the same *wailing notes*, and was much affected by them. It was during the famine of 1845–6. In all the songs of the slaves, there was ever some expression in praise of the great house farm; something which would flatter the pride of the owner, and, possibly, draw a favorable glance from him.

> "I am going away to the great house farm,
>   O yea! O yea! O yea!
> My old master is a good old master,
>   O yea! O yea! O yea!"

This they would sing, with other words of their own improvising —jargon to others, but full of meaning to themselves. I have sometimes thought, that the mere hearing of those songs would do more to impress truly spiritual-minded men and women with the soul-crushing and death-dealing character of slavery, than the reading of whole volumes of its mere physical cruelties. They speak to the heart and to the soul of the thoughtful. I cannot better express my sense of them now, than ten years ago, when, in sketching my life, I thus spoke of this feature of my plantation experience:

"I did not, when a slave, understand the deep meanings of those rude, and apparently incoherent songs. I was myself within the circle, so that I neither

saw nor heard as those without might see and hear. They told a tale which
was then altogether beyond my feeble comprehension; they were tones, loud,
long and deep, breathing the prayer and complaint of souls boiling over with
the bitterest anguish. Every tone was a testimony against slavery, and a prayer
to God for deliverance from chains. The hearing of those wild notes always
depressed my spirits, and filled my heart with ineffable sadness. The mere recurrence, even now, afflicts my spirit, and while I am writing these lines, my
tears are falling. To those songs I trace my first glimmering conceptions of the
dehumanizing character of slavery. I can never get rid of that conception.
Those songs still follow me, to deepen my hatred of slavery, and quicken my
sympathies for my brethren in bonds. If any one wishes to be impressed with
a sense of the soul-killing power of slavery, let him go to Col. Lloyd's plantation, and, on allowance day, place himself in the deep, pine woods, and there
let him, in silence, thoughtfully analyze the sounds that shall pass through the
chambers of his soul, and if he is not thus impressed, it will only be because
'there is no flesh in his obdurate heart.'"

The remark is not unfrequently made, that slaves are the most
contented and happy laborers in the world. They dance and sing,
and make all manner of joyful noises—so they do; but it is a great
mistake to suppose them happy because they sing. The songs of the
slave represent the sorrows, rather than the joys, of his heart; and he
is relieved by them, only as an aching heart is relieved by its tears.
Such is the constitution of the human mind, that, when pressed to
extremes it often avails itself of the most opposite methods. Extremes meet in mind as in matter. When the slaves on board of the
"Pearl" were overtaken, arrested, and carried to prison—their hopes
for freedom blasted—as they marched in chains they sang, and found
. . . a melancholy relief in singing. The singing of a man cast
away on a desolate island, might be as appropriately considered an
evidence of his contentment and happiness, as the singing of a
slave. Sorrow and desolation have their songs, as well as joy and peace.
Slaves sing more to *make* themselves happy, than to express their
happiness.

It is the boast of slaveholders, that their slaves enjoy more of the
physical comforts of life than the peasantry of any country in the
world. My experience contradicts this. The men and the women slaves
on Col. Lloyd's farm, received, as their monthly allowance of food,
eight pounds of pickled pork, or their equivalent in fish. The pork
was often tainted, and the fish was of the poorest quality—herrings,
which would bring very little if offered for sale in any northern market. ith their pork or fish, they had one bushel of Indian meal—
unbolted—of which quite fifteen per cent was fit only to feed pigs.
With this, one pint of salt was given; and this was the entire monthly
allowance of a full grown slave, working constantly in the open field,

from morning until night, every day in the month except Sunday and living on a fraction more than a quarter of a pound of meat per day, and less than a peck of corn-meal per week. There is no kind of work that a man can do which requires a better supply of food to prevent physical exhaustion, than the field-work of a slave. So much for the slave's allowance of food; now for his raiment. The yearly allowance of clothing for the slaves on this plantation, consisted of two tow-linen shirts—such linen as the coarsest crash towels are made of; one pair of trowsers of the same material, for summer, and a pair of trowsers and a jacket of woolen, most slazily put together, for winter; one pair of yarn stockings, and one pair of shoes of the coarsest description. The slave's entire apparel could not have cost more than eight dollars per year. The allowance of food and clothing for the little children, was committed to their mothers, or to the older slave-women having the care of them. Children who were unable to work in the field, had neither shoes, stockings, jackets nor trowsers given them. Their clothing consisted of two coarse tow-linen shirts—already described—per year; and when these failed them, as they often did, they went naked until the next allowance day. Flocks of little children from five to ten years old, might be seen on Col. Lloyd's plantation, as destitute of clothing as any little heathen on the west coast of Africa; and this, not merely during the summer months, but during the frosty weather of March. The little girls were no better off than the boys; all were nearly in a state of nudity. . . .

In the month of August, 1833, when I had almost become desperate under the treatment of Master Thomas, and when I entertained more strongly than ever the oft-repeated determination to run away, a circumstance occurred which seemed to promise brighter and better days for us all. At a Methodist camp-meeting, held in the Bay Side, (a famous place for camp-meetings,) about eight miles from St. Michael's, Master Thomas came out with a profession of religion. He had long been an object of interest to the church, and to the ministers, as I had seen by the repeated visits and lengthy exhortations of the latter. He was a fish quite worth catching, for he had money and standing. In the community of St. Michael's he was equal to the best citizen. He was strictly temperate; *perhaps*, from principle, but most likely, from interest. There was very little to do for him, to give him the appearance of piety, and to make him a pillar in the church. Well, the camp-meeting continued a week; people gathered from all parts of the county, and two steamboat loads came from Baltimore. The ground was happily chosen; seats were arranged; a stand erected; a rude altar fenced in, fronting the preachers' stand, with a straw in it for the accommodation of mourners. This latter would hold at least one hundred persons. In front, and on the sides of the preachers' stand, and outside the long rows of seats, rose the first class of stately tents, each vieing with the other in strength, neatness, and capacity for accommodating its inmates. Behind this first circle of tents was another, less imposing, which reached round the camp-ground to the speakers' stand. Outside this second class of tents were covered wagons, ox carts, and vehicles of every shape and size. These served as tents to their owners. Outside of these, huge fires were burning, in all directions, where roasting, and boiling, and frying, were going on, for the benefit of those who were attending to their own spiritual welfare within the circle. *Behind* the preachers' stand, a narrow space was marked out for the use of the colored people. There were no seats provided for this class of persons; the preachers addressed them, *"over the left,"* if they addressed them at all. After the preaching was over, at every service, an invitation was given to mourners to come into the pen; and, in some cases, ministers went out to persuade men and women to come in. By one of these ministers, Master Thomas Auld was persuaded to go inside the pen. I was deeply interested in that matter, and followed; and, though colored people were not allowed either in the pen or in front of the preachers' stand, I ventured to take my stand at a sort of half-way place between the blacks and whites, where I could distinctly see the movements of mourners, and especially the progress of Master Thomas. . . .

Mr. Covey was not content with the cold style of family worship, adopted in these cold latitudes, which begin and end with a simple prayer. No! the voice of praise, as well as of prayer, must be heard in his house, night and morning. At first, I was called upon to bear some part in these exercises; but the repeated flogging given me by Covey, turned the whole thing into mockery. He was a poor singer, and mainly relied on me for raising the hymn for the family, and when I failed to do so, he was thrown into much confusion. I do not think that he ever abused me on account of these vexations. His religion was a thing altogether apart from his worldly concerns. He knew nothing of it as a holy principle, directing and controlling his daily life, making the latter conform to the requirements of the gospel. . . .

But with all our caution and studied reserve, I am not sure that Mr. Freeland did not suspect that all was not right with us. It *did* seem that he watched us more narrowly, after the plan of escape had been conceived and discussed amongst us. Men seldom see themselves as others see them; and while, to ourselves, everything connected with our contemplated escape appeared concealed, Mr. Freeland may have, with the peculiar prescience of a slaveholder, mastered the huge thought which was disturbing our peace in slavery.

I am the more inclined to think that he suspected us, because, prudent as we were, as I now look back, I can see that we did many silly things, very well calculated to awaken suspicion. We were, at times, remarkably buoyant, singing hymns and making joyous exclamations, almost as triumphant in their tone as if we had reached a land of freedom and safety. A keen observer might have detected in our repeated singing of

> "O Canaan, sweet Canaan,
> I am bound for the land of Canaan,"

something more than a hope of reaching heaven. We meant to reach the *north*—and the north was our Canaan.

> "I thought I heard them say,
> There were lions in the way,
> I don't expect to stay
>   Much longer here.
> Run to Jesus—shun the danger—
> I don't expect to stay
>   Much longer here,"

was a favorite air, and had a double meaning. In the lips of some, it meant the expectation of a speedy summons to a world of spirits; but, in the lips of *our* company, it simply meant a speedy pilgrimage toward a free state, and deliverance from all the evils and dangers of slavery.

15. LEWIS W. PAINE

➤➤➤ A native of Providence County in Rhode Island, Lewis W. Paine (1819–?) went to Georgia in 1841 "for the purpose of starting and running some machinery in a factory." At the beginning of his book, *Six Years in a Georgia Prison* (New York, 1851), Paine states that he "had grown from youth to manhood with a full conviction that slavery was wrong." He was not an abolitionist, however, and after moving to the South made efforts to get along peacefully with the people in the community in which he lived. In 1845, Paine was approached by the slave Samson—a good blacksmith, "powerful," and endowed with "a keen intelligent eye"—with regard to providing help in an escape plot. Convinced that Samson's struggle was a just one, Paine helped the slave to escape, was caught in the process, and sentenced to "seven years of hard labor in the State Prison." According to the judge who sentenced Paine, he had committed "a crime of the blackest dye."

When Paine was released from prison, with a year off for good behavior, he wrote his autobiography. Upon the advice of some friends, he added a few chapters about slavery, one of which, entitled "Amusements," contains considerable information about music practices on the plantation. ◄◄◄

From *Six Years in a Georgia Prison* [1851] †

Under all these restrictions, privations, restraints and wrongs, it must be evident to all, that the slaves can have but little time or opportunity for amusement; but where they have a chance they make the best possible use of it. They most emphatically "Throw dull care away," and enter into their sports with every demonstration of joy.

They are generally allowed to make such use of Sunday as they please. Some hunt; others fish; some work for themselves; some go to see their friends; some sleep all day, and a few go to meeting. Their principal sports are Log-rolling, Corn Shucking, or what the Northern farmers call Husking, and at Christmas. The log-rollings and shuck-

† Text: The original edition (New York, 1851), pp. 177–86.

ings are always participated in by the whites. These sports are episodes in their lives. They are like oases to the weary traveler of the desert; they help to enliven the sad journey of life; they are faint rays that shine over their dark voyage, and enable them to keep their course; they are stars which relieve them from eternal night.

Log-rollings are commonly in vogue during the winter season. After a farmer has cleared a piece of land, and gathered all but the large logs, he gives an invitation to his neighbors to come and help him roll the remaining logs into large piles, for the purpose of being burnt. They go by the principle that many hands make light work. They all accept the invitation with pleasure. The white men will go, and take two or three of their slaves; and by the time all have arrived there will be quite a collection.

They take a hand-spike, about four or five feet long, to lift, carry, and roll the logs with. Every one, whether black or white, strives to excel the others in feats of activity and strength, and especially jokes. To the one that can "tote" the largest log, lift the heaviest butt, or roll the log the highest on the pile, is awared the palm. They always have aplenty of whisky, or peach brandy, to make them lively. They are full of sport and fun, and bandy round all kinds of jokes.

They generally so arrange matters, as to get done before night, when they take up their line of march for the house; and, on arriving there, take a drink all round. Then commence their gymnastic exercises. They wrestle, jump, and run foot-races. Black and white all take part in the sport, and he who comes off victorious has an extra sip of the "white eye." After indulging in these exercises as long as they wish, some one calls for a fiddle—but if one is not to be found, some one "pats juber." This is done by placing one foot a little in advance of the other, raising the ball of the foot from the ground, and striking it in regular time, while, in connection, the hands are struck slightly together, and then upon the thighs. In this way they make the most curious noise, yet in such perfect order, it furnishes music to dance by. All indulge in the dance. The slaves, as they become excited, use the most extravagant gestures—the music increases in speed—and the Whites soon find it impossible to sustain their parts, and they retire. This is just what the slaves wish, and they send up a general shout, which is returned by the Whites, acknowledging the victory.

Then they all sing out,

"Now show de white man what we can do!"

And with heart and soul they dive into the sport, until they fairly exceed themselves. It is really astonishing to witness the rapidity of their motions, their accurate time, and the precision of their music and dance. I have never seen it equaled in my life.

After the dance is over, they all take supper, and start for home, well pleased with their sport.

But the shucking frolic is considered by them as a far greater jubilee. A farmer will haul up from his field a pile of corn from ten to twenty rods long, from ten to twenty feet wide, and ten feet high. This pile consists of nothing but ears. They always break the ears from the stalk, and never cut it at the ground, as the Northern farmers do. It is so arranged that this can be on a moonlight evening. The farmer then gives a general "invite" to all the young ladies and gentlemen in the neighborhood, to come and bring their slaves; for it takes no small number to shuck such a pile of corn.

The guests begin to arrive about dark, and in a short time, they can be heard in all directions, singing the plantation songs, as they come to the scene of action. When they have all arrived, the Host makes the following propositions to his company, "You can shuck the pile, or work till eleven o'clock, or divide the pile and the hands, and try a race."

The last offer is generally accepted. Each party selects two of the shrewdest and best singers among the slaves, to mount the pile and sing, while all join in the chorus.The singers also act the part of sentinels, to watch the opposite party—for it is part of the game for each party to try to throw corn on the other's pile.

As soon as all things are ready, the word is given, and they fall to work in good earnest. They sing awhile, then tell stories, and joke and laugh awhile. At last they get to making all the different noises the human voice is capable of, all at the same time—each one of each party doing his best to win the victory. One unacquainted with such scenes would think that Bedlam *had* broken loose, and all its inmates were doing their best to thunder forth their uproarious joy.

This is continued till the task is finished. They have plenty of liquor to keep up the excitement.

The victorious party peal forth their shouts and jests in a deafening volley, and the negroes seem fairly beside themselves. They jump, roll, and tumble about, as though "kingdom come" was already in their possession. As soon as the pile is finished, the slaves keep a sharp eye on the Host, lest he should slip out of their sight, and get to the house; for it is a rule with them at corn-shuckings, always to tote their Host to the house, on their heads; and the moment he gives the word to proceed to the house, he expects his doom—and, by dodging and running, he tries to escape it. But a dozen stalwart negroes pounce upon him, and it is always understood that he is not to hurt them, but prevent them, if he can, by wrestling and running;

but when the negroes get their iron gripe on him, it is useless to struggle. If he should get angry, it will make no difference; the masters of the slaves will run to their rescue, and order them to seize him; and nothing suits them better than this. They lay hold of him, and down he comes, and on to their heads he goes, in just no time at all; and they bear him off in triumph to the house, where he receives the jokes and gibes of the young ladies, and of his family.

On arriving at the house they find that the young ladies have not been idle; for the long tables smoke and groan with the loads of poultry, pigs, and all kinds of eatables, which would make a Lord Mayor and all his Aldermen smile with a peculiar emphasis. They sit down to the table with the appetites of alligators; for they have been sharpened by active exercise, and by the play of good humor and jokes, that have circulated freely all the while. After each one has hid no inconsiderable portion of what *was* before him, they rise from the table with the roundness of a drum, and the tightness of one of its heads.

As soon as the table is cleared the girls give a wink; and in a trice the room is stripped of every thing but the bed. Two or three men take hold of this, and set it out of the room. The negro fiddler then walks in; and the dance commences. After they have enjoyed their sport sufficiently, they give way to the negroes, who have already supplied themselves with torch-lights, and swept the yard. The fiddler walks out, and strikes up a tune; and at it they go in a regular tear-down dance; for here they are at home. The sound of a fiddle makes them crazy; and I do believe that if they were in the height of an insurrection, and any one should go among them, and play on a violin, they would all be dancing in five minutes. I never saw a slave in my life but would stop as if he were shot at the sound of a fiddle; and if he has a load of two hundred pounds on his head, he will begin to dance. One would think they had steam engines inside of them, to jerk them about with so much power; for they go through with more motions in a minute, than you could shake two sticks at in a month; and of all comic actions, ludicrous sights, and laughable jokes, and truly comic songs, there is no match for them. It is useless to talk about Fellows' Minstrels, or any other band of merely artificial "Ethiopians;" for they will bear no comparison with the plantation negroes. The latter, by frequenting these places of amusement in the capacity of entertainers, become actors, and that of a high order, for in this way they cultivate the faculties most necessary to success in that profession—ideality, marvelousness, and imitation—all of which greatly predominate in the negro character; while tune or the sense of harmony bears off the palm; for if there is a people whom,

above all others, the gods themselves have made musical, they are entitled to the distinction. They hold the mirror up to nature; nay, it is
nature's self displayed so fully, and with such graphic power, that in
spite of himself the gravest will burst out in the most uproarious
laughter. They keep up the dance till all are fairly tired out, and then
disperse for their homes.

But Christmas is their time of times. They are generally allowed
several days at Christmas, from two to seven, according to the disposition of their masters. They all have to do something special for this
carnival. They get leave to plat a little patch of cotton, corn, rice,
tobacco, pease, potatoes, or whatever they choose. Some make brooms,
mats, tubs, pails, chairs, or horse-collars; and they have all these for
sale about Christmas. Their plans are all matured beforehand. Some
go to see their relations; some to parties; some to dances; some to
one place, and some to another; and some go nowhere, have nothing, care for nothing, and get nothing. Some lay up their money;
some drink it up; some gamble it away; and some buy themselves
clothes.

They spend the time as they please, till the period expires for
which their pass was given. They know that this is their greatest time,
and they make the most of it; and having staid till the last moment,
they return to take their stations of labor, and begin a new year's
work.

Thus, year in and year out, they go through with the same monotonous course, till old age brings them to the grave.

16. SOLOMON NORTHUP

≫≫ The slave autobiography represented a very popular genre in nineteenth-century American literature, reaching its greatest vogue during the 1850s. By some estimates, several hundred such narratives were published during the middle years of the century. The first example of the genre appeared as early as 1760—an autobiography published at Boston for one Briton Hammond. The most successful of the eighteenth-century narratives, however, was *The Interesting Narrative of the Life of Olaudah Equiano, or Gustavus Vassa, the African. Written by Himself* (London, 1789). The last notable example of the form was Booker T. Washington's *Up from Slavery* (1903). The memoir of Solomon Northup (1808–63) was published in 1853, at the peak of the vogue, and sold 27,000 copies during the first two years after its publication. The title page stated *Twelve Years a Slave* to be a "Narrative of Solomon Northup, A Citizen of New York, Kidnapped in Washington City in 1841, and Rescued in 1853 from a Cotton Plantation near the Red River in Louisiana."

Northup's story (edited by David Wilson) has several unusual aspects. He began life as a *free* man, was kidnapped into slavery, and later regained his freedom. Although it was not uncommon during the period for free blacks to be kidnapped and sold into slavery, few of those unfortunate persons were actually born free; most had either escaped to freedom or had purchased it. Consequently, the loss of this freedom thrust them back into tragic, but nonetheless familiar, circumstances. But Northup, having lived only as a free man before his capture, entered slavery with little preparation for its brutalizing impact on the mind and soul. He was able to perceive slavery, therefore, both as an outsider and as one who suffered directly from its evil.

Northup's book is especially useful because he was a musician who had depended upon music as a source of income in the North. Early in his narration, Northup informs the reader that playing on the violin was "the ruling passion of [his] youth." As an adult, Northup won a wide reputation as a dance fiddler, and it was this that led directly to his abduction. "Two gentlemen of respectable appearance" accosted Northup on the streets of his home town, Saratoga Springs (New York), and engaged him to travel with them to provide music for their exhibitions. They finally lured Northup to Washington, D.C., where they sold him into slavery. ≪≪

From *Twelve Years a Slave* [1853] †

One morning, towards the latter part of the month of March, 1841, having at that time no particular business to engage my attention, I was walking about the village of Saratoga Springs, thinking to myself where I might obtain some present employment, until the busy season should arrive. Anne,¹ as was her usual custom, had gone over to Sandy Hill, a distance of some twenty miles, to take charge of the culinary department at Sherrill's Coffee House, during the session of the court. Elizabeth, I think, had accompanied her. Margaret and Alonzo were with their aunt at Saratoga.

On the corner of Congress street and Broadway, near the tavern, then, and for aught I know to the contrary, still kept by Mr. Moon, I was met by two gentlemen of respectable appearance, both of whom were entirely unknown to me. I have the impression that they were introduced to me by some one of my acquaintances, but who, I have in vain endeavored to recall, with the remark that I was an expert player on the violin.

At any rate, they immediately entered into conversation on that subject, making numerous inquiries touching my proficiency in that respect. My responses being to all appearances satisfactory, they proposed to engage my services for a short period, stating, at the same time, I was just such a person as their business required. . . . They were connected, as they informed me, with a circus company, then in the city of Washington; that they were on their way thither to rejoin it, having left it for a short time to make an excursion northward, for the purpose of seeing the country, and were paying their expenses by an occasional exhibition. They also remarked that they had found much difficulty in procuring music for their entertainments, and that if I would accompany them as far as New York, they would give me one dollar for each day's services, and three dollars in addition for every night I played at their performances, besides sufficient to pay the expenses of my return from New York to Saratoga.

I at once accepted the tempting offer, both for the reward it promised, and from a desire to visit the metropolis. They were anxious to leave immediately. Thinking my absence would be brief, I did not deem it necessary to write to Anne whither I had gone; in fact supposing that my return, perhaps, would be as soon as hers. So taking a change of linen and my violin, I was ready to depart.

† Text: The original edition (Cincinnati, 1853), pp. 12–20, 51–52, 136–37, 163–69, 218–22.

1. Northup's wife. [*Editor*]

The carriage was brought round—a covered one, drawn by a pair of noble bays, altogether forming an elegant establishment. Their baggage, consisting of three large trunks, was fastened on the rack, and mounting to the driver's seat, while they took their places in the rear, I drove away from Saratoga on the road to Albany, elated with my new position, and happy as I had ever been, on any day in all my life.

We passed through Ballston, and striking the ridge road, as it is called, if my memory correctly serves me, followed it direct to Albany. We reached that city before dark, and stopped at a hotel southward from the Museum.

This night I had an opportunity of witnessing one of their performances—the only one, during the whole period I was with them. Hamilton was stationed at the door; I formed the orchestra, while Brown provided the entertainment. It consisted in throwing balls, dancing on the rope, frying pancakes in a hat, causing invisible pigs to squeal, and other like feats of ventriloquism and legerdemain. The audience was extraordinarily sparse, and not of the selectest character at that, and Hamilton's report of the proceeds presented but a "beggarly account of empty boxes."

Early next morning we renewed our journey. The burden of their conversation was now the expression of an anxiety to reach the circus without delay. They hurried forward, without again stopping to exhibit, and in due course of time, we reached New York, taking lodgings at a house on the west side of the city, in a street running from Broadway to the river. I supposed my journey was at an end, and expected in a day or two at least, to return to my friends and family at Saratoga. Brown and Hamilton, however, began to importune me to continue with them to Washington. They alleged that immediately on their arrival, now that the summer season was approaching, the circus would set out for the north. They promised me a situation and high wages if I would accompany them. Largely did they expatiate on the advantages that would result to me, and such were the flattering representations they made, that I finally concluded to accept the offer. . . . [Northup went with them to Washington.]

Then did the idea begin to break upon my mind, at first dim and confused, that I had been kidnapped. But that I thought was incredible. There must have been some misapprehension—some unfortunate mistake. It could not be that a free citizen of New York, who had wronged no man, nor violated any law, should be dealt with thus inhumanly. The more I contemplated my situation, however, the more I became confirmed in my suspicions. It was a desolate thought, indeed. I felt there was no trust or mercy in unfeeling man;

and commending myself to the God of the oppressed, bowed my head upon my fettered hands, and wept most bitterly. . . .

[In the next excerpt, Northup is in New Orleans.]

The very amiable, pious-hearted Mr. Theophilus Freeman, a partner or consignee of James H. Burch, and keeper of the slave pen in New Orleans, was out among his animals early in the morning. With an occasional kick of the older men and women, and many a sharp crack of the whip about the ears of the younger slaves, it was not long before they were all astir, and wide awake. Mr. Theophilus Freeman bustled about in a very industrious manner, getting his property ready for the sales-room, intending, no doubt, to do that day a rousing business.

In the first place we were required to wash thoroughly, and those with beards, to shave. We were then furnished with a new suit each, cheap, but clean. The men had hat, coat, shirt, pants and shoes; the women frocks of calico, and handkerchiefs to bind about their heads. We were now conducted into a large room in the front part of the building to which the yard was attached, in order to be properly trained, before the admission of customers. The men were arranged on one side of the room, the women on the other. The tallest was placed at the head of the row, then the next tallest, and so on in the order of their respective heights. Emily was at the foot of the line of women. Freeman charged us to remember our places; exhorted us to appear smart and lively,—sometimes threatening, and again, holding out various inducements. During the day he exercised us in the art of "looking smart," and of moving to our places with exact precision.

After being fed in the afternoon, we were again paraded and made to dance. Bob, a colored boy, who had some time belonged to Freeman, played on the violin. Standing near him, I made bold to inquire if he could play the "Virginia Reel." He answered he could not, and asked me if I could play. Replying in the affirmative he handed me the violin. I struck up a tune, and finished it. Freeman ordered me to continue playing, and seemed well pleased, telling Bob that I far excelled him—a remark that seemed to grieve my musical companion very much.

Next day many customers called to examine Freeman's "new lot." The latter gentleman was very loquacious, dwelling at much length upon our several good points and qualities. He would make us hold up our heads, walk briskly back and forth, while customers would feel of our hands and arms and bodies, turn us about, ask us what we could do, make us open our mouths and show our teeth, precisely as a jockey examines a horse which he is about to barter for or purchase. Sometimes a man or woman was taken back to the small house in the yard, stripped, and inspected more minutely. Scars upon a slave's back were considered evidence of a rebellious or unruly spirit, and hurt his sale.

One old gentleman who said he wanted a coachman, appeared to take a fancy to me. From his conversation with Burch, I learned he was a resident in the city. I very much desired that he would buy me, because I conceived it would not be difficult to make my escape from New Orleans on some northern vessel. Freeman asked him fifteen hundred dollars for me. The old gentleman insisted it was too much, as times were very hard. Freeman, however, declared that I was sound and healthy, of good constitution, and intelligent. He made it a point to enlarge upon my musical attainments. . . .

[After living under several masters, Northup was finally sold to Edwin Epps, a planter of Bayou Boeuf, Louisiana. Northup's name was changed to Platt.]

During the two years Epps remained on the plantation at Bayou Huff Power, he was in the habit, as often as once in a fortnight at least, of coming home intoxicated from Holmesville. The shooting-matches almost invariably concluded with a debauch. At such times he was boisterous and half-crazy. Often he would break the dishes, chairs, and whatever furniture he could lay his hands on. . . .

At other times he would come home in a less brutal humor. Then there must be a merry-making. Then all must move to the measure of a tune. Then Master Epps must needs regale his melodious ears with the music of a fiddle. Then did he become buoyant, elastic, gaily "tripping the light fantastic toe" around the piazza and all through the house.

Tibeats, at the time of my sale, had informed him I could play the violin. He had received this information from Ford. Through the importunities of Mistress Epps, her husband had been induced to purchase me one during a visit to New Orleans. Frequently I was called into the house to play before the family, mistress being passionately fond of music.

All of us would be assembled in the large room of the great house, whenever Epps came home in one of his dancing moods. No matter how worn out and tired we were, there must be a general dance. When properly stationed on the floor, I would strike up a tune.

"Dance you d—d niggers, dance," Epps would shout.

Then there must be no halting or delay, no slow or languid movements; all must be brisk, and lively, and alert. "Up and down, heel and toe, and away we go," was the order of the hour. Epps' portly form mingled with those of his dusky slaves, moving rapidly through all the mazes of the dance.

Usually his whip was in his hand, ready to fall about the ears of the presumptuous thrall, who dared to rest a moment, or even stop to catch his breath. When he was himself exhausted, there would be a brief cessation, but it would be very brief. With a slash, and crack, and flourish of the whip, he would shout again, "Dance, niggers dance," and away they would go once more, pell-mell, while I, spurred by an occasional sharp touch of the lash, sat in a corner, extracting from my violin a marvelous quick-stepping tune. The mistress often upbraided him, declaring she would return to her father's house at Cheneyville; nevertheless, there were times she could not restrain a burst of laughter, on witnessing his uproarious pranks. Frequently, we were thus detained until almost morning. Bent with excessive toil—actually suffering for a little refreshing rest, and feeling rather as if we could cast ourselves upon the earth and weep, many a night in the house of Edwin Epps have his unhappy slaves been made to dance and laugh. . . .

The only respite from constant labor the slave has through the whole year, is during the Christmas holidays. Epps allowed us three —others allow four, five and six days, according to the measure of their generosity. It is the only time to which they look forward with any interest or pleasure. They are glad when night comes, not only because it brings them a few hours repose, but because it brings them one day nearer Christmas. It is hailed with equal delight by the old and the young; even Uncle Abram ceases to glorify Andrew Jackson, and Patsey forgets her many sorrows, amid the general hilarity of the holidays. It is the time of feasting, and frolicking, and fiddling—the carnival season with the children of bondage. They are the only days when they are allowed a little restricted liberty, and heartily indeed do they enjoy it.

It is the custom for one planter to give a "Christmas supper," inviting the slaves from neighboring plantations to join his own on the occasion; for instance, one year it is given by Epps, the next by Marshall, the next by Hawkins, and so on. Usually from three to five hundred are assembled, coming together on foot, in carts, on horseback, on mules, riding double and triple, sometimes a boy and girls, at others a girl and two boys, and at others again a boy, a girl and an old woman. Uncle Abram astride a mule, with Aunt Phebe and Patsey behind him, trotting towards a Christmas supper, would be no uncommon sight on Bayou Boeuf.

Then, too, "of all days i' the year," they array themselves in their best attire. The cotton coat has been washed clean, the stump of a tallow candle has been applied to the shoes, and if so fortunate as to possess a rimless or a crownless hat, it is placed jauntily on the head. They are welcomed with equal cordiality, however, if they come bare-headed and bare-footed to the feast. . . .

The table is spread in the open air, and loaded with varieties of meat and piles of vegetables. Bacon and corn meal at such times are dispensed with. . . .

When the viands have disappeared, and the hungry maws of the children of toil are satisfied, then, next in the order of amusement, is the Christmas dance. My business on these gala days always was to play on the violin. The African race is a music-loving one, proverbially; and many there were among my fellow-bondsmen whose organs of tune were strikingly developed, and who could thumb the banjo with dexterity; but at the expense of appearing egotistical, I must, nevertheless, declare, that I was considered the Ole Bull of Bayou Boeuf. My master often received letters, sometimes from a distance of ten miles, requesting him to send me to play at a ball or festival of the whites. He received his compensation, and usually I also returned with many picayunes jingling in my pockets—the extra contributions of those to whose delight I had administered. In this manner I became more acquainted than I otherwise would, up and down the bayou. The young men and maidens of Holmesville always knew there was to be a jollification somewhere, whenever Platt Epps was seen passing through the town with his fiddle in his hand. "Where are you going now, Platt?" and "What is coming off tonight, Platt?" would be interrogatories issuing from every door and window, and many a time when there was no special hurry, yielding to pressing importunities, Platt would draw his bow, and sitting astride his mule, perhaps, discourse musically to a crowd of delighted children, gathered around him in the street.

Alas! had it not been for my beloved violin, I scarcely can conceive how I could have endured the long years of bondage. It introduced me to great houses—relieved me of many days' labor in the field—supplied me with conveniences for my cabin—with pipes and tobacco, and extra pair of shoes, and oftentimes led me away from the presence of a hard master, to witness scenes of jollity and mirth. It was my companion—the friend of my bosom—triumphing loudly when I was joyful, and uttering its soft, melodious consolations when I was sad. Often, at midnight, when sleep had fled affrighted from the cabin, and my soul was disturbed and troubled with the contemplation of my fate, it would sing me a song of peace. On holy Sabbath days, when an hour or two of leisure was allowed, it would accompany me to some quiet place on the bayou bank, and, lifting up its voice, discourse kindly and pleasantly indeed. It heralded my name round the country—made me friends, who, otherwise would not have noticed me—gave me an honored seat at the yearly feasts, and secured the loudest and heartiest welcome of them all at the Christmas dance. The Christmas dance! Oh, ye pleasure-seeking sons and daughters of idleness, who moved with measured step, listless and snail-like, through the slow winding cotillon, if ye wish to look upon the celerity, if not the "poetry of motion"—upon genuine happiness, rampant and unrestrained—go down to Louisiana and see the slaves dancing in the starlight of a Christmas night. . . .

One "set" off another takes its place, he or she remaining on the floor longest receiving the most uproarious commendation, and so the dancing continues until broad daylight. It does not cease with the sound of the fiddle, but in that case they set up a music peculiar to themselves. This is called "patting," accompanied with one of those unmeaning songs, composed rather for its adaptation to a certain tune or measure, than for the purpose of expressing any distinct idea. The patting is performed by striking the hands on the knees, then striking the hands together, then striking the right shoulder with one hand, the left with the other—all the while keeping time with the feet, and singing, perhaps, this song:

> "Harper's creek and roarin' ribber,
> Thar, my dear, we'll live forebber;
> Den we'll go to de Ingin Nation,
> All I want in dis creation,
> Is pretty little wife and big plantation.
> *Chorus.* Up dat oak and down dat ribber,
> Two overseers and one little nigger"

Or, if these words are not adapted to the time called for, it may be that "Old Hog Eye" *is*—a rather solemn and startling specimen of versification, not, however, to be appreciated unless heard at the South. It runneth as follows:

> "Who's been here since I've been gone?
> Pretty little gal wid a josey on.
> Hog eye!
> Old Hog Eye!
> And Hosey too!
> Never see de like since I was born,
> Here comes a little gal wid a josey on
> Hog eye!
> Old Hog Eye!
> And Hosey too!"

Or, maybe the following, perhaps, equally nonsensical, but full of melody, nevertheless, as it flows from the negro's mouth:

"Ebo Dick and Jurdan's Jo,
Them two niggers stole my yo'.
Chorus. Hop Jim along,
Walk Jim along,
Talk Jim along," &c.
"Old black Dan, as black as tar,
He dam glad he was not dar.
Hop Jim along," &c.

During the remaining holidays succeeding Christmas, they are provided with passes, and permitted to go where they please within a limited distance, or they may remain and labor on the plantation, in which case they are paid for it. It is very rarely, however, that the latter alternative is accepted. They may be seen at these times hurrying in all directions, as happy looking mortals as can be found on the face of the earth. They are different beings from what they are in the field; the temporary relaxation, the brief deliverance from fear, and from the lash, producing an entire metamorphosis in their appearance and demeanor. In visiting, riding, renewing old friendships, or, perchance, reviving some old attachment or pursuing whatever pleasure may suggest itself, the time is occupied. Such is "southern life as it is," *three days in the year*, as I found it—the other three hundred and sixty-two being days of weariness, and fear, and suffering, and unremitting labor. . . .

It was Christmas morning [1852]—the happiest day in the whole year for the slave. That morning he need not hurry to the field, with his gourd and cotton-bag. Happiness sparkled in the eyes and overspread the countenances of all. The time of feasting and dancing had come. The cane and cotton fields were deserted. That day the clean dress was to be donned—the red ribbon displayed; there were to be re-unions, and joy and laughter, and hurrying to and fro. It was to be a day of *liberty* among the children of Slavery. Wherefore they were happy, and rejoiced.

After breakfast Epps and Bass sauntered about the yard, conversing upon the price of cotton, and various other topics.

"Where do your niggers hold Christmas?" Bass inquired.

"Platt is going to Tanners to-day. His fiddle is in great demand. They want him at Marshall's Monday, and Miss Mary McCoy, on the old Norwood plantation, writes me a note that she wants him to play for her niggers Tuesday."

"He is rather a smart boy, ain't he?" said Bass. "Come here, Platt," he added, looking at me as I walked up to them, as if he had never thought before to take any special notice of me.

"Yes," replied Epps, taking hold of my arm and feeling it, "there isn't a bad joint in him. There ain't a boy on the bayou worth more than he is—perfectly sound, and no bad tricks. D—n him, he isn't like other niggers; doesn't look like 'em—don't act like 'em. I was offered seventeen hundred dollars for him last week."

"And didn't take it?" Bass inquired, with an air of surprise.

"Take it—no; devilish clear of it. Why, he's a reg'lar genius; can make a plough beam, wagon tongue—anything, as well as you can. Marshall wanted to put up one of his niggers agin him and raffle for them, but I told him I would see the devil have him first."

"I don't see anything remarkable about him," Bass observed.

"Why, just feel of him, now," Epps rejoined. "You don't see a boy very often put together any closer than he is. He's a thin-skin'd cuss, and won't bear as much whipping as some; but he's got the muscle in him, and no mistake."

Bass felt of me, turned me round, and made a thorough examination, Epps all the while dwelling on my good points. But his visitor seemed to take but little interest finally in the subject, and consequently it was dropped. Bass soon departed, giving me another sly look of recognition and significance, as he trotted out of the yard.

When he was gone I obtained a pass, and started for Tanner's— not Peter Tanner's, of whom mention has previously been made, but a relative of his. I played during the day and most of the night, and spending the next day, Sunday, in my cabin. Monday I crossed the bayou to Douglass Marshall's, all Epps' slaves accompanying me, and on Tuesday went to the old Norwood place, which is the third plantation above Marshall's, on the same side of the water. . . .

Tuesday concluded the three holidays Epps yearly allowed us. On my way home, Wednesday morning, while passing the plantation of William Pierce, that gentleman hailed me, saying he had received a line from Epps, brought down by William Varnell, permitting him to detain me for the purpose of playing for his slaves that night. It was the last time I was destined to witness a slave dance on the shores of Bayou Boeuf. The party at Pierce's continued their jollification, until broad daylight, when I returned to my master's house; somewhat wearied with the loss of rest, but rejoicing with the possession of numerous bits and picayunes, which the whites, who were pleased with my musical performances, had contributed.

[Aided by Samuel Bass and others, Northup regained his freedom in January, 1853.]

17. FREDRIKA BREMER

>>> A leading novelist of the nineteenth century and highly honored in her native Sweden, Fredrika Bremer (1801–65) was born into a wealthy family and began writing at an early age. Following an extensive tour of Europe with her family in 1820–21 she published anonymously her first book, *Sketches of Everyday Life*. Bremer began a career as a woman-of-letters after her father's death in 1830, traveling widely and publishing novels and travel accounts, many of which were translated into English. Her visit to the United States during the years 1849–50 was followed by the publication of *Homes of the New World: Impressions of America* (New York, 1853). While in America, Bremer eagerly sought opportunities to come into contact with both free and enslaved blacks. Some of her descriptions of Negro folkways—and of other American folkways, as well—are superb. Her book consists of diary entries and letters written to friends in Europe. <<<

From *Homes of the New World* [1853] †

» [Letter] . . . Macon, Vineville [Georgia], May 7th, 1850 «

Nay, I did not go to Savannah the day I thought of, but went—on an excursion, to which I invite you to accompany me, but without telling you whither we go. We drive to the rail-road, we enter one of the carriages: Mrs. W. H., an agreeable young man—I have the pleasure of introducing Mr. R. to you—and myself; and now you will accompany us. Away we go, through forest and field, eighteen miles from Charleston. It is late in the afternoon and very warm. We stop; it is in the middle of a thick wood. There is wood on all sides, and not a house to be seen. We alight from the carriages and enter a fir-wood. After we have walked for an hour along unformed paths, the wood begins to be very animated. It swarms with people, in particular with blacks, as far as we can see among the lofty tree-stems. In

† Text: The 1854 New York edition, II, 156–60, 174.

the middle of the wood is an open space, in the centre of which rises
a great long roof, supported by pillars, and under which stand
benches in rows, affording sufficient accommodation for four or five
thousand people. In the middle of this tabernacle is a lofty, square
elevation, and in the middle of this is a sort of chair or pulpit. All
round the tabernacle, for so I call the roofed-in space supported on
pillars, hundreds of tents, and booths of all imaginable forms and
colors, are pitched and erected in a vast circle, and are seen shining
out white in the wood to a great distance, and everywhere, on all
sides, near and afar off, may be seen groups of people, mostly black,
busied at small fires, roasting and boiling. Children are running
about or sitting by the fires; horses stand and feed beside the carriages they have drawn thither. It is a perfect camp, with all the
varied party-colored life of a camp, but without soldiers and arms.
Here everything looks peaceful and festive, although not exactly joyful.

By degrees the people begin to assemble within the tabernacle,
the white people on one side, the black on the other; the black
being considerably more numerous than the white. The weather is
sultry; thunder-clouds cover the heavens, and it begins to rain. Not a
very agreeable prospect for the night, my little darling, but there is
nothing for it, we must pass the night here in the wild wood. We
have no other resource. But stop; we have another resource. That
excellent young Mr. R. employs his eloquence, and a tent is opened
for us, and we are received into it by a comfortable bookseller's family. The family are red-hot Methodists, and not to be objected to.
Here we have coffee and supper.

After this meal I went to look around me, and was astonished by a
spectacle which I shall never forget. The night was dark with the
thunder-cloud, as well as with the natural darkness of night; but the
rain had ceased, excepting for a few heavy drops, which fell here
and there, and the whole wood stood in flames. Upon eight fire-
altars, or fire-hills, as they are called—a sort of lofty table raised on
posts, standing around the tabernacle—burned, with a flickering
brilliance of flame, large billets of fire-wood, which contains a great
deal of resin, while on every side in the wood, far away in its most
remote recesses, burned larger or smaller fires, before tents or in
other places, and lit up the lofty fir-tree stems, which seemed like
columns of an immense natural temple consecrated to fire. The vast
dome above was dark, and the air was so still that the flames rose
straight upward, and cast a wild light, as of a strange dawn upon
the fir-tree tops and the black clouds.

Beneath the tabernacle an immense crowd was assembled, certainly from three to four thousand persons. They sang hymns—a

magnificent choir! Most likely the sound proceeded from the black portion of the assembly, as their number was three times that of the whites, and their voices are naturally beautiful and pure. In the tower-like pulpit, which stood in the middle of the tabernacle, were four preachers, who, during the intervals between the hymns addressed the people with loud voices, calling sinners to conversion and amendment of life. During all this, the thunder pealed, and fierce lightning flashed through the wood like angry glances of some mighty invisible eye. We entered the tabernacle, and took our seats among the assembly on the side of the whites.

Round the elevation, in the middle of which rose the pulpit, ran a sort of low counter, forming a wide square. Within this, seated on benches below the pulpit, and on the side of the whites, sat the Methodist preachers, for the most part handsome tall figures, with broad, grave foreheads; and on the side of the blacks their spiritual leaders and exhorters, many among whom were mulattoes, men of a lofty, noticeable, and energetic exterior.

The later it grew in the night, the more earnest grew the appeals; the hymns short, but fervent, as the flames of the light-wood ascended, like them, with a passionate ardor. Again and again they arose on high, like melodious, burning sighs from thousands of harmonious voices. The preachers increase in the fervor of their zeal; two stand with their faces turned toward the camp of the blacks, two toward that of the whites, extending their hands, and calling on the sinners to come, come, all of them, *now* at this time, at this moment, which is perhaps the last, the only one which remains to them in which to come to the Savior, to escape eternal damnation! Midnight approaches, the fires burn dimmer, but the exaltation increases and becomes universal. The singing of hymns mingles with the invitations of the preachers, and the exhortations of the class-leaders with the groans and cries of the assembly. And now, from among the white people, rise up young girls and men, and go and throw themselves, as if overcome, upon the low counter. These are met on the other side by the ministers, who bend down to them, receive their confessions, encourage and console them. In the camp of the blacks is heard a great tumult and a loud cry. Men roar and bawl out; women screech like pigs about to be killed; many, having fallen into convulsions, leap and strike about them, so that they are obliged to be held down. It looks here and there like a regular fight; some of the calmer participants laugh. Many a cry of anguish may be heard, but you distinguish no words excepting, "Oh, I am a sinner!" and "Jesus! Jesus!"

During all this tumult the singing continues loud and beautiful, and the thunder joins in with its pealing kettle-drum. . . .

It was now past midnight; the weather had cleared, and the air was so delicious and the spectacle so beautiful, that I was compelled to return to the tent to tell Mrs. Howland, who at once resolved to come out with me. The altar-fires now burned low, and the smoke hung within the wood. . . . Some oppressed souls still lay bowed upon the counter, and still were the preachers giving consolation either by word or song. By degrees the people assembled in the tabernacle dispersed, scattered themselves through the woods, or withdrew to their tents. . . . Mr. R. had now joined us, and accompanied by him we went the round of the camp, especially on the black side. And here all the tents were still full of religious exaltation, each separate tent presenting some new phasis. We saw in one a zealous convert, male or female, as it might be, who with violent gesticulations gave vent to his or her newly-awakened feelings, surrounded by devout auditors; in another we saw a whole crowd of black people on their knees, all dressed in white, striking themselves on the breast, and crying out and talking with the greatest pathos; in a third women were dancing "the holy dance" for one of the newly-converted. This dancing, however, having been forbidden by the preachers, ceased immediately on our entering the tent. I saw merely a rocking movement of women, who held each other by the hand in a circle, singing the while. In a fourth, a song of the spiritual Canaan was being sung excellently. In one tent we saw a fat Negro member walking about by himself and breathing hard; he was hoarse, and sighing, he exclaimed to himself, "Oh! I wish I could hollo!" In some tents people were sitting around the fires, and here visits were received, greetings were made, and friendly, cheerful talk went on, while everywhere prevailed a quiet, earnest state of feeling, which we also experienced whenever we stopped to talk with the people. These black people have a something warm and kind about them which I like much. One can see that they are children of the warm sun. The state of feeling was considerably calmer in the camp of the whites. One saw families sitting at their covered tables eating and drinking. . . .

At sunrise I heard something which resembled the humming of an enormous wasp caught in a spider's web. It was an alarm which gave the sign for the general rising. At half-past five I was dressed and out. The hymns of the Negroes, which had continued through the night, were still to be heard on all sides. The sun shone powerfully—the air was oppressive. People were cooking and having breakfast by the fires, and a crowd already began to assemble on the benches under the tabernacle. At seven o'clock the morning sermon and worship commenced. . . .

The principal sermon of the day was preached about eleven o'clock by a lawyer from one of the neighboring states, a tall, thin gentleman, with strongly-marked, keen features, and deep-set, brilliant eyes. He preached about the Last Judgment, and described in a most lively manner "the fork-like cloven flames, the thunder, the general destruction of all things," and described it as possibly near at hand. "As yet, indeed," exclaimed he, "I have not felt the earth tremble under my feet; it yet seems to stand firm," and he stamped vehemently on the pulpit floor; "and as yet I hear not the rolling of the thunder of doom; *but* it may, nevertheless, be at hand," and so on; and he admonished the people, therefore, immediately to repent and be converted.

Spite of the strength of the subject, and spite of the power in the delineation, there was a something dry and soulless in the manner in which it was presented, which caused it to fail of its effect with the congregation. People seemed to feel that the preacher did not believe, or, rather, did not livingly feel that which he described and preached. A few cries and groans were heard, it is true, and some sinners came forth; but the assembly, upon the whole, continued calm, and was not agitated by the thunders of the Last Judgment. The hymns were, as on the former occasion, fervent and beautiful on the side of the negroes' camp. This people seem to have a keen perception of the most beautiful doctrines of religion, and understand particularly well how to apply them. Their musical talents are remarkable. Most of the blacks have beautiful, pure voices, and sing as easily as we whites talk.

After this service came the hour of dinner, when I visited various tents in the black camp, and saw tables covered with dishes of all kinds of meat, with puddings and tarts; there seemed to be a regular superfluity of meat and drink. Several of the tents were even furnished like rooms, with capital beds, looking-glasses, and such like.

The people seemed gay, happy, and gentle. These religious camp-meetings—my little heart, thou hast now been at a camp-meeting!—are the saturnalia of the negro slaves. In these they luxuriate both soul and body, as is their natural inclination to do; but on this occasion every thing was carried on with decency and befitting reverence. . . .

» [Diary entry] Columbia, South Carolina, May 25th, 1850 «

When at home with Mr. B., I heard the negroes singing, it having been so arranged by Hannah L. I wished rather to have heard their own *naïve* songs, but was told that they "dwelt with the Lord," and sang only hymns. I am sorry for this exclusiveness; nevertheless, their hymns sung in quartette were glorious. It would be impossible to have more exquisite or better singing. They had notebooks before them, and seemed to be singing from them; but my friends laughed, doubting whether they were for actual use. In the midst of the singing a cock began to crow in the house, and kept on crowing incessantly. From the amusement this occasioned, I saw that there was more in it than appeared. Nor was it, in reality, a cock that crowed, but a young negro from a neighboring court, who, being possessed of the cock's ability to crow, chose to make one in the concert.

After this, another young Negro, who was not so evangelical as the rest, came and sang with his banjo several of the negro songs [i.e., minstrel songs] universally known and sung in the South by the negro people, whose product they are, and in the Northern States by persons of all classes, because they are extremely popular. The music of these songs is melodious, *naïve*, and full of rhythmical life, and the deepest, tenderest sentiment. Many of these songs remind me of Haydn's and Mozart's simple, *naïve* melodies; for example, "Rosa Lee," "Oh, Susannah," "Dearest May," "Carry me back to old Virginny," "Uncle Ned," and "Mary Blane," all of which are full of the most touching pathos, both in words and melody. The words, however, are frequently inferior to the music; they are often childish, and contain many repetitions both of phrases and imagery; but frequently, amid all this, expressions and turns of thought which are in the highest degree poetical, and with bold and happy transitions, such as we find in the oldest songs of our Northern people. These negro songs are also not uncommonly ballads, or, more properly, little romances, which contain descriptions of their love affairs and their simple life's fate. There is no imagination, no gloomy background, rich with saga or legend, as in our songs; but, on the other hand, much sentiment, and a *naïve*, and often humorous seizing upon the moment and its circumstances. These songs have been made on the road; during the journeyings of the slaves; upon the rivers, as they paddled their canoes along or steered the raft down the stream; and, in particular, at the corn-huskings, which are to the negroes what the harvest-home is to our peasants, and at which they sing impromptu whatever is uppermost in their hearts or in their brain. Yes, all these songs are peculiarly improvisations, which have taken root in the mind of the people, and are listened to and sung to the whites, who, possessed of a knowledge of music, have caught and noted them down. And this improvisation goes forward every day. People hear new songs continually; they are the offspring of nature and of accident, produced from the joys and the sorrows of a childlike race. The rhyme comes as it may, sometimes clumsily, sometimes no rhyme at all, sometimes most wonderfully fresh and perfect; the rhythm is excellent, and the descriptions have local coloring and distinctness. Alabama, Louisiana, Tennessee, Carolina, "Old Virginny," all the melodious names of the Southern States and places there, the abodes of the slaves, are introduced into their songs, as well as their love histories, and give a local interest and coloring not only to the song, but to the state and to the place which they sing about. Thus these songs are like flowers and fragrance from the negro life in those states—like flowers cast upon the waves of the river, and borne hither and thither by the wind—like fragrance from the flowers of the wilderness in their summer life, because there is no bitterness, no gloomy spirit in these songs. They are the offspring of life's summer day, and bear witness to this. And if bitterness and the condition of slavery were to cease forever in the free land of the United States, these songs would still live, and bear witness to the light of life, even as the phosphorescent beam of the fire-fly shines, though the glow-worm may be crushed.

The young negro whom I heard sing this evening, sang among other songs one of which I would that I could give you an idea, so fresh was the melody, and so peculiar the key. Of the words I only remember this first verse:

> I am going to the old Pedee!
> And there on the old Pedee,
>   On a summer's night,
>   When the moon shines bright,
> My Sally I shall see!

The last syllable of the first and last verse is long drawn out. The little romance describes how the lover and Sally will be married and settle themselves down, and live happily all on the banks of the old Pedee. A heartfelt, charming Southern idyll.

The banjo is an African instrument, made from the half of a fruit called the calabash, or gourd, which has a very hard rind. A thin skin or piece of bladder is stretched over the opening, and over this one or two strings are stretched, which are raised on a bridge. The banjo is the negroes' guitar, and certainly it is the first-born among stringed instruments.

» [Diary entry] Charleston [South Carolina], June 10, 1850 «

One evening which I spent at Mr. G.'s I was present at the evening worship of the negroes, in a hall which that good, right-thinking minister had allowed them to use for that purpose. The first speaker, an old negro, was obliged to give place to another, who said he was so full of the power of the word that he could not possibly keep silence, and he poured forth of his eloquence for a good hour, but said the same thing over and over again. These negro preachers were far inferior to those which I heard in Savannah.

Finally, he admonished one of the sisters "to pray." On this, an elderly, sickly woman began immediately to pray aloud, and her evident fervor in thanksgiving for the consolation of the Gospel of Christ, and her testimony on behalf of its powers, in her own long and suffering life, was really affecting. But the prayer was too long; the same thing was repeated too often, with an incessant thumping on the bench with her fists, as an accompaniment to every groan of prayer. At the close of this, and when another sister was admonished to pray, the speaker added, "But make it short, if you please!"

This sister, however, did not make it short, but longer even than the first, with still more circumlocution, and still more thumping on the bench.

A third sister, who was admonished to pray, received the short, definite injunction, "But *short*." And when she lost herself in the long bewilderment of prayer, she was interrupted without ceremony by the wordy preacher, who could no longer keep silence, but must hear himself talk on for another good hour. Nor was it until the singing of one of the hymns composed by the negroes themselves, such as they sing in their canoes, and in which the name "Jerusalem" is often repeated, that the congregation became really alive. They sang so that it was a pleasure to hear, with all their souls and with all their bodies in unison; for their bodies wagged, their heads nodded, their feet stamped, their knees shook, their elbows and their hands beat time to the tune and the words which they sang with evident delight. One must see these people singing if one is rightly to understand their life. I have seen their imitators, the so-called "Sable Singers," who travel about the country painted up as negroes, and singing negro songs in the negro manner, and with negro gestures, as it is said; but nothing can be more radically unlike, for the most essential part of the resemblance fails—namely, *the life*.

One of my pleasures here has been to talk with an old negro called Romeo, who lives in a little house in a garden near, and which said garden he takes care of, or rather neglects, according to his pleasure. He is the most good-tempered, merriest old man that any one can imagine, and he has a good deal of natural wit. He was, in the prime of his life, stolen from Africa and brought hither, and he tells stories about that event in the most *naïve* manner. I asked him one day what the people in his native land believed respecting life after death! He replied "that the good would go to the God of heaven who made them." "And what of the bad?" asked I. "They go out into the wind," and he blew with his mouth around him on all sides.

I got him to sing me an Ethiopian death-song, which seemed to consist of a monotone vibration upon three semi-tones; and after that an African love-song, which seemed to be tolerably rude, and which convulsed the old fellow with laughter. I have his portrait in my album, but he laughed and was so shame-faced while I made the sketch, that it was difficult for me to catch the likeness. He is dressed in his slave garments, gray clothes, and knitted woolen cap.

The negro people and the primeval forest have made a peculiarly living impression upon me, and have extended my vision as regards the richness of those forms in which the Creator expresses his life. The earth seems to me as a great symbolic writing, a grand epic, in which the various species of man, of vegetable productions and animals, water and land, form groups of separate songs and paragraphs which we have to read, and from which to learn the style of the Great Master, His design, and His system. My soul, in this view, spreads forth her wings and flies—alas! only in spirit—around the whole world; across the deserts and the paradise of Africa; across the icy tracts of Siberia; over the mountain land of the Himalayas—every where between the poles and the equator, where man lives, and animals breathe, and vegetation ascends toward the light; and I endeavor involuntarily to group and arrange the dissimilar forms into harmonious constellations around one central, all-illuminating Sun; but—all is yet only anticipation, glimpses, flashes of light into my soul—merely the dawn, the morning watch! Perhaps at length the perfect day may appear; perhaps in the native land of runes, in my own silent home, I may be enabled to expound these runes of the earth, and that runic song which has been given me to ponder upon. . . .

» [Letter to the Rev. P. J. Böklin] Cincinnati, Ohio, November 27th, 1850 «

Not a little is done in the free states for the instruction and elevation of the negroes; but still I can not convince myself that the Americans are doing this in the best way. They endeavor to form this human race so different to themselves, according to their own methods and institutions. When I see those frolicsome negro children in their school sit down like white children on benches and before desks, I am quite distressed. I am convinced that these children ought to learn their lessons standing, or dancing amid games and songs, and that their divine worship ought to be conducted with singing and dancing; and I will answer for it, that their songs and dances would have more life, beauty, and intelligence in them than those of the

Shaker community. But who shall teach them thus! None but a negro can teach the negroes, and only one of their own people can become the deliverer of the people in the highest sense. But this captive Israel yet waits for its Moses.

That, however, which very much prevents the redemption of this people from captivity, is their own want of national spirit. Already split into tribes in Africa, where they were at war, and where they enslaved one another, it is difficult to take hold of any more widely extended interests than those of family and local society. I have spoken with many freemen of this people in good circumstances here, also with some young mulattoes who have studied and taken degrees at the Oberlin Institution in this state, and I have found them particularly lukewarm toward the interests of their captive brethren, and especially so as regards colonization in Liberia. Frederick Douglas [sic] is as yet the only strong champion among them for their own people.

But if any thing can awake within them a more comprehensive feeling for the whole people, it is assuredly that common slavery on the soil of America, and perhaps, more than any thing else at this moment, the bill which allows the recapture of fugitive slaves. I awoke to this thought to-day during a visit to a free negro church, where I had no occasion to lament any want of interest in the national affairs, either in the negro preacher or the congregation.

I had in the forenoon visited a negro Baptist Church belonging to the Episcopal creed. There were but few present, and they of the negro aristocracy of the city. The mode of conducting the divine service was quiet, very proper, and a little tedious. The hymns were beautifully and exquisitely sung. The sermon, which treated of "Love without dissimulation; how hard to win, how impossible without the influence of God and the communication of his power," was excellent. The preacher was a fair mulatto, with the features and demeanor of the white race, a man of very good intellect and conversational power, with whom I had become already acquainted in my Cincinnati home.

In the afternoon I went to the African Methodist Church in Cincinnati, which is situated in the African quarter. In this district live the greater number of the free colored people of the city; and the quarter bears the traces thereof. The streets and the houses have, it is true, the Anglo-American regularity; but broken windows and rags hanging from them, a certain neglected, disorderly aspect, both of houses and streets, testified of negro management. I found in the African Church African ardor and African life. The church was full to overflowing, and the congregation sang their own hymns. The singing ascended and poured forth like a melodious torrent, and the heads, feet, and elbows, of the congregation moved all in unison with it, amid evident enchantment and delight in the singing, which was in itself exquisitely pure and full of melodious life.

The hymns and psalms which the negroes have themselves composed have a peculiar *naïve* character, childlike, full of imagery and life. Here is a specimen of one of their popular church hymns:

"What ship is this that's landed at the shore?
　　　Oh, glory halleluiah!
　　It's the old ship of Zion, halleluiah,
　　It's the old ship of Zion, halleluiah,
　Is the mast all sure, and the timber all sound?
　　　Oh, glory halleluiah!
　　She's built of gospel timber, halleluiah,
　　She's built, &c.

"What kind of men does she have on board?
　　　Oh, glory halleluiah!
　　They're all true-hearted soldiers, halleluiah,
　　They're all, &c.

"What kind of Captain does she have on board?
　　　Oh, glory halleluiah!
　　King Jesus is the Captain, halleluiah,
　　King Jesus, &c.

"Do you think she will be able to land us on the shore?
　　　Oh, glory halleluiah!
　　I think she will be able, halleluiah,
　　I think, &c.

"She has landed over thousands, and can land as many more.
　　　Oh, glory, halleluiah!" &c., &c.

After the singing of the hymns, which was not led by any organ or musical instrument, whatever, but which arose like burning melodious sighs from the breasts of the congregation, the preacher mounted the pulpit. He was a very black negro, young, with a very retreating forehead, and the lower portion of the countenance protruding; upon the whole, not at all good-looking. But when he began to speak, the congregation hung upon his words, and I could not but admire his flowing eloquence. He admonished the assembly to reflect on the present need of their brethren; to pray for the fugitive slaves, who must now, in great multitudes, leave their acquired homes, and seek a shelter out of the country against legal violence and legal injustice. He exhorted them also to pray for that nation which, in its blindness, would pass such laws and oppress the innocent! This exhortation was received with deep groans and lamenting cries.

After this the preacher drew a picture of the death of "Sister Bryant," and related the history of her beautiful Christian devotion, and applied to her the words of the Book of Revelation, of those "who come out of great afflictions." The intention of suffering on earth, the glorious group of the children of suffering in their release, and thanksgiving-song as represented in so divine and grand a manner in the pages of Scripture, were placed by the negro preacher in the light as of noonday, and as I had never before heard from the lips of any ordinary ministers. After this the preacher nearly lost himself in the prayer for the sorrowing widower and his children, and their "little blossoming souls." Then came the sermon proper.

The preacher proposed to the congregation the question, "Is God with us?" "I speak of our nation, my brethren," said he; "I regard our nationality. Let us examine the matter." And with this he drew a very ingenious parallel between the captivity of the Israelites in Egypt and the negroes in America, and those trials by which Providence evinced His especial solicitude about the chosen people. After having represented the fate of the Israelites under Pharaoh and Moses, he went on to contemplate the fate of the negro people.

"How shall we know that God is with us? Let me look at the question thus."

He then boldly sketched out a picture of an enslaved people as oppressed in every way, but not the less "increasing in numbers and improving themselves, purchasing their own freedom from slavery (cries of 'Yes! yes!' 'Oh, glory!' throughout the church); purchasing land (shouts of joy); ever more and more land (increasing shouts); buying houses, large houses, larger and still larger houses (increasing jubilation and stamping of feet); building churches (still louder cries); still more and larger churches (louder and still louder cries, movement, stamping of feet, and clapping of hands); the people increasing still in number, in property, in prosperity, and in understanding, so that the rulers of the land began to be terrified, and to say, 'They are becoming too strong for us; let us send them over to Liberia!' (Violent fermentation and excitement.) This, then, will show us, my brethren, that God is with us. Let us not forsake Him; for He will lead us out of captivity, and make of us a great people!" (extreme delight and joy, with the cry of 'Amen!' 'Yes, yes!' 'Oh, glory!' and so on). The whole congregation was for several minutes like a stormy sea. The preacher's address had been a rushing tempest of natural eloquence. I doubt, however, whether his patriotism extended much beyond the moment of inspiration and of his pulpit; he was not a new Moses. Old Moses was slow of speech; he was a man of action.

This preacher was, however, the first negro from whom I had heard any distinct sentiment of nationality. The bill against fugitive slaves must mind what it is about, and what it may lead to. . . .

» [Diary entry] Noah's Ark [i.e. the steamer Belle Key], December 18th, 1850 «

I must tell you of a pleasure which he [Lerner H.] prepared for me one evening on the Ohio. He asked me whether I should like to hear the negroes of the ship sing, and led me for this purpose to the lowest deck, where I beheld a strange scene. The immense engine-fires are all on this deck, eight or nine apertures all in a row; they are like yawning fiery throats, and beside each throat stood a negro naked to his middle, who flung in fire-wood. Pieces of wood were passed onward to these feeders by other negroes, who stood up aloft on a large open place between them and a negro, who, standing on a lofty stack of fire-wood, threw down with vigorous arms food for the monsters on deck. Lerner H. encouraged the negroes to sing; and the negro up aloft on the pile of fire-wood began immediately an improvised song in stanzas, and at the close of each the negroes down below joined in vigorous chorus. It was a fantastic and grand sight to see these energetic black athletes lit up by the wildly flashing flames from the fiery throats, while they, amid their equally fantastic song, keeping time most exquisitely, hurled one piece of fire-wood after another into the yawning fiery gulf. Every thing went on with so much life, and so methodically, and the whole scene was so accordant and well arranged, that it would have produced a fine effect upon any theatre whatever. . . .

18. The Slave Narrative Collection

⇥⇥⇥ During the years 1936–38, the Federal Writer's Project produced a huge collection of narratives obtained by white interviewers from ex-slaves living in thirteen southern states. The Writer's Unit of the Library of Congress Project processed and assembled a large amount of material left over from the state projects, ending up with a collection that contains over 2,000 ex-slave narratives, white-informant narratives, photographs, records of sales, and slave advertisements—a veritable folk history of slavery. B. A. Botkin, chief editor of the Library of Congress Slave Narrative Collection, wrote in 1941: "For the first and the last time, a large number of surviving slaves have been permitted to tell their own story, in their own way. In spite of obvious limitations—bias and fallibility of both informants and interviewers, the use of leading questions, unskilled techniques, and insufficient controls and checks—this saga must remain the most authentic and colorful source of our knowledge of the lives and thoughts of thousands of slaves. . . .

"To the white myth of slavery must be added the slaves' own folklore and folk-say of slavery. . . . The patterns they reveal are folk and regional patterns—the patterns of field hand, house and body servant, and artisan; the patterns of kind and cruel master or mistress; the patterns of Southeast and Southwest, lowland and upland, tidewater and inland, small and larger plantations, and racial mixture (including Creole and Indian).

"The narratives belong also to folk literature. Rich not only in folk songs, folk tales, and folk speech but also in folk humor and poetry, crude or skilful in dialect, uneven in tone and treatment, they constantly reward one with earthy imagery, salty phrase, and sensitive detail." ⇤⇤⇤

From the Slave Narrative Collection [1941] †

GUS FEASTER (UNION, SOUTH CAROLINA)

We had Saturday afternoons to do our work and to wash. We had all de holidays off and a big time Christmas and July 4th.

Going to funerals we used all Marse's wagons. Quick as de funeral

† Text: From microfilm copies of the Slave Narrative Collection. Courtesy of the Schomburg Collection, the New York Public Library.

start, de preacher give out a funeral hymn. All in de procession took up de tune and as de wagons move along with de mules at a slow walk, everybody sing dat hymn. When it was done, another was lined out, and dat kept up 'till we reach de graveyard. Then de preacher pray and we sung some mo'. In dem days funerals was slow for both de white and de black folks. Now they is so fast, you is home again before you gets dar good.

On de way home from de funeral, de mules would perk up a little in dey walk and a faster hymn was sung on the way home. When we got home, we was in a good mood from singing de faster hymns and de funeral soon be forgot. . . .

Ma sung some of de oldest hymns dat I is ever heard: (She sang) "O Zion, O Zion, O Zion, wanta get home at last". (father) "Is you over, Is you over, Is you over" (and the bass come back) "Yes thank God, Yes thank God, Yes thank God, I is over." "How did you cross?" "At de ferry, at de ferry, at de ferry. Yes, thank God I is over." If I sing dem now folks laughs at me, ma sho' teached dem to her children. . . . Our work song was, "John Henry was a man; he worked all over dis town." They still uses dat song. In slavery, some holler when dey be in de field like owls; some like crows; and some like pea-fowls [a reference to "field hollers"].

C. B. BURTON (NEWBERRY, SOUTH CAROLINA)

We danced and had jigs. Some played de fiddle and some made whistles from canes, having different lengths for different notes, and blowed 'em like mouth organs.

JASPER BATTLE (ATHENS, GEORGIA)

When us got de corn up from de fields, niggers came from far and nigh to Marster's cornshucking. Dat cornshucking work was easy with everybody singing and having a good time together whilst dey made dem shucks fly. De cornshucking captain led all de singing, and he set right up on top of de highest pile of corn.

PEGGY GRIGSBY (NEWBERRY, SOUTH CAROLINA)

The old folk had corn-shuckings, frolics, pender pullings, and quiltings. . . . When dey danced, dey always used fiddles to make the music.

ANDY BRICE (WINNSBORO, SOUTH CAROLINA)

One day I see Marse Thomas a twistin' de ears on a fiddle and rosinin' de bow. Then he pull dat bow 'cross de belly of dat fiddle. Something bust loose in me and sing all thru my head and tingle in

my fingers. I made up my mind, right then and dere, to save and
buy me a fiddle. I got one dat Christmas, bless God! I learnt and
been playin' de fiddle ever since. I pat one foot while I'm playin'. I
kept on playin' and pattin' dat foot for thirty years. I lose dat foot in
a smash-up wid a highway accident, but [when] I play de old tunes
on dat fiddle at night, dat foot seem to be dere at de end of dat
leg and pats just de same. Sometime I ketch myself lookin' down to
see if it have come back and joined itself up to dat leg, from de
very charm of de music I makin' wid de fiddle and de bow.

. . . Who I marry? I marry Ellen Watson, as pretty a ginger
cake nigger as ever fried a batter cake or rolled her arms up in a wash
tub. How I git her? I never get her; dat fiddle get her. I play for
all de white folks dances down at Cedar Shades, up at Blackstock.
De money roll in when someone pass 'round de hat and say: 'De
fiddler?' Ellen had more beaux 'round her than her could shake a
stick at but de beau she like best was de beau dat could draw music
out of them five strings, and draw money into dat hat, dat jingle in
my pocket de next day when I go to see her. . . .

What church I belong to? None. Dat fiddle draws down from
heaven all de sermons dat I understand. I sings de hymns in de way
I praise and glorify de Lord.

Louisa Brown (Waverly Mills, South Carolina)

At night when de meeting dun busted till next day was when de
darkies really did have dey freedom o' spirit. And de wagon be creeping along in de late hours o' moonlight and de darkies would raise a
tune. Den de air soon be filled with the sweetest tune as us rode on
home and sung all de old hymns dat us loved. It was always some
big black nigger with a deep bass voice like a frog dat would start
up de tune. Den de other men join in, followed up by de fine little
voices o' de gals and de cracked voices of de old women and de
grannies. When us reach near de big house us soften down to a deep
hum dat de missus like! Sometime she listen up de window and
tell us [to] sing *Swing Low Sweet Chariot* for her and de visiting
guests. Dat all we want to hear. Us open up and de niggers near de
big house dat hadn't been to church would wake up and come out to
de cabin door and join in de refrain. From dat we'd swing on into all
de old spirituals dat us love so well and dat us knowed how to sing.
Missus often allow dat her darkies could sing with heaven's inspiration. Now and den some old mammie would fall out'n de wagon a
shoutin' "Glory" and "Hallelujah" and "Amen!" After dat us went
off to lay down for de night.

W. L. Bost (Asheville, North Carolina)

Us niggers never have chance to go to Sunday School and church. The white folks feared for niggers to get any religion and education, but I reckon somethin' inside just told us about God and that there was a better place hereafter. We would sneak off and have prayer meetin'. Sometimes the paddyrollers catch us and beat us good but that didn't keep us from tryin'. I remember one old song we use to sing when we went down in the woods back of the barn. My mother she sing an' pray to the Lord to deliver us out o' slavery. She always say she thankful she was never sold from her children, and that our Massa not so mean as some of the others. But the old song it went something like this:

> Oh, mother, lets go down, lets go down, lets go down,
>   lets go down.
>
> Oh, mother, lets go down, down in the valley to pray.
> As I went down in the valley to pray
> Studyin' about that good ole way
> Who shall wear that starry crown.

Joseph Holmes Prichard (near Mobile, Alabama)

Den come cornshucking time. My goodness, I would just love to be dar now. De corn would be piled up high and one man would git on dat pile. It was usually a kinda foreman who could sing and get de work out of de slaves. Dis foreman would sing a verse something like dis:

> Polk and Clay went to war,
> Polk come back with a broken jaw.

Then all de niggers would sing back at him with a kinda shouting sound. Near about all de times de foreman made up his own songs, by picking dem out of de shucking.

Isaac Stier (Nachez, Mississippi)

De best time I can remember always came around de Fourth of July. Dat was always de beginning of camp meeting. Ain't nothing like dat in these days. . . .

Us slaves sang mostly hymns and psalms. But I remember one song about a frog pond and one about *Jump, Mr. Toad*. I's too word-less to sing 'em now, but dey was funny. Us danced plenty too. Some of de men clogged and pigeoned, but when us had dances dey was real cotillions, like de white folks had. Dere was always a fiddler and,

on Christmas and other holidays, de slaves was allowed to invite dey
sweethearts from other plantations. I use to call out de figgers:

> Ladies sasshay, Gents to de left, now all swing.

Everybody like my calls, and de dancers sho' moved smooth and
pretty.

JAMES SINGLETON (SIMPSON COUNTY, MISSISSIPPI)

We didn't have no dancing dat I remember, but had plenty log-
rollings. Had fiddling and all would join in singing songs, like *Run
nigger run, Pattyrollers ketch you, Run nigger run, It's breaking day.*
I still fiddle dat tune. Well, you see, dey just rolled up all de old
dead logs and trees in a big pile, and burned it at night.

JAMES CALHART JAMES (BALTIMORE, MARYLAND)

One of the songs sung by the slaves on the plantation I can remember part of it. They sang it with great feeling of happiness.

> Oh where shall we go when de great day comes
> And de blowing of de trumpets and de banging of de drums.
> When General Sherman comes.
> No more rice and cotton fields
> We will hear no more crying
> Old master will be sighing

I can't remember the tune. People sang it according to their own
tune.

JAMES DEANE (BALTIMORE, MARYLAND)

After work was done, the slaves would smoke, sing, tell ghost
stories and tales, dance, [and make] music, [with] homemade fiddles.
Saturday was work day like any other day. We had all legal holidays.
Christmas morning we went to the big house and got presents and
had a big time all day.

At corn shucking all the slaves from other plantations would
come to the barn, the fiddler would sit on top of the highest barrel
of corn, and play all kinds of songs; [there was] a barrel of cider, jug
of whiskey, [with] one man to dish out a drink of liquor each hour,
cider when wanted. We had supper at twelve, roast pig for everybody,
apple sauce, hominy, and corn bread. We went back to shucking. The
carts from other farms would be there to haul it to the corn crib,
[the] dance would start after the corn was stored, [and] we danced
until daybreak.

The only games we played [as children] were marbles, mumble peg and ring play. We sang *London Bridge*.

When we wanted to meet at night we had an old conk; we blew that. We all would meet on the bank of the Potomac River and sing across the river to the slaves in Virginia, and they would sing back to us.

VI. Music in the Cities in the Nineteenth Century

19. ROBERT WALN (PETER ATALL)

→» Son of a wealthy Quaker merchant, Robert Waln (1794–1825) wrote a satire on the fashionable life of Philadelphia in *The Hermit in America on a Visit to Philadelphia* (Philadelphia, 1819), under the pseudonym Peter Atall, Esq. To Waln we are indebted for the earliest report on the activities of the renowned black composer and bandleader Frank Johnson (1792–1844). In 1819 Johnson was on the threshold of a career that won for him the reputation of "one of the best performers in the country on the bugle and the French horn" and earned his band a rating among the cognoscenti just below that of the Royal Band of London and the Band of the National Guards at Paris. Eventually Johnson's talent took him to England, where he gave a command performance at Buckingham Palace and was presented with a silver bugle by Queen Victoria. «←

From *The Hermit in America* [1819] †

THE COTILLION PARTY

The coach stopped at the door of the Masonic Hall in Chestnut Street. It was raining, and the snow that during the day had been gradually melting, was now almost incorporated with the water. It was precisely in that situation in which it is least desirable to walk therein in full dress; but the regulations of the Hall were not to be contravened, and my friend Mr. Atall and myself were constrained to undergo this hardship in common with all the *ladies* and gentlemen of the party. The hall is situated a goodly distance from the street, and there is an especial entrance and outlet for the use of carriages: I was informed by my friend that their non-admittance, by which so much inconvenience could be avoided, was founded upon economical motives, the bricks of the carriage-way being of a remarkably soft and perishable nature. This irresistibly reminded me of the care-

† Text: The original edition (Philadelphia, 1819), pp. 151–55, 178–80.

ful landlord, who, in his zeal to prevent the dropping of the spigot, lost the contents of the cask out of the bung-hole.

We entered the room, pretty much in the same manner as I should have entered the theatre, or any other place of public amusement. Mr. C. having been prevented from accompanying me, and I not having the honour of the manager's acquaintance, it was not to be supposed they should have penetration enough to distinguish a stranger. Had such been the case, common civility would of course have required a reception of some kind or other. Mr. Atall separated himself from me the moment we entered, very innocently thinking, no doubt, I was old enough to shift for myself.

The room was about half filled with a most splendid collection of belles and beaux, the greater part engaged in dancing cotillions, after the fashion of my country. The decorations of the saloon, independent of certain dark-looking figures (apparently in bronze), which are placed at certain intervals around, are plain, but neat and ornamental. The figures alluded to have the most comical effect imaginable, and are, no doubt, placed there for the purpose;—seeing that no place is better adapted to the free and admissible use of the risible muscles, than a ball-room. The ingenious managers deserve credit for this invention, for I believe it is indisputably original.

Mr. Atall returned just in time to prevent the execution of a resolution deliberately formed, to make the best of my way back to the Washington Hall hotel. He had paid his respects to the "few ladies," to use his own expressions, "with whom he was remarkably solicitous to continue his acquaintance," and returned to dedicate the remainder of the evening to me.

"Is not the orchestra rather elevated?" I enquired.

"A great part of the sound is lost, but it is an evil not to be remedied.——You observe the leader of the band. He is a descendant of Africa, and possesses a most respectable share of musical talents.—Among other follies of our young ladies, it is quite a fashionable one, to be 'enchanted' with this fiddler. He is indeed a prominent character in the gay world, and happy the lady, in whose ear, at the midnight hour, he pours the dulcet notes of love!"

"Sir?" said I, starting.

"Be not alarmed. Music, you know, is the food of love, and many of our young lovers are in the habit of feasting their mistresses most luxuriously. I have even heard it whispered, that two or three have been so unfortunately overpowered by a surfeit, as not to recover their senses until the ensuing morning. This fiddler is the presiding deity on such occasions, and although a tawny one, is not the less fervently invoked on that account. In fine, he is leader of the band at all balls, public and private; sole director of all serenades, acceptable and not acceptable; inventor-general of cotillions; to which add, a remarkable taste in distorting a sentimental, simple, and beautiful song, into a reel, jig, or country-dance;—and you have a pretty correct idea of the favoured little J—ns—n."

"An important personage, certainly. . . ."

The first act [i.e., the supper after the dancing] had commenced, in which the whole strength of the company was elucidated; and the oysters were vanishing with inconceivable rapidity. The sameness of the action and length of the scene was somewhat tiresome, more especially as it belonged to that class of spectacles, denominated pantomimes, so universally and worthily detested: every mouth was kept in constant motion, without the utterance of a syllable.

"There is our friend, Mr. Quotem," whispered Atall, "very busily employed; we must endeavor to avoid him: he has many friends here, and if he puts them on the scent, we shall be quizzed most unmercifully. You are a stranger, and will have no quarters."

"I am very willing to defend myself," I replied.

The calls of hunger being appeased, many of the gentlemen seceded from the tables, and stood before the stoves, or wandered about the room, enjoying their "Woodville yellows" with infinite *gusto*. Their brethren, supping at the tables, did not appear at all incommoded, when the white smoke might be seen sailing around their heads. "Practice makes perfect," but it would require a long time to accustom me to sup on an alternate mouthful of oysters and tobacco smoke!

At length the cloths were removed, and the tables cleared.

"Stop your fiddling there."—"Let us have none of your cursed scraping."—"Rest your cat-gut."—"No more talk up in the gallery there"—was bawled out by a dozen voices to the indefatigable musicians, who had been playing sundry marches and sentimental songs, probably to rest their elbows from the fatigues attendant upon reels and jigs.

"Aye! aye! sir;" replied the little man of music, greatly rejoiced, as he was anxious to comply with a fortuitous engagement. One or two of the younger dandies had demonstrated to his satisfaction, that, "inasmuch as he was then up, and not gone to bed, and the band was assembled, without the trouble of assembling it, and all their fingers were in tune, without the pains of putting them so, he ought not to charge full price for a serenade." Half-price was accordingly agreed upon, and the young gentlemen triumphantly departed with the negroes at their heels, to seal the slumbers of some fair damsels, already resting (beyond the probability of discomposure) from the fatigues of the evening.

20. SAMUEL MORDECAI

⋙ In 1800 the population of Richmond, Virginia, was 5,300, divided almost equally between whites and blacks. It was this period of Richmond's history that Samuel Mordecai discussed in his book, *Richmond in By-Gone Days* (Richmond, 1856). Although an apologist for slavery, Mordecai nevertheless provides useful information about the roles played by black musicians in the social life of the town. ⋘

From *Richmond in By-Gone Days* [1856] †

The most prominent member of the black aristocracy of my early years was *Sy. Gilliat* (probably Simon, or Cyrus), the leading violinist, (fiddler was then the word,) at the balls and dancing parties. He traced his title to position to the days of vice royalty, having held office under Lord Botetourt, when governor, but whether behind his chair or his coach, is in the mist of obscurity.

Sy. Gilliat flourished in Richmond in the first decade of this century, and I know not how many of the last. He was tall, and even in his old age, (if he ever grew old,) erect and dignified. When he appeared officially in the orchestra, his dress was an embroidered silk coat and vest of faded lilac, small clothes, (he would not say breeches,) and silk stockings, (which rather betrayed the African prominence of the shin-bone,) terminating in shoes fastened or decorated with large buckles. This court-dress being of the reign of Lord Botetourt, and probably part of the fifty suits which, according to the inventory he made, constituted his wardrobe; to complete this court costume, Sy. wore a brown wig, with side curls, and a long cue appended. His manners were as courtly as his dress, and he elbowed himself and his fiddle-stick through the world with great propriety and harmony. . . .

Gentlemen of town and country formed the Jockey Clubs, which

† Text: The original edition (Richmond, 1856), pp. 310–11, 178–80, 296–97.

held the Spring and Fall races at Richmond and Petersburg, and perhaps elsewhere. They and their friends came to town in their coaches and four, in their phaetons, chariots, and gigs, bringing their wives and daughters: a very convenient time for the Spring and Fall fashions. . . . The race week was a perfect carnival. The streets were thronged with equipages, and the shops with customers. Not only taverns and boarding-houses were filled, but private families opened their hospitable doors to their country friends. Among the amusements of the week was the *Race Ball,* which (as well as the regular dancing assemblies of the winter) was held in the large ball-room of the Eagle. Boots and pants in those days were proscribed. Etiquette required shorts and silks, and pumps with buckles, and powdered hair. The ball was opened by one of the managers and the lady he thought proper to distinguish, with a *minuet de la Cour,* putting the grace and elegance of the couple to a severe ordeal.

Such bowing and curtseying, tiptoeing and tipfingering, backing and filling, advancing and retreating, attracting and repelling, all in the figures of Z or X, to a tune which would have served for a dead march! A long silken train following the lady, like a sunset shadow; and the gentleman holding a cocked hat under his arm, or in his hand, until at last the lady permitted the gentleman, at full armslength, to hand her, by the very tips of her fingers to a seat, when, with a most profound bow, he retreated backward to seek one for himself.

Then commenced the reel, like a storm after a calm—all life and animation. No solemn walking of the figure to a measured step—but pigeon-wings fluttered, and all sorts of capers were cut to the music of Sy. Gilliat's fiddle, and the flute or clarionet of his blacker comrade, London Brigs.

Contra dances followed, and sometimes a congo, or a hornpipe; and when "the music grew fast and furious," and the most stately of the company had retired, a jig would wind up the evening, which, by-the-by, commenced about eight o'clock.

The waltz and the polka were as great strangers to the ball-room floor, as were Champaign and Perigord pies to the supper-table. . . .

On the spot where it [i.e. a church] stood, is now erected a tobacco factory large enough for a Cathedral, and not only by the belfry which surmounts it, but also by the sounds that proceed from within its walls, might it be mistaken for one, as might several other similar establishments; for many of the negroes, male and female, employed in the factories, have acquired such skill in psalmody and have generally such fine voices, that it is a pleasure to listen to the sacred music with which they beguile the hours of labour. Besides the naturally fine voice and ear for music which seems to have been given to the black race, (perhaps to enable them "to whistle and to sing for want of thought,") many of the slaves in Richmond have acquired some knowledge of music by note, and may be seen, even in the factories, with their books of psalmody open on the work-bench. How much worse off are they than operatives in a factory in Old, or even in New England?

At the foot also of Church Hill, on Main and Twenty-sixth streets, was erected a Catholic church, too large for the small number of worshipers when it was built, some thirty or forty years ago, and too small for the large number of later years. It was converted to Presbyterianism, and after adhering to this church for some years, it fell, (as a witty friend tells me,) "into the seré and yellow leaf," and became devoted to tobacco. It is now a tobacco factory, and its original dimensions are trebled, if not quadrupled in size. A host of blacks now work there in twisting tobacco where *the sacred Host* was formerly elevated by the priest. A solution of liquorice has taken the place of holy water; but possibly the establishment may be employed in the manufacture of "Christian's Comfort," a commodity rarely mentioned. Here also fine psalmody may be heard, as of yore, and the organ loft is still occupied by a choir, but one whose music *ceases* on Sabbaths and Holy days.

21. GEORGE G. FOSTER

>>> Little is known about George G. Foster (d. 1850), a local historian of the city of New York, who wrote one of the earliest reports on black dance bands in New York. Foster's *New York by Gas Light with Here and There a Streak of Sunshine* (New York, 1850) refers to this music in two chapters, one entitled "The Points at Midnight" and the other "The Dance House." The latter subject had been made famous by the English author Charles Dickens, who visited it in 1842 and wrote about his experiences in *Notes on America* (New York, 1842). At that time the dance hall was called Almack's, and its music was furnished by a "corpulent black fiddler" and a man playing the tambourine. The special attraction of the night was the world-renowned black dancer "Master Juba" (William Henry Lane, ca. 1825–53). After Dickens' visit, the name of the night club was changed to Dickens' Place. <<<

From *New York by Gas Light* [1850] †

THE DANCE-HOUSE

PETE WILLIAMS'S, OR DICKENS'S PLACE

It is an especially dark and muggy night, and we could not wish for a more favorable opportunity of visiting the celebrated dance-house of Pete Williams, known ever since the visit of a distinguished foreigner to this country, as "Dickens's Place." The old building was burnt down or gutted in a fire some three or four years ago; but so popular a resort as this could not remain long unbuilt, and in a few months it resumed its wonted aspect—though perhaps a trifle cheerfuler—and reëchoed its wonted sounds of festive jollification. You may have read recently in the newspapers—for since the telegraph has taken the news out of the inkstands of the editors, they are turning their attention to all sorts of abstruse and æsthetic subjects —long and dreary dissertations on architecture, from which you learned

† Text: The original edition (New York, 1850), pp. 72–76.

exactly all the writers knew—nothing. But however extensive may have been your reading or observation on the subject, it would puzzle you to find an appropriate designation for the style of architecture in which Dickens's Place is built. The outside is of boards, discolored in various places and mismatched—as if they had been gathered together from the remnants of some pig-pen wrecked in a barn-yard. Jack-plane nor ruler never violated their mottled surfaces, and as to grooving and smoothedging, they are as innocent of it as a wrangling couple. The door is fastened with a wooden pin stuck in a hole by the side, like a country stable—although on occasion a stout padlock stands sentry over the premises. But it is a gala night, and the door is invitingly open—the faithful pin hanging to its post by a string. We pay a shilling at the door and enter. No tickets nor presentations are required. No master of ceremonies tortures you with inconvenient questions, nor director of the floor struts round with all the women in the room under his wing, doling them out, one by one, as he sees fit. You are here—you pay your shilling at the door—and you are "hunk."

It is Saturday night, and the company begins assembling early, for Saturday night is a grand time for thieves, loafers, prostitutes and rowdies, as well as for honest, hard-working people. Already the room —a large, desolate-looking place, with white-washed walls garnished with wooden benches—is half full of men and women, among whom the latter at this hour predominate. Later there will be pretty nearly a numerical equilibrium established—for the "friends of the house" are out in all directions picking up recruits.

In the middle of one side of the room a shammy platform is erected, with a trembling railing, and this is the "orchestra" of the establishment. Sometimes a single black fiddler answers the purpose; but on Saturday nights the music turns out strong, and the house entertains, in addition, a trumpet and a bass drum. With these instruments you may imagine that the music at Dickens's Place is of no ordinary kind. You cannot, however, begin to imagine *what* it is. You cannot *see* the red-hot knitting-needles spirted out by that red-faced trumpeter, who looks precisely as if he were blowing glass, which needles aforesaid penetrating the tympanum, pierce through and through your brain without remorse. Nor can you perceive the frightful mechanical contortions of the bass-drummer as he sweats and deals his blows on every side, in all violation of the laws of rhythm, like a man beating a baulky mule and showering his blows upon the unfortunate animal, now on this side, now on that. If you could, it would be unnecessary for us to write.

Probably three quarters of the women assembled here, and who frequent this place, are negresses, of various shades and colors. And the truth compels us to say that, on the whole, they are more tidy and presentable—or rather less horribly disgusting—than their white companions. Such bleared-eyed, idiotic, beastly wretches as these latter it is difficult to imagine and impossible to describe. The orchestra have taken their places, ready to begin. The "bar" is crowded by motley and thirsty souls, refreshing themselves for the severe exercises about to commence, and the ladies are all agog for the fun to commence. Each gentleman, by a simultaneous and apparently preconcerted movement, now "drawrs" his "chawr" of tobacco, and depositing it carefully in his trowsers pocket, flings his arms about his buxom inamorata and salutes her whisky-breathing lips with a chaste kiss, which extracts a scream of delight from the delicate creature, something between the whoop of an Indian and the neighing of a horse. And now the orchestra strikes up "Cooney in de Holler" and the company "cavorts to places." Having taken their positions and saluted each other with the most ludicrous exaggeration of ceremony, the dance proceeds for a few moments in tolerable order. But soon the excitement grows—the dancers begin contorting their bodies and accelerating their movements, accompanied with shouts of laughter and yells of encouragement and applause, until all observance of the figure is forgotten and every one leaps, stamps, screams and hurras on his or her own hook. Affairs are now at their hight. The black leader of the orchestra increases the momentum of his elbow and calls out the figure in convulsive efforts to be heard, until shining streams of perspiration roll in cascades down his ebony face; the dancers, now wild with excitement, like Ned Buntline at Astor Place, leap frantically about like howling dervishes, clasp their partners in their arms, and at length conclude the dance in hot confusion and disorder. As soon as things have cooled off a little each cavalier walks up to the bar, pays his shilling for the dance, and the floor is cleared for a new set; and so goes on the night. . . .

It would be scarcely fair to dismiss so important an "institution," (if the American Art-Union will pardon us for presuming to use a word to which they seem to claim exclusive right,) as Dicken's Place, without a few words respecting its landlord and proprietor. Pete Williams, Esq. is then a middle-aged, well-to-do, coal-black negro, who has made an immense amount of money from the profits of his dance-house—which, unfortunately, he regularly gambles away at the sweat-cloth or the roulette-table as fast as it comes in. He glories in being a bachelor—although there are something under a dozen "yel-low-boys" in the neighborhood who have a very strong resemblance to Pete, and for whom he appears to entertain a particular fondness

—frequently supplying them with sucks of candy, penny worths of peanuts, and other similar luxuries for the most part enjoyed only in dreams by the juvenile population of the Points. Pete is a great admirer of the drama, and is in fact a first-rate amateur and critic of things theatrical. Whenever there is anything "high" going on at either of the theaters, you may be sure Pete, is there; and although we never heard it positively asserted that he furnished theatrical criticisms to the newspapers, yet from the tone and peculiar collocation observable in many of them, we should not be at all surprised to hear that they were the product of his classic pen. He of course abominates Macready but "hollers" on Forrest and goes his death for "our Charlotte," whom he always prophesied would turn out some pumpkins and nothing else! He delights in the Ravels and luxuriates over the ballet. He has been heard to express opinions very much in favor of Miss Mary Taylor's *Marie* in "the Child of the Regiment," (why not translate it "female child of the Regiment," by way of perspicuity?)—and it is even whispered that he has been seen burrowing like a beaver round the back seats of the amphitheater at Astor Place. Such is a brief description of Pete Williams and Dickens's Place. We trust that our readers will not draw "oderous" comparisons between our humble and unpretending statement of facts and the elaborate and artistic picture of the place given by Dickens after a single visit. We both have written to the same end—to interest the reader: but while the great artist has summoned the aid of all his well-prepared colors to fascinate the imagination with harmonious hues, graceful proportions and startling contrasts, the unambitious reporter contents himself with sketching human nature as it is and as all may see it.

22. JAMES M. TROTTER

⇛ In 1878, the first survey on the activities of black concert musicians, *Music and Some Highly Musical People*, was written by James Monroe Trotter (1844–?), one of the first Negro officers in the Post Office at Boston, and later Recorder of Deeds for the District of Columbia. Although an amateur, Trotter devoted much time to musical pursuits and enjoyed wide contacts among black musicians of his time. He succeeded in producing a well-documented book—including press notices, pictures, and a small anthology of works by black composers—that is a milestone in the history of black American music. ⇚

From *Music and Some Highly Musical People* [1881] †

PREFACE

The purposes of this volume will be so very apparent to even the most casual observer, as to render an extended explanation here unnecessary. The author will therefore only say, that he has endeavored faithfully to perform what he was convinced was a much-needed service, not so much, perhaps, to the cause of music itself, as to some of its noblest devotees and the race to which the latter belong.

The inseparable relationship existing between music and its worthy exponents gives, it is believed, full showing of propriety to the course hereinafter pursued,—that of mingling the praises of both. But, in truth, there was little need to speak in praise of music. Its tones of melody and harmony require only to be heard in order to awaken in the breast emotions the most delightful. And yet who can speak at all of an agency so charming in other than words of warmest praise? Again: if music be a thing of such consummate beauty, what else can be done but to tender an offering of praise, and even of gratitude, to those, who, by the invention of most pleasing combinations of tones, melodies, and harmonies, or by great skill in vocal or instrumental per-

† Text: The original edition (Boston, 1878), pp. 3–4, 285–88, 324–28.

formance, so signally help us to the fullest understanding and enjoyment of it?

As will be seen by a reference to the introductory chapters, in which the subject of music is separately considered, an attempt has been made not only to form by them a proper setting for the personal sketches that follow, but also to render the book entertaining to lovers of the art in general.

While grouping, as has here been done, the musical celebrities of a single race; while gathering from near and far these many fragments of musical history, and recording them in one book,—the writer yet earnestly disavows all motives of a distinctively clannish nature. But the haze of complexional prejudice has so much obscured the vision of many persons, that they cannot see (at least, there are many who affect not to see) that musical faculties, and power for their *artistic* development, are not in the exclusive possession of the fairer-skinned race, but are alike the beneficent gifts of the Creator to all his children. Besides, there are some well-meaning persons who have formed, for lack of the information which is here afforded, erroneous and unfavorable estimates of the art-capabilities of the colored race. In the hope, then, of contributing to the formation of a more just opinion, of inducing a cheerful admission of its existence, and of aiding to establish between both races relations of mutual respect and good feeling; of inspiring the people most concerned (if that be necessary) with a greater pride in their own achievements, and confidence in their own resources, as a basis for other and even greater acquirements, as a landmark, a partial guide, for a future and better chronicler; and, finally, as a sincere tribute to the winning power, the noble beauty, of music, a contemplation of whose own divine harmony should ever serve to promote harmony between man and man,—with these purposes in view, this humble volume is hopefully issued.

» [Part First includes a discussion of the best-known concert performers of the period, as is indicated by the following selective list of chapter headings:] «

Elizabeth Taylor Greenfield, the Famous Songstress; often called the "Black Swan"

The "Luca Family," Vocalists and Instrumentalists

Henry F. Williams, Composer, Band-Instructor, Etc.

Justin Holland, the Eminent Author and Arranger

Thomas J. Bowers, Tenor-Vocalist; often styled the "American Mario"

James Gloucester Demarest, Guitar and Violin

Thomas Greene Bethune, otherwise known as "Blind Tom," the Wonderful Pianist

Anna Madah and Emma Louise Hyers, Vocalists and Pianists

Frederick Elliot Lewis, Pianist, Organist, Violinist, Etc.
Nellie E. Brown, the Favorite New Hampshire Vocalist
Samuel E. Jamieson, the Brilliant Young Pianist
Joseph White, the Eminent Violinist and Composer
The Colored American Opera Company
The Famous Jubilee Singers of Fisk University
The Georgia Minstrels

PART SECOND

*Other Remarkable Musicians, and
the Music-Loving Spirit of Various Localities*

On the following pages I shall make mention in collective form,
and somewhat briefly, of a number of artists whose histories, although
not less important than those by which they are preceded, could not,
owing to various causes, be placed in the first part of this book.

The true value of musical proficiency does not consist alone in the
power it gives one to win the applause of great audiences, and thereby
to attain to celebrity: it consists also in its being a source of refine-
ment and pleasure to the possessor himself, and by which he may add
to the tranquillity, the joys, of his own and the home life of his neighbors and friends. And here will be found, therefore, a brief mention of
those, who, although they are not public performers, are yet sincere
devotees of the art of music, who possess decided talent, and who in
their attainments present instances of a character so noticeable as to
render the same well worthy of record.

It is considered proper to say, also,—a caution which perhaps may
not be necessary,—that I shall here make mention by name of none
but persons of scientific musical culture; of none but those who read
the printed music page, and can give its contents life and expression,
generally, too, with a fine degree of excellence, either with voice or
instrument; and who evince by their studies and performances the true
artistic spirit. The singer or player "by ear" merely, however well fa-
vored by nature, will not be mentioned. This course will be followed,
not because persons of the latter class are regarded contemptuously,—
not by any means; but because it is intended that the list here given
shall be, as far as it goes, a true record of what pertains to the higher
reach and progress of a race, which, always considered as *naturally*
musical, has yet, owing to the blighting influences of the foul system
of slavery, been hitherto prevented from obtaining, as generally as
might be, a *scientific* knowledge of music.

Nor must the list of names furnished be understood as an exhaus-
tive one. Had the author the time in which to collect more names, or

had he here the space for printing the same, he assures the reader of this only partial chronicle that one could be furnished which would be many times larger. And moreover, if any meritorious musician shall complain because his name does not here appear, I ask him to pardon the omission, made not from choice, nor with the purpose of giving personal offence.

If the first edition of this book shall be received with such favor as to warrant the issuing of a second one, I shall, if it be found necessary, take the time and pains to supply in it such omissions as appear to be made in this one. If it be found necessary, I say; for I am inclined to opine that ere long,—judging from a "view of the field" that I have lately taken, and after witnessing there the many delightful evidences of musical love and culture,—that ere long neither such lists as this, nor just such books as this, will be considered as necessary.

Nevertheless, the writer requests all who are interested in the more general cultivation of music by the people to send him such names as have been here left out, together with all facts that may additionally illustrate the subject treated in these pages; all names and statements to be accompanied by as strong confirmation as can possibly be procured. These will be published in case other editions of the book are issued.

It is hoped that the persons here mentioned, on seeing that their present achievements in art are regarded as of so much value in indicating the aesthetic taste and musical capacity of their race, may be impelled thereby to put forth even greater efforts, and to thus attain to that still higher state of usefulness and distinction, which, it is believed, their talents and present accomplishments show is quite possible.

In the city of Boston, which is the acknowledged great art centre of this country, the amplest facilities for the study of music are afforded. There the doors of conservatories and other music schools, among the finest of any in the world, are thrown open to *all*; the cost of admission being, considering the many advantages afforded, quite moderate. A love of the "divine art" pervades all classes in Boston; and there the earnest student and the skilful in music, of whatever race he may be, receives ready recognition and full encouragement. It is, in fact, almost impossible for one to live in that city of melody, and not become either a practical musician, or at least a lover of music.

It need not, then, be a matter of surprise that so many of the most finely-educated artists mentioned in this book are found to have been residents of the city mentioned. Affected by its all-pervading, its infectious, so to say, musical spirit, they eagerly embraced the many opportunities offered for culture; and their noble achievements are only such as would have been made by others of the same race residing in other sections of the country, had the latter enjoyed there (as, alas! mostly on account of the depressing, the vile spirit of caste that prevailed, they did not) the same advantages as the former. . . .

Some Musical People of the South

The colored people of the South are proverbially musical. They might well be called, in that section of the country, a race of troubadours, so great has ever been their devotion to and skill in the delightful art of music. Besides, it is now seen, and generally acknowledged, that in certain of their forms of melodic expression is to be found our only distinctively *American* music; all other kinds in use being merely the echo, more or less perfect, of music that originated in the Old World. All who have listened to the beautiful melody and harmony of the songs sung by those wonderful minstrels, the "Jubilee Singers," will readily admit that scarcely ever before the coming of the latter had they been so melted, so swayed, so entirely held captive, by a rendering of music; nor will they fail to admit that in these "slave-songs" of the South was to be found a new musical idea, forming, as some are wont to term it, a *"revelation."*

And if it were necessary to prove that music is a language by which, in an elevated manner, is expressed our thoughts and emotions, what stronger evidence is needed than that found in this same native music of the South? for surely by its tones of alternate moaning and joyousness—tones always weird, but always full of a ravishing sweetness, and ever replete with the expression of deepest pathos—may be plainly read the story of a race once generally languishing in bondage, yet hoping at times for the coming of freedom.

Of the character of this music, and of its effect upon those who hear it, no one speaks more clearly than does Longfellow in the following lines from his poem, "The Slave singing at Midnight:"—

> "And the voice of his devotion
> Filled my soul with strange emotion;
> For its tones by turns were glad,
> Sweetly solemn, wildly sad."

Mrs. Kemble, in writing of life on a Southern plantation, tells how on many an occasion she listened as one entranced to the strangely-pleasing songs of the bond-people. Often she wished that some great musician might be present to catch the bewitching melodies, and weave them into a beautiful opera; for she thought them well worthy of such treatment.

It is often said that the colored race is naturally musical. Certainly it is as much so as other races. More than this need not be, nor do I think can be, claimed. It is, however, very remarkable, that a people who have for more than two hundred years been subjected, as they have, to a system of bondage so well calculated, as it would seem, to utterly quench the fire of musical genius, and to debase the mind generally, should yet have originated and practised continually certain forms of melody which those skilled in the science consider the very soul of music. Moreover, one is made to wonder how a race subjected to such cruelties could have had the heart to sing at all; much more that they could have sung so sweetly throughout all the dark and dismal night of slavery. Here is seen, it must be admitted, what appears very much like genius in the melody-making power. Something it is, undoubtedly, that shows an innate comprehension, power in expression, and love of harmony, in a degree that is simply intense. The history of the colored race in this country establishes the fact, too, that no system of cruelty, however great or long inflicted, can destroy that sympathy with musical sounds that is born with the soul. Only death itself can end it here on earth, while we are taught that for ever and ever heaven shall be rich in harmony formed by the songs of the redeemed. Perhaps other races, under the same terribly trying circumstances, would have shown a power to resist the mind-destroying influences of those circumstances equal to that which has been so fully shown by the colored race. But, be that as it may, the latter has actually been subjected to the awful test; and the sequel has proved, that, to say the least, it may be considered as the equal naturally of any of the other "musical" races composing the human family.

But the music of which I have been speaking was never cradled, so to say, in the lap of science; although, in its strangely-fascinating sweetness, soulfulness, and perfect rhythmic flow, it has often quite disarmed the scientific critic. It is a kind of natural music. Until quite recently no attempt was made to write it out, and place its melodies upon the printed music-page. Slavery, of course, prevented that. And this vile system, although it could not stamp out the "vocal spark," the germ of great musical ideas, could still prevent such growth of the same, such elaboration, as would have been secured by education in a state of freedom. Yet, since the war, many of the religious slave-songs of the South, words and music, have been printed. It has been found that they are as subject to the laws of science as are others; that they were not, as many persons have supposed, merely a barbarous confusion of sounds, each warring, as it were, against the other. For a proof of this (if there be those who doubt), the reader is referred to the "History of the Jubilee Singers of Fisk University," in which he will find printed the music of many songs like those to which I have alluded.

Thus have we considered, in part, the native minstrelsy of the South.

Notwithstanding their lack of a scientific knowledge of music, colored men, as instrumentalists, have long furnished most of the best music that has been produced in nearly all of the Southern States. At the watering-places, orchestras composed of colored musicians were always to be found; in fact, at such places their services were considered indispensable. Many of them could not read music; but they seemed naturally full of it, and possessed a most remarkable faculty for "catching" a tune from those of their associates who learned it from the written or printed notes: in truth, the facility of all in executing some of the most pleasing music in vogue was so great, that, when these little orchestras played, it was almost impossible to discover the slightest variation from the music as found on the printed page.

"A good many years ago," writes a correspondent from the White Sulphur Springs of Virginia, "the statesman Henry Clay was here, enjoying a respite from his arduous government duties. Being present at a grand reception where dancing was in progress, Mr. Clay wished to have played the music for a 'Virginia Reel;' but, to his great surprise, he learned that the colored musicians present did not know the necessary tune. Not to be cheated out of an indulgence in this, his favorite dance, Mr. Clay took the band over to a corner of the room, and *whistled* the music to them. In a very few minutes they 'caught' it perfectly; and, returning to their places, the enterprising statesman and his friends enjoyed themselves in dancing the 'Virginia Reel' just as though nothing unusual had occurred." At levees, at other public festive gatherings, and at the receptions given in the homes of the wealthy, these orchestras were nearly always present, adding to the enjoyments of the hour by discoursing the most delightful music. In short, they were to be found everywhere, always receiving that warm welcome with which a music-loving people ever greet the talented musician.

But, besides the associations of which I have just been speaking,—associations composed in part of those who understood music as a science, and in part of those who did not,—there has always been a goodly number of other persons of the same race, who, in spite of obstacles that would seem to be insurmountable, have obtained a fair musical education, and who have exhibited an artistic skill and general aesthetic love and taste that would be creditable to many of those who have enjoyed far greater advantages for culture.

VII. General Characteristics of Slave Music

23. William Francis Allen

➤➤➤ In 1867 the epoch-making *Slave Songs of the United States*, edited by William Francis Allen (1830–99), Lucy McKim Garrison (1842–77), and Charles Pickard Ware (1840–1921), was published in New York. Allen wrote the introduction to this collection of 137 songs, giving descriptions of the music and of performance practices. A graduate of Harvard who had studied further in Europe, Allen was a well-known scholar of the period. During the war years he worked with ex-slaves living in contraband camps on the Sea Islands off the coast of Georgia. A talented amateur musician who played both piano and flute, Allen had considerable experience in writing down folksongs before he collaborated with Ware and Garrison to produce the 1867 collection.

Lucy McKim Garrison was a well-trained pianist, whose enthusiasm for songs of the slaves was thoroughly aroused when she accompanied her father, James Miller McKim, on a mission in 1862 to the contraband camps of the Port Royal Islands and other islands off the coast of South Carolina and Georgia.* She wrote down the melodies for several songs, and upon returning to her home in New Jersey wrote a letter to *Dwight's Journal of Music* in which she described the singing of the slaves and published two of the songs she had transcribed, *Roll, Jordan, Roll* and *Poor Rosy*. An excerpt from this letter appears in Allen's introduction.

Charles Ware, a cousin of Allen's, was an avid collector of slave songs and made the largest personal contribution to the collection. ◄◄◄

From *Slave Songs of the United States* [1867] †

The musical capacity of the negro race has been recognized for so many years that it is hard to explain why no systematic effort has hitherto been made to collect and preserve their melodies. More than thirty years ago those plantation songs made their appearance which were so extraordinarily popular for a while; and if "Coal-black Rose," "Zip Coon" and "Ole Virginny nebber tire" have been suc-

* See Dena J. Epstein, *Lucy McKim Garrison, American Musician*, Bulletin of the New York Public Library, 67 (1963), No. 8.
† Text: The original edition (New York, 1867), pp. i–xxiii.

ceeded by spurious imitations, manufactured to suit the somewhat sentimental taste of our community, the fact that these were called "negro melodies" was itself a tribute to the musical genius of the race.[1]

The public had well-nigh forgotten these genuine slave songs, and with them the creative power from which they sprung, when a fresh interest was excited through the educational mission to the Port Royal islands, in 1861. The agents of this mission were not long in discovering the rich vein of music that existed in these half-barbarous people, and when visitors from the North were on the islands, there was nothing that seemed better worth their while than to see a "shout" or hear the "people" sing their "sperichils." A few of these last, of special merit,[2] soon became established favorites among the whites, and hardly a Sunday passed at the church on St. Helena without "Gabriel's Trumpet," "I hear from Heaven to-day," or "Jehovah Hallelujah." The last time I myself heard these was at the Fourth of July celebration, at the church, in 1864. All of them were sung, and then the glorious shout, "I can't stay behind, my Lord," was struck up, and sung by the entire multitude with a zest and spirit, a swaying of the bodies and nodding of the heads and lighting of the countenances and rhythmical movement of the hands, which I think no one present will ever forget.

Attention was, I believe, first publicly directed to these songs in a letter from Miss McKim, of Philadelphia, to *Dwight's Journal of Music*, Nov. 8, 1862, from which some extracts will presently be given. At about the same time, Miss McKim arranged and published two of them, "Roll Jordan" (No. 1) and "Poor Rosy" (No. 8)— probably on all accounts the two best specimens that could be selected. Mr. H. G. Spaulding not long after gave some well-chosen specimens of the music in an article entitled "Under the Palmetto" in the *Continental Monthly* for August, 1863, among them, "O Lord, remember me" (No. 15) and "The Lonesome Valley" (No. 7). Many other persons interested themselves in the collection of words and tunes, and it seems time at last that the partial collections in the possession of the editors, and known by them to be in the possession of others, should not be forgotten and lost, but that these relics of a state of society which has passed away should be preserved while it is still possible.[3]

---

1. It is not generally known that the beautiful air "Long time ago," or "Near the lake where drooped the willow," was borrowed from the negroes, by whom it was sung to words beginning, "Way down in Raccoon Hollow."

2. The first seven spirituals in this collection, which were regularly sung at the church.

3. Only this last spring a valuable collection of songs made at Richmond, Va., was lost in the *Wagner* [a ship]. No copy had been made from the original manuscript, so

The greater part of the music here presented has been taken down by the editors from the lips of the colored people themselves; when we have obtained it from other sources, we have given credit in the table of contents. The largest and most accurate single collection in existence is probably that made by Mr. Charles P. Ware, chiefly at Coffin's Point, St. Helena Island. We have thought it best to give this collection in its entirety, as the basis of the present work; it includes all the hymns as far as No. 43. Those which follow, as far as No. 55, were collected by myself on the Capt. John Fripp and neighboring plantations, on the same island. In all cases we have added words from other sources and other localities, when they could be obtained, as well as variations of the tunes wherever they were of sufficient importance to warrant it. Of the other hymns and songs we have given the locality whenever it could be ascertained.

The difficulty experienced in attaining absolute correctness is greater than might be supposed by those who have never tried the experiment and we are far from claiming that we have made no mistakes. I have never felt quite sure of my notation without a fresh comparison with the singing, and have then often found that I had made some errors. I feel confident, however, that there are no mistakes of importance. What may appear to some to be an incorrect rendering, is very likely to be a variation; for these variations are endless, and very entertaining and instructive.

Neither should any one be repelled by any difficulty in adapting the words to the tunes. The negroes keep exquisite time in singing, and do not suffer themselves to be daunted by any obstacle in the words. The most obstinate Scripture phrases or snatches from hymns they will force to do duty with any tune they please, and will dash heroically through a trochaic tune at the head of a column of iambs with wonderful skill. We have in all cases arranged one set of words carefully to each melody; for the rest, one must make them fit the best he can, as the negroes themselves do.

The best that we can do, however, with paper and types, or even with voices, will convey but a faint shadow of the original. The voices of the colored people have a peculiar quality that nothing can imitate; and the intonations and delicate variations of even one singer cannot be reproduced on paper. And I despair of conveying any notion of the effect of a number singing together, especially in a complicated shout, like "I can't stay behind, my Lord" (No. 8), or "Turn, sinner, turn O!" (No. 48). There is no singing in *parts*,[4] as

that the labor of their collection was lost. We had hoped to have the use of them in preparing the present work.

4. "The high voices, all in unison, and the admirable time and true accent with which their responses are made, always make me wish that some great musical composer could hear these semi-savage performances. With a very little skilful adaptation and instrumenta-

we understand it, and yet no two appear to be singing the same thing—the leading singer starts the words of each verse, often improvising, and the others, who "base" him, as it is called, strike in with the refrain, or even join in the solo, when the words are familiar. When the "base" begins, the leader often stops, leaving the rest of his words to be guessed at, or it may be they are taken up by one of the other singers. And the "basers" themselves seem to follow their own whims, beginning when they please and leaving off when they please, striking an octave above or below (in case they have pitched the tune too low or too high), or hitting some other note that chords, so as to produce the effect of a marvellous complication and variety, and yet with the most perfect time, and rarely with any discord. And what makes it all the harder to unravel a thread of melody out of this strange network is that, like birds, they seem not infrequently to strike sounds that cannot be precisely represented by the gamut, and abound in "slides from one note to another, and turns and cadences not in articulated notes." "It is difficult," writes Miss McKim, "to express the entire character of these negro ballads by mere musical notes and signs. The odd turns made in the throat, and the curious rhythmic effect produced by single voices chiming in at different irregular intervals, seem almost as impossible to place on the score as the singing of birds or the tones of an Æolian Harp." There are also apparent irregularities in the time, which it is no less difficult to express accurately, and of which Nos. 10, 130, 131, and (eminently) 128, are examples.

Still, the chief part of the negro music is *civilized* in its character —partly composed under the influence of association with the whites, partly actually imitated from their music. In the main it appears to be original in the best sense of the word, and the more we examine the subject, the more genuine it appears to us to be. In a very few songs, as Nos. 19, 23, and 25, strains of familiar tunes are readily traced; and it may easily be that others contain strains of less familiar music, which the slaves heard their masters sing or play.[5]

On the other hand there are very few which are of an intrinsically barbaric character, and where this character does appear, it is chiefly in short passages, intermingled with others of a different character. Such passages may be found in perhaps Nos. 10, 12, and 18; and "Becky Lawton," for instance (No. 29), "Shall I die?" (No. 52), "Round the corn, Sally" (No. 87), and "O'er the crossing" (No. 93)

---

tion. I think one or two barbaric chants and choruses might be evoked from them that would make the fortune of an opera."—*Mrs. Kemble's "Life on a Georgian Plantation," p.* 218.

5. We have rejected as spurious "Give me Jesus," "Climb Jacob's Ladder," (both sung at Port Royal), and "I'll take the wings of the morning," which we find in Methodist hymn-books. A few others, the character of which seemed somewhat suspicious, we have not felt at liberty to reject without direct evidence.

may very well be purely African in origin. Indeed, it is very likely that if we had found it possible to get at more of their secular music, we should have come to another conclusion as to the proportion of the barbaric element. A gentleman in Delaware [John McKim, uncle of Lucy McKim Garrison] writes:

"We must look among their non-religious songs for the purest specimens of negro minstrelsy. It is remarkable that they have themselves transferred the best of these to the uses of their churches—I suppose on Mr. Wesley's principle that 'it is not right the Devil should have all the good tunes.' Their leaders and preachers have not found this change difficult to effect; or at least they have taken so little pains about it that one often detects the profane *cropping out*, and revealing the origin of their most solemn 'hymns,' in spite of the best intentions of the poet and artist. Some of the best *pure negro* songs I have ever heard were those that used to be sung by the black stevedores, or perhaps the crews themselves, of the West India vessels, loading and unloading at the wharves in Philadelphia and Baltimore. I have stood for more than an hour, often, listening to them, as they hoistèd and lowered the hogsheads and boxes of their cargoes; one man taking the burden of the song (and the slack of the rope) and the others striking in with the chorus. They would sing in this way more than a dozen different songs in an hour; most of which might indeed be warranted to contain 'nothing religious'—a few of them, 'on the contrary, quite the reverse'—but generally rather innocent and proper in their language, and strangely attractive in their music; and with a volume of voice that reached a square or two away. That plan of labor has now passed away, in Philadelphia at least, and the songs, I suppose, with it. So that these performances are to be heard only among black sailors on their vessels, or 'long-shore men in out-of-the-way places, where opportunities for respectable persons to hear them are rather few."

These are the songs that are still heard upon the Mississippi steamboats—wild and strangely fascinating—one of which we have been so fortunate as to secure for this collection. This, too, is no doubt the music of the colored firemen of Savannah, graphically described by Mr. Kane O'Donnel, in a letter to the Philadelphia *Press*, and one of which he was able to contribute for our use. Mr. E. S. Philbrick was struck with the resemblance of some of the rowing tunes at Port-Royal to the boatmen's songs he had heard upon the Nile.

The greater number of the songs which have come into our possession seem to be the natural and original production of a race of remarkable musical capacity and very teachable, which has been long enough associated with the more cultivated race to have become im-

bued with the mode and spirit of European music—often, nevertheless, retaining a distinct tinge of their native Africa.

The words are, of course, in a large measure taken from Scripture, and from the hymns heard at church; and for this reason these
religious songs do not by any means illustrate the full extent of the
debasement of the dialect. Such expressions as "Cross Jordan," "O
Lord, remember me," "I'm going home," "There's room enough in
Heaven for you," we find abundantly in Methodist hymn-books; but
with much searching I have been able to find hardly a trace of the
tunes. The words of the fine hymn, "Praise, member" (No. 5), are
found, with very little variation, in "Choral Hymns" (No. 138). The
editor of this collection informs us, however, that many of his songs
were learned from negroes in Philadelphia, and Lt.-Col. Trowbridge
tells us that he heard this hymn, before the war, among the colored
people of Brooklyn.[6] For some very comical specimens of the way
in which half-understood words and phrases are distorted by them, see
Nos. 22, 23. Another illustration is given by Col. Higginson.[7]

"The popular camp-song of 'Marching Along' was entirely new
to them until our quartermaster taught it to them at my request.
The words 'Gird on the armor' were to them a stumbling-block,
and no wonder, until some ingenious ear substituted 'Guide on de
army,' which was at once accepted and became universal. 'We'll guide
on de army, and be marching along,' is now the established version
on the Sea Islands."

I never fairly heard a secular song among the Port Royal freedmen, and never saw a musical instrument among them. The last
violin, owned by a "worldly man," disappeared from Coffin's Point
"de year gun shoot at Bay Pint." [8] In other parts of the South,
"fiddle-sings," "devil-songs," "corn-songs," "jig-tunes," and what not,
are common; all the world knows the banjo, and the "Jim Crow"
songs of thirty years ago. We have succeeded in obtaining only a
very few songs of this character. Our intercourse with the colored
people has been chiefly through the work of the Freedman's Commission, which deals with the serious and earnest side of the negro
character. It is often, indeed, no easy matter to persuade them to sing
their old songs, even as a curiosity, such is the sense of dignity with
has come with freedom. It is earnestly to be desired that some person,
who has the opportunity, should make a collection of these now,

6. We have generally preserved the words as sung, even where clearly nonsensical, as
in No. 89; so "Why don't you move so slow?" (No. 22). We will add that "Paul and
Silas, bound in jail" (No. 4), is often sung "Bounden Cyrus born in jail," and the words
of No. 11 would appear as "I take my tex in Matchew and by de Revolutions–I know you
by your gammon," &c.; so "Ringy Rosy Land" for "Ring Jerusalem."

7. *Atlantic Monthly*, June, 1867.

8. *i.e.*, November, 1861, when Hilton Head was taken by Admiral Dupont—a great
date on the islands.

before it is too late.

In making the present collection, we have only gleaned upon the surface, and in a very narrow field. The wealth of material still awaiting the collector can be guessed from a glance at the localities of those we have, and from the fact, mentioned above, that of the first forty-three of the collection most were sung upon a single plantation, and that it is very certain that the stores of this plantation were by no means exhausted. Of course there was constant intercourse between neighboring plantations; also between different States, by the sale of slaves from one to another. But it is surprising how little this seems to have affected local songs, which are different even upon adjoining plantations. The favorite of them all, "Roll, Jordan" (No. 1) is sung in Florida, but not, I believe, in North Carolina. "Gabriel's Trumpet" (No. 4) and "Wrestle on, Jacob" (No. 6) probably came from Virginia, where they are sung without much variation from the form usual at Port Royal; No. 6 is also sung in Maryland.[9] "John, John of the Holy Order" (No. 22) is traced in Georgia and North Carolina, and "O'er the Crossing" (No. 93) appears to be the Virginia original, variations of which are found in South Carolina, Georgia, and Tennessee. As illustrations of the slowness with which these songs travel, it may be mentioned that the "Graveyard" (No. 21) which was frequently sung on Capt. John Fripp's plantation in the winter of 1863–4, did not reach Coffin's Point (five miles distant) until the following Spring. I heard it myself at Pine Grove, two miles from the latter place, in March. Somewhere upon this journey this tune was strikingly altered, as will be seen from the variation given, which is the form in which I was accustomed to hear it. Nos. 38, 41, 42, 43, 118, 119, 122, 123, were brought to Coffin's Point after Mr. Ware left, by refugees returning to the plantation from "town" and the Main. No. 74, likewise, "Nobody knows the trouble I see," which was common in Charleston in 1865, has since been carried to Coffin's Point, very little altered.

These hymns will be found peculiarly interesting in illustrating the feelings, opinions and habits of the slaves. Of the dialect I shall presently speak at some length. One of their customs, often alluded to in the songs (as in No. 19), is that of wandering through the woods and swamps, when under religious excitement, like the ancient bacchantes. To get religion is with them to "fin' dat ting." Molsy described thus her sister's experience in searching for religion: "Couldn't fin' dat leetle ting—hunt for 'em—huntin' for 'em all de time—las' foun' 'em." And one day, on our way to see a "shout," we

9. It is worthy of notice that a song much resembling "Poor Rosy" was heard last Spring from the boat hands of an Ohio River steamboat—the only words caught being "Poor Molly, poor gal."

asked Bristol whether he was going:—"No, ma'am, wouldn't let me in—hain't foun' dat ting yet—hain't been on my knees in de swamp." Of technical religious expressions, "seeker," "believer," "member," &c., the songs are full.

The most peculiar and interesting of their customs is the "shout," an excellent description of which we are permitted to copy from the N. Y. *Nation* of May 30, 1867:

"This is a ceremony which the white clergymen are inclined to discountenance, and even of the colored elders some of the more discreet try sometimes to put on a face of discouragement; and although, if pressed for Biblical warrant for the shout, they generally seem to think 'he in de Book,' or 'he dere-da in Matchew,' still it is not considered blasphemous or improper if 'de chillen' and 'dem young gal' carry it on in the evening for amusement's sake, and with no well-defined intention of 'praise.' But the true 'shout' takes place on Sundays or on 'praise'-nights through the week, and either in the praise-house or in some cabin in which a regular religious meeting has been held. Very likely more than half the population of the plantation is gathered together. Let it be the evening, and a light-wood fire burns red before the door of the house and on the hearth. For some time one can hear, though at a good distance, the vociferous exhortation or prayer of the presiding elder or of the brother who has a gift that way, and who is not 'on the back seat,'—a phrase, the interpretation of which is, 'under the censure of the church authorities for bad behavior;'—and at regular intervals one hears the elder 'deaconing' a hymn-book hymn, which is sung two lines at a time, and whose wailing cadences, borne on the night air, are indescribably melancholy. But the benches are pushed back to the wall when the formal meeting is over, and old and young men and women, sprucely-dressed young men, grotesquely half-clad fieldhands—the women generally with gay handkerchiefs twisted about their heads and with short skirts—boys with tattered shirts and men's trousers, young girls barefooted, all stand up in the middle of the floor, and when the 'sperichil' is struck up, begin first walking and by-and-by shuffling round, one after the other, in a ring. The foot is hardly taken from the floor, and the progression is mainly due to a jerking, hitching motion, which agitates the entire shouter, and soon brings out streams of perspiration. Sometimes they dance silently, sometimes as they shuffle they sing the chorus of the spiritual, and sometimes the song itself is also sung by the dancers. But most frequently a band, composed of some of the best singers and of tired shouters, stand at the side of the room to 'base' the others, singing the body of the song and clapping their hands together or on the knees. Song and dance are alike extremely energetic, and often, when the shout lasts into the middle of the night, the monotonous thud, thud of the feet prevents sleep within half a mile of the praise-house."

In the form here described, the "shout" is probably confined to South Carolina and the States south of it. It appears to be found in Florida, but not in North Carolina or Virginia. It is, however, an interesting fact that the term "shouting" is used in Virginia in reference to a peculiar motion of the body not wholly unlike the Carolina shouting. It is not unlikely that this remarkable religious ceremony is a relic of some native African dance, as the Romaika is of the classical Pyrrhic. Dancing in the usual way is regarded with great horror by the people of Port Royal, but they enter with infinite zest into the movements of the "shout." It has its connoisseurs, too. "Jimmy great shouter," I was told; and Jimmy himself remarked to me, as he looked patronizingly on a ring of young people. "Dese yere worry deyseff—we don't worry weseff." And indeed, although the perspiration steamed copiously down his shiny face, he shuffled round the circle with great ease and grace.

The shouting may be to any tune, and perhaps all the Port Royal hymns here given are occasionally used for this purpose; so that our cook's classification into "sperichils" and "runnin' sperichils" (shouts), or the designation of certain ones as sung "just sittin' round, you know," will hardly hold in strictness. In practice, however, a distinction is generally observed. The first seven, for instance, favorite hymns in the St. Helena church, would rarely, if ever, be used for shouting; while probably on each plantation there is a special set in common use. On my plantation I oftenest heard "Pray all de member" (No. 47), "Bell da ring" (No. 46), "Shall I die?" (No. 52), and "I can't stay behind, my Lord" (No. 8). The shouting step varied with the tune; one could hardly dance with the same spirit to "Turn, sinner," or "My body rock 'long fever," as to "Rock o' Jubilee," or "O Jerusalem, early in de morning." So far as I can learn, the shouting is confined to the Baptists [10]; and it is, no doubt, to the overwhelming preponderance of this denomination on the Sea Islands that we owe the peculiar richness and originality of the music there.

The same songs are used for rowing as for shouting. I know only one pure boat-song, the fine lyric, "Michael row the boat ashore" (No. 31); and this I have no doubt is a real spiritual—it being the archangel Michael that is addressed. Among the most common rowing tunes were Nos. 5, 14, 17, 27, 28, 29, 30, 31, 32, 33, 36, 46. "As I have written these tunes," says Mr. Ware, "two measures are to be

---

10. From the vantage point of the present, we realize this is not true. Black Methodists, for example, participated in the shout early in the nineteenth century (see p. 62). [*Editor*]

sung to each stroke, the first measure being accented by the beginning of the stroke, the second by the rattle of the oars in the row-locks. On the passenger boat at the [Beaufort] ferry, they rowed from sixteen to thirty strokes a minute; twenty-four was the average. Of the tunes I have heard, I should say that the most lively were 'Heaven bell a-ring' (No. 27), 'Jine 'em' (No. 28), 'Rain fall' (No. 29), 'No man' (No. 14, 'Bell da ring' (No. 46), and 'Can't stay behind;' and that 'Lay this body down' (No. 26), 'Religion so sweet' (No. 17), and 'Michael row' (No. 31), were used when the load was heavy or the tide was against us. I think that the long hold on 'Oh,' in 'Rain fall,' was only used in rowing. When used as a 'shout' I am quite sure that it occupied only one measure, as in the last part of the verse. One noticeable thing about their boat-songs was that they seemed often to be sung just a trifle behind time; in 'Rain fall,' for instance, 'Believer cry holy' would seem to occupy more than its share of the stroke, the 'holy' being prolonged till the very beginning of the next stroke; indeed, I think Jerry often hung on his oar a little just there before dipping it again." [11]

As to the composition of these songs, "I always wondered," says Col. Higginson, "whether they had always a conscious and definite origin in some leading mind, or whether they grew by gradual accretion, in an almost unconscious way. On this point I could get no information, though I asked many questions, until at last, one day when I was being rowed across from Beaufort to Ladies' Island, I found myself, with delight, on the actual trail of a song. One of the oarsmen, a brisk young fellow, not a soldier, on being asked for his theory of the matter, dropped out a coy confession. 'Some good sperituals,' he said, 'are start jess out o' curiosity. I been a-raise a sing, myself, once.'

"My dream was fulfilled, and I had traced out, not the poem alone, but the poet. I implored him to proceed.

" 'Once we boys,' he said, 'went for tote some rice, and de nigger-driver, he keep a-callin' on us; and I say, 'O, de ole nigger-driver!' Den anudder said, 'Fust ting my mammy told me was, notin' so bad as nigger-drivers.' Den I made a sing, just puttin' a word, and den anudder word.'

"Then he began singing, and the men, after listening a moment, joined in the chorus as if it were an old acquaintance, though they evidently had never heard it before. I saw how easily a new 'sing' took root among them."

A not inconsistent explanation is that given on page 12 of an "Address delivered by J. Miller McKim, in Sansom Hall, Philadelphia,

11. For another curious circumstance in rowing, see note to "Rain fall," No. 29.

July 9, 1862."

"I asked one of these blacks—one of the most intelligent of them [Prince Rivers, Sergeant 1st Reg. S. C. V.]—where they got these songs. 'Dey make 'em, sah.' 'How do they make them?' After a pause, evidently casting about for an explanation, he said: 'I'll tell you, it's dis way. My master call me up, and order me a short peck of corn and a hundred lash. My friends see it, and is sorry for me. When dey come to de praise-meeting dat night dey sing about it. Some's very good singers and know how; and dey work in it—work it in, you know, till they get it right; and dat's de way.' A very satisfactory explanation; at least so it seemed to me."

We were not so fortunate as Col. Higginson in our search for a poet. Cuffee at Pine Grove did, to be sure, confess himself the author of "Climb Jacob's Ladder;"—unfortunately, we afterwards found it in a Northern hymn book. And if you try to trace out a new song, and ask, "Where did you hear that?" the answer will be, "One strange man come from Eding's las' praise-night and sing 'em in praise-house, and de people catch 'em;" or "Titty 'Mitta [sister Amaritta] fetch 'em from Polawana, where she tuk her walk gone spend Sunday. Some of her fahmly sing 'em yonder." "But what does 'Ringy rosy land' [Ring Jerusalem, No. 21] mean?" "Me dunno."

Our title, "Slave Songs," was selected because it best described the contents of the book. A few of those here given (Nos. 64, 59) were, to be sure, composed since the proclamation of emancipation, but even these were inspired by slavery. "All, indeed, are valuable as an expression of the character and life of the race which is playing such a conspicuous part in our history. The wild, sad strains tell, as the sufferers themselves could, of crushed hopes, keen sorrow, and a dull, daily misery, which covered them as hopelessly as the fog from the rice swamps. On the other hand, the words breathe a trusting faith in rest for the future—in 'Canaan's air and happy land,' to which their eyes seem constantly turned."

Our original plan hardly contemplated more than the publication of the Port Royal spirituals, some sixty in all, which we had supposed we could obtain, with perhaps a few others in an appendix. As new materials came into our hands, we enlarged our plan to the present dimensions. Next to South Carolina, we have the largest number from Virginia; from the other States comparatively few. Few as they are, however, they appear to indicate a very distinct character in different States. Contrary to what might be expected, the songs from Virginia are the most wild and strange. "O'er the Crossing" (No. 93) is peculiarly so; but "Sabbath has no end" (No. 89), "Hypocrite and Concubine" (No. 91), "O shout away" (No. 92), and

"Let God's saints come in" (No. 99), are all distinguished by odd intervals and a frequent use of chromatics. The songs from North Carolina are also very peculiar, although in a different way, and make one wish for more specimens from that region. Those from Tennessee and Florida are most like the music of the whites.

We had hoped to obtain enough secular songs to make a division by themselves; there are, however, so few of these that it has been decided to intersperse them with the spirituals under their respective States. They are highly characteristic, and will be found not the least interesting of the contents of this work.

It is, we repeat, already becoming difficult to obtain these songs. Even the "spirituals" are going out of use on the plantations, superseded by the new style of religious music, "closely imitated from the white people, which is solemn, dull and nasal, consisting in repeating two lines of a hymn and then singing it, and then two more, *ad infinitum*. They use for this sort of worship that one everlasting melody, which may be remembered by all persons familiar with Western and Southern camp-meetings, as applying equally well to long, short or common metre. This style of proceeding they evidently consider the more dignified style of the two, as being a closer imitation of white, genteel worship—having in it about as little soul as most stereotyped religious forms of well instructed congregations." [12]

It remains to speak of points connected with the typography of the songs.

We have aimed to give all the characteristic variations which have come into our hands, whether as single notes or whole lines, or even longer passages; and of words as well as tunes. Many of these will be found very interesting and instructive. The variations in words are given as foot-notes—the word or group of words in the note, to be generally substituted for that which precedes the mark: and it may be observed, although it seems hardly necessary, that these variations are endless; such words as "member," "believer," "seeker," and all names, male and female, may be brought in wherever appropriate. We have not always given all the sets of words that we have received often they are improvised to such an extent that this would be almost impracticable. In Nos. 16, 17, 19, etc., we have given them very copiously, for illustration; in others we have omitted the least interesting ones. In spelling, we proposed to ourselves the rule well stated by Col. Higginson at the commencement of his collection: "The words will be here given, as nearly as possible, in the original dialect; and if the spelling seems sometimes inconsistent, or the misspelling insufficient, it is because I could get no nearer."

12. Mrs. H. B. Stowe, in *Washington and Reflector*, April, 1867.

As the negroes have no part-singing, we have thought it best to print only the melody; what appears in some places as harmony is really variations in single notes. And, in general, a succession of such notes turned in the same direction indicates a single longer variation. Words in a parenthesis, with small notes, (as "Brudder Sammy" in No. 21), are interjaculatory; it has not, however, been possible to maintain entire consistency in this matter. Sometimes, as "no man" and "O no man," in No. 14, interchangeable forms are put, for convenience sake, in different parts of the tune.

It may sometimes be a little difficult, for instance in Nos. 9, 10, 20 and 27, to determine precisely which part of the tune each verse belongs to; in these cases we have endeavored to indicate it as clearly as is in our power. However much latitude the reader may take in all such matters, he will hardly take more than the negroes themselves do. In repeating, it may be observed that the custom at Port Royal is to repeat the first part of the tune over and over, it may be a dozen times, before passing to the "turn," and then to do the same with that. In the Virginia songs, on the other hand, the chorus is usually sung twice after each verse—often the second time with some such interjaculatory expression as "I say now," "God say you must," as given in No. 99.

We had some thought of indicating with each the *tempo* of the different songs, but have concluded to print special directions for singing by themselves. It should be remarked, however, that the same tune varied in quickness on different occasions. "As the same songs," writes Miss McKim, "are sung at every sort of work, of course the *tempo* is not always alike. On the water, the oars dip 'Poor Rosy' to an even *andante*; a stout boy and girl at the hominy mill will make the same 'Poor Rosy' fly, to keep up with the whirling stone; and in the evening, after the day's work is done, 'Heab'n shall-a be my home' peals up slowly and mournfully from the distant quarters. One woman, a respectable house-servant, who had lost all but one of her twenty-two children, said to me: 'Pshaw! don't har to dese yer chil'en, missee. Dey just rattles it off—dey don't know how for sing it. I likes 'Poor Rosy' better dan all de songs, but it can't be sung widout *a full heart and a troubled sperrit.*"

The rests, by the way, do not indicate a cessation in the music, but only in part of the singers. They overlap in singing, as already described, in such a degree that at no time is there any complete pause. In "A House in Paradise" (No. 40) this overlapping is most marked. . . .

It remains for the Editors to acknowledge the aid they have received in making this compilation. To Col. T. W. Higginson, above all others, they are indebted for friendly encouragement and for direct and indirect contributions to their original stock of songs. From first to last he has manifested the kindest interest in their undertaking, constantly suggesting the names of persons likely to afford them information, and improving every opportunity to procure them material. As soon as his own valuable collection had appeared in the *Atlantic Monthly*, he freely made it over to them with a liberality which was promptly confirmed by his publishers, Messrs. Ticknor & Fields. It is but little to say that without his co-operation this *Lyra Africana* would have lacked greatly of its present completeness and worth. Through him we have profited by the cheerful assistance of Mrs. Charles J. Bowen, Lieut.-Colonel C. T. Trowbridge, Capt. James S. Rogers, Rev. Horace James, Capt. Geo. S. Barton, Miss Lucy Gibbons, Mr. William A. Baker, Mr. T. E. Ruggles, and Mr. James Schouler. Our thanks are also due for contributions, of which we have availed ourselves, to Dr. William A. Hammond, Mr. Geo. H. Allan, Lt.-Col. Wm. Lee Apthorp, Mr. Kane O'Donnel, Mr. E. J. Snow, Miss Charlotte L. Forten, Miss Laura M. Towne, and Miss Ellen Murray; and for criticisms, suggestions, communications, and unused but not unappreciated contributions, to Mr. John R. Dennett, Miss Annie Mitchell, Mr. Reuben Tomlinson, Mr. Arthur Sumner, Mr. N. C. Dennett, Miss Mary Ellen Pierce, Maj.-Gen. Wager Swayne, Miss Maria W. Benton, Prof. J. Silsby, Rev. John L. McKim, Mr. Albert Griffin, Mr. A. S. Jenks, Mr. E. H. Hawkes, Rev. H. C. Trumbull, Rev. J. K. Hosmer, Rev. F. N. Knapp, Brev. Maj.-Gen. Truman Seymour, Maj.-Gen. James H. Wilson, Mr. J. H. Palmer, and others; and, finally, to the editors of various newspapers who gratuitously announced the forthcoming volume.

Conscious of many imperfections in this, the result of not inconsiderable joint labor for nearly a year, the Editors submit it, nevertheless, to the public judgment, in the belief that it will be pronounced deserving of even greater pains and of permanent preservation.

William Francis Allen,
Charles Pickard Ware,
Lucy McKim Garrison.

Contents

DIRECTIONS FOR SINGING

In addition to those already given in the Introduction, the following explanations may be of assistance:

Where all the words are printed with the music, there will probably be little difficulty in reading the songs; but where there are other words printed below the music, it will often be a question to which part of the tune these words belong, and how the refrain and the chorus are to be brought in.

It will be noticed that the words of most of the songs arrange themselves into stanzas of four lines each. Of these some are *refrain*, and some are *verse* proper. The most common arrangement gives the second and fourth lines to the refrain, and the first and third to the verse; and in this case the third line may be a repetition of the first, or may have different words. Often, however, the refrain occupies only one line, the verse occupying the other three; while in one or two songs the verse is only one line, while the refrain is three lines in length. The refrain is repeated with each stanza: the words of the verse are changed at the pleasure of the leader, or fugleman, who sings either well-known words, or, if he is gifted that way, invents verses as the song goes on.

In addition to the stanza, some of the songs have a chorus, which usually consists of a fixed set of words, though in some of the songs the chorus is a good deal varied. The refrain of the main stanza often appears in the chorus. The stanza can always be distinguished from the chorus, in those songs which have more than one stanza, by the figure "1" placed before the stanza which is printed with the music; the verses below being numbered on "2," "3," "4," &c. In a few cases the first verse below the music is numbered "3;" this occurs when two verses have been printed above in the music, instead of the first verse being repeated. When the chorus has a variety of words, the additional verses are printed below without numbers. . . .

» [Some of the songs are provided with footnotes that describe performance practices. A few examples follow.] «

No. 8   *I Can't Stay Behind*

This "shout" is very widely spread, and variously sung. In Charleston it is simpler in its movement, and the refrain is "I can't stay away." In Edgefield it is expostulating: "Don't stay away, my mudder." Col. Higginson gives the following version, as sung in his regiment:

"O, my mudder is gone! my mudder is gone!
My mudder is gone into heaven, my Lord!
    I can't stay behind!
Dere's room in dar, room in dar.
Room in dar, in de heaven, my Lord!
    I can't stay behind!
Can't stay behind, my dear,
    I can't stay behind!

"O, my fader is gone! &c.

"O, de angels are gone! &c.

"O, I 'se been on de road! I 'se been on de road!
I 'se been on de road into heaven, my Lord!
     I can't stay behind!
O, room in dar, room in dar,
Room in dar, in de heaven, my Lord!
     I can't stay behind!"

No. 26   *Lay Dis Body Down*

This is probably the song heard by W. H. Russell of the London *Times*, as described in chapter xviii. of "My Diary North and South." The writer was on his way from Pocotaligo to Mr. Trescot's estate on Barnwell Island, and of the midnight row thither he says:

"The oarsmen, as they bent to their task, beguiled the way by singing in unison a real negro melody, which was unlike the works of the Ethiopian Serenaders as anything in song could be unlike another. It was a barbaric sort of madrigal, in which one singer beginning was followed by the others in unison, repeating the refrain in chorus, and full of quaint expression and melancholy:—

'Oh your soul! oh my soul! I'm going to the churchyard
     To lay this body down;
Oh my soul! oh your soul! we're going to the churchyard
     To lay this nigger down.'

And them some appeal to the difficulty of passing the 'Jawdam' constituted the whole of the song, which continued with unabated energy during the whole of the little voyage. To me it was a strange scene. The stream, dark as Lethe, flowing between the silent, houseless, rugged banks, lighted up near the landing by the fire in the woods, which reddened the sky—the wild strain, and the unearthly adjurations to the singers' souls, as though they were palpable, put me in mind of the fancied voyage across the Styx."

We append with some hesitation the following as a variation; the words of which we borrow from Col. Higginson. Lt. Col. Trowbridge says of it that it was sung at funerals in the night time—one of the most solemn and characteristic of the customs of the negroes. He attributes its origin to St. Simon's Island, Georgia:

I   know moon-light, I   know star-light; I   lay dis bod-y   down.

2 I walk in de moonlight, I walk in de starlight;
     I lay dis body down.

3 I know de graveyard, I know de graveyard,
  When I lay dis body down.

No. 58   *Early in the Morning*

This shout is accompanied by the peculiar shuffling dance, except in the chorus, where they walk around in slow time, keeping step to their song.—J. S. R.

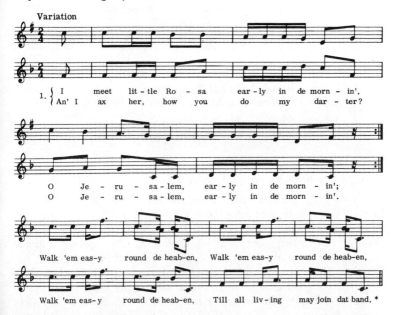

1. { I meet lit - tle Ro - sa ear - ly in de morn - in',
   { An' I ax her, how you do my dar - ter?

O Je - ru - sa - lem, ear - ly in de morn - in';
O Je - ru - sa - lem, ear - ly in de morn - in'.

Walk 'em eas-y round de heab-en, Walk 'em eas-y round de heab-en,

Walk 'em eas-y round de heab-en, Till all liv-ing may join dat band. *

*O shout glory till 'em join dat ban'.

2 I meet my mudder early in de mornin',
  An' I ax her, how you do my mudder?
  Walk 'em easy, etc.

3 I meet brudder Robert early in de mornin';
  I ax brudder Robert, how you do, my sonny?

4 I meet titta-Wisa [Louisa] early in de mornin';
  I ax titta-Wisa, how you do, my darter?

No. 62   *Good-Bye Brother*

Sung at the breaking up of a midnight meeting after the death of a soldier. These midnight *wails* are very solemn to me, and exhibit the sadness of the present mingled with the joyful hope of the future. I have known the negroes to get together in groups of six or eight around a small fire, and sing and pray alternately from nine o'clock till three the next morning, after the death of one of their number.—J. S. R.

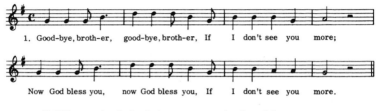

1. Good-bye, broth-er, good-bye, broth-er, If I don't see you more;

Now God bless you, now God bless you, If I don't see you more.

2 We part in de body but we meet in de spirit,
   We'll meet in de heaben in de blessed kingdom.

3 So good-bye, brother, good-bye, sister;
   Now God bless you, now God bless you.

No. 74   *Nobody Knows de Trouble I've Had*

This song was a favorite in the colored schools of Charleston in 1865; it has since that time spread to the Sea Islands, where it is now sung with the variation noted above. An independent transcription of this melody, sent from Florida by Lt. Col. Apthorp, differed only in the ictus of certain measures, as has also been noted above. The third verse was furnished by Lt. Col. Apthorp. Once when there had been a good deal of ill feeling excited, and trouble was apprehended, owing to the uncertain action of Government in regard to the confiscated lands on the Sea Islands, Gen. Howard was called upon to address the colored people earnestly and even severely. Sympathizing with them, however, he could not speak to his own satisfaction; and to relieve their minds of the ever-present sense of injustice, and prepare them to listen, he asked them to sing. Immediately an old woman on the outskirts of the meeting began "Nobody knows the trouble I've had," and the whole audience joined in. The General was so affected by the plaintive words and melody, that he found himself melting into tears and quite unable to maintain his official sternness.

No-bod-y knows de trou-ble I've had, No-bod-y knows but

Foot Tapping

Hand Clapping

Je-sus, No-bod-y knows de trou-ble I've had, (Sing) Glo-ry hal-le-

lu! One morn-ing I was a-walk-ing down, O yes,

Lord! I saw some ber-ries a-hang-ing down, O yes, Lord!

2. I pick de berry and I suck de juice, O yes, Lord!
   Just as sweet as the honey in de comb, O yes, Lord!
3. Sometimes I'm up, sometimes I'm down,
   Sometimes I'm almost on de groun'.
4. What make ole Satan hate me so?
   Because he got me once and he let me go.

No. 111   *I'm Gwine to Alabamy*

A very good specimen, so far as notes can give one, of the strange barbaric songs that one hears upon the Western steamboats.

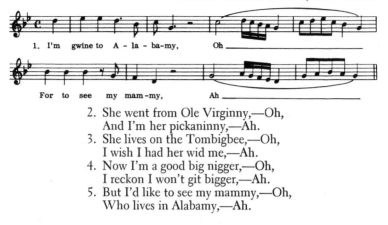

1. I'm gwine to A - la - ba-my,   Oh _____

For to see my mam -my,   Ah _____

2. She went from Ole Virginny,—Oh,
   And I'm her pickaninny,—Ah.
3. She lives on the Tombigbee,—Oh,
   I wish I had her wid me,—Ah.
4. Now I'm a good big nigger,—Oh,
   I reckon I won't git bigger,—Ah.
5. But I'd like to see my mammy,—Oh,
   Who lives in Alabamy,—Ah.

No. 112   *My Father, How Long?*

For singing this "the negroes had been put in jail at Georgetown, S.C., at the outbreak of the Rebellion. 'We'll soon be free' was too dangerous an assertion, and though the chant was an old one, it was no doubt sung with redoubled emphasis during the new events. 'De Lord will call us home,' was evidently thought to be a symbolical verse; for, as a little drummer boy explained it to me, showing all his white teeth as he sat in the moonlight by the door of my tent, 'Dey tink *de Lord* mean for say *de Yankees.*' "—T. W. H.

My * fa - ther, how ___ long,   My   fa - ther, how   long,   My

fa - ther, how   long,   Poor   sin - ner   suf - fer   here?

1. And it won't be   long,   And it won't_ be ___ long,   And it

won't_ be   long,   Poor   sin - ner   suf - fer   here.

*mother, etc.

2 We'll soon be free, (*ter*)
   De Lord will call us home.

3 We'll walk de miry road
   Where pleasure never dies.

4 We'll walk de golden streets
   Of de New Jerusalem.

    5 My brudders do sing
      De praises of de Lord.

    6 We'll fight for liberty
      When de Lord will call us home.

No. 124   *These Are All My Father's Children*

This is interesting as being probably the original of "Trouble of the world" (No. 10) and peculiarly so from the following custom, which is described by a North Carolina negro as existing in South Carolina. When a *pater-familias* dies, his family assemble in the room where the coffin is, and, ranging themselves round the body in the order of age and relationship, sing this hymn, marching round and round. They also take the youngest and pass him first over and then under the coffin. Then two men take the coffin on their shoulders and carry it on the run to the grave.

No. 136   *Musieu Bainjo*

The seven . . . songs [of this type] were obtained from a lady who heard them sung, before the war, on the "Good Hope" plantation, St. Charles Parish, Louisiana. The language, evidently a rude corruption of French, is that spoken by the negroes in that part of the State; and it is said that it is more difficult for persons who speak French to interpret this dialect, than for those who speak English to understand the most corrupt of the ordinary negro-talk. The pronunciation of this negro-French is indicated, as accurately as possible, in the versions given here, which furnish, also, many interesting examples of the peculiar phrases and idioms employed by this people. The frequent omission of prepositions, articles, and auxiliary verbs, as well as of single letters, and the contractions constantly occurring, are among the most noticeable peculiarities. Some of the most difficult words are: *mo* for *me, mon, je*; *li* for *lui, le la, il, elle*; *mouin* for *moi*; *yé* for *ils, leur*; *aine, dé,* for *un, deux*; *té* for *été, était*; *ya, yavé* for *il y a,* etc.; *ouar* for *voir* and its inflections; *oulé* for *vouloir,* etc.; *pancor* for *pas encore*; *michié* for *monsieur*; *inpé* for *un peu.* The words are, of course, to be pronounced as if they were pure French.

Four of these songs, Nos. 130, 131, 132 and 133, were sung to a simple dance, a sort of minuet, called the *Coonjai*; the name and the dance are probably both of African origin. When the *Coonjai* is danced, the music is furnished by an orchestra of singers, the leader of whom—a man selected both for the quality of his voice and for his skill in improvising—sustains the solo part, while the others afford him an opportunity, as they shout in chorus, for inventing some neat verse to compliment some lovely *danseuse,* or celebrate the deeds of some plantation hero. The dancers themselves never sing, as in the case of the religious "shout" of the Port Royal negroes; and the usual musical accompaniment, besides that of the singers, is that furnished by a skilful performer on the barrel-head-drum, the jaw-bone and key, or some other rude instrument.

No. 134. The "calinda" was a sort of contra-dance, which has now passed entirely out of use. Bescherelle describes the two lines as "avançant et reculant en cadence, et faisant des contorsions fort singulières et des gestes fort lascifs."

The first movement of No. 135, "Lolotte," has furnished M. Gottschalk with the theme of his "Ballade Créole," "La Savane," op. 3 de la Louisiane.

In 136, we have the attempt of some enterprising negro to write a French song; he is certainly to be congratulated on his success.

It will be noticed that all these songs are "seculars"; and that while the words of most of them are of very little account, the music is as peculiar, as interesting, and, in the case of two or three of them, as difficult to write down, or to sing correctly, as any that have preceded them.

24. THOMAS W. HIGGINSON

>>> Abolitionist, clergyman, author, and army officer, Thomas Wentworth Higginson (1823–1911) served as a colonel in command of the first slave regiment, the South Carolina Volunteers, mustered into the service of the Union army during the Civil War. It was entirely appropriate that Higginson should have been given such a command. A graduate of Harvard College and the Harvard Divinity School, he had left the ministry of a Unitarian church in Massachusetts after a three-year period to work in the anti-slavery movement. His activities as an abolitionist involved him with the Underground Railroad and with the struggles of John Brown, the noted martyr to the cause of abolition. Higginson's fascination with the songs sung by the ex-slaves of his regiment led him to write an article on the subject for the *Atlantic Monthly*, XIX (June, 1867), which was later incorporated as Chapter IX into his book, *Army Life in a Black Regiment* (Boston, 1870). <<<

From *Army Life in a Black Regiment* [1870] †

CAMP DIARY

December 3, 1862.—7 P.M.
What a life is this I lead! It is a dark, mild, drizzling evening, and as the foggy air breeds sand-flies, so it calls out melodies and strange antics from this mysterious race of grown-up children with whom my lot is cast. All over the camp the lights glimmer in the tents, and as I sit at my desk in the open doorway, there come mingled sounds of stir and glee. Boys laugh and shout,—a feeble flute stirs somewhere in some tent, not an officer's,—a drum throbs far away in another,—wild kildeer-plover flit and wail above us, like the haunting souls of dead slave-masters,—and from a neighboring cook-fire comes the monotonous sound of that strange festival, half

† Text: The original edition (Boston, 1870), pp. 16–19, 22–25, 130–34, 197–222.

pow-wow, half prayer-meeting, which they know only as a "shout." These fires are usually enclosed in a little booth, made neatly of palm-leaves and covered in at top, a regular native African hut, in short, such as is pictured in books, and such as I once got up from dried palmleaves for a fair at home. This hut is now crammed with men, singing at the top of their voices, in one of their quaint, monotonous, endless, negro-Methodist chants, with obscure syllables recurring constantly, and slight variations interwoven, all accompanied with a regular drumming of the feet and clapping of the hands, like castanets. Then the excitement spreads: inside and outside the enclosure men begin to quiver and dance, others join, a circle forms, winding monotonously round some one in the centre; some "heel and toe" tumultuously, others merely tremble and stagger on, others stoop and rise, others whirl, others caper sideways, all keep steadily circling like dervishes; spectators applaud special strokes of skill; my approach only enlivens the scene; the circle enlarges, louder grows the singing, rousing shouts of encouragement come in, half bacchanalian, half devout, "Wake 'em, brudder!" "Stan' up to 'em, brudder!"—and still the ceaseless drumming and clapping, in perfect cadence, goes steadily on. Suddenly there comes a sort of *snap*, and the spell breaks, amid general sighing and laughter. And this not rarely and occasionally, but night after night, while in other parts of the camp the soberest prayers and exhortations are proceeding sedately.

A simple and lovable people, whose graces seem to come by nature, and whose vices by training. Some of the best superintendents confirm the first tales of innocence, and Dr. Zachos told me last night that on his plantation, a sequestered one, "they had absolutely no vices." Nor have these men of mine yet shown any worth mentioning; since I took command I have heard of no man intoxicated, and there has been but one small quarrel. I suppose that scarcely a white regiment in the army shows so little swearing. Take the "Progressive Friends" and put them in red trousers, and I verily believe they would fill a guard-house sooner than these men. If camp regulations are violated, it seems to be usually through heedlessness. They love passionately three things besides their spiritual incantations: namely, sugar, home, and tobacco. This last affection brings tears to their eyes, almost, when they speak of their urgent need of pay; they speak of their last-remembered quid as if it were some deceased relative, too early lost, and to be mourned forever. As for sugar, no white man can drink coffee after they have sweetened it to their liking.

I see that the pride which military life creates may cause the plantation trickeries to diminish. For instance, these men make the most admirable sentinels. It is far harder to pass the camp lines at

night than in the camp from which I came; and I have seen none of
that disposition to connive at the offences of members of one's own
company which is so troublesome among white soldiers. Nor are they
lazy, either about work or drill; in all respects they seem better material for soldiers than I had dared to hope.

There is one company in particular, all Florida men, which I
certainly think the finest-looking company I ever saw, white or black;
they range admirably in size, have remarkable erectness and ease of
carriage, and really march splendidly. Not a visitor but notices them;
yet they have been under drill only a fortnight, and a part only two
days. They have all been slaves, and very few are even mulattoes.

December 5, 1862.

Give these people their tongues, their feet, and their leisure, and
they are happy. At every twilight the air is full of singing, talking,
and clapping of hands in unison. One of their favorite songs is full
of plaintive cadences; it is not, I think, a Methodist tune, and I wonder where they obtained a chant of such beauty.

> "I can't stay behind, my Lord, I can't stay behind!
> O, my father is gone, my father is gone,
> My father is gone into heaven, my Lord!
>   I can't stay behind!
> Dere's room enough, room enough,
> Room enough in de heaven for de sojer:
>   Can't stay behind!"

It always excites them to have us looking on, yet they sing these
songs at all times and seasons. I have heard this very song dimly
droning on near midnight, and, tracing it into the recesses of a cook-
house, have found an old fellow coiled away among the pots and
provisions, chanting away with his "Can't stay behind, sinner," till
I made him leave his song behind.

This evening, after working themselves up to the highest pitch, a
party suddenly rushed off, got a barrel, and mounted some man
upon it, who said, "Gib anoder song, boys, and I 'se gib you a speech."
After some hesitation and sundry shouts of "Rise de sing, somebody,"
and "Stan' up for Jesus, brudder," irreverently put in by the juveniles,
they got upon the John Brown song, always a favorite, adding a jubilant verse which I had never before heard,—"We'll beat Beauregard
on de clare battlefield." Then came the promised speech, and then
no less than seven other speeches by as many men, on a variety of
barrels, each orator being affectionately tugged to the pedestal and
set on end by his special constituency. Every speech was good, without exception; with the queerest oddities of phrase and pronuncia-

tion, there was an invariable enthusiasm, a pungency of statement, and an understanding of the points at issue, which made them all rather thrilling. Those long-winded slaves in "Among the Pines"[1] seemed rather fictitious and literary in comparison. The most eloquent, perhaps, was Corporal Prince Lambkin, just arrivee from Fernandina, who evidently had a previous reputation among them. His historical references were very interesting. He reminded them that he had predicted this war ever since Fremont's time, to which some of the crowd assented; he gave a very intelligent account of that Presidential campaign, and then described most impressively the secret anxiety of the slaves in Florida to know all about President Lincoln's election, and told how they all refused to work on the fourth of March, expecting their freedom to date from that day. He finally brought out one of the few really impressive appeals for the American flag that I have ever heard. "Our mas'rs dey hab lib under de flag, dey got dere wealth under it, and ebryting beautiful for dere chilen. Under it dey hab grind us up, and put us in dere pocket for money. But de fus' minute dey tink dat ole flag mean freedom for we colored people, dey pull it right down, and run up de rag ob dere own." (Immense applause). "But we'll neber desert de ole flag, boys, neber; we hab lib under it for *eighteen hundred sixty-two years*, and we'll die for it now." With which overpowering discharge of chronology-at-long-range, this most effective of stump-speeches closed. I see already with relief that there will be small demand in this regiment for harangues from the officers; give the men an empty barrel for a stump, and they will do their own exhortation.

                                                   December 11, 1862.

Haroun Alraschid,[2] wandering in disguise through his imperial streets, scarcely happened upon a greater variety of groups than I, in my evening strolls among our own camp-fires .

Beside some of these fires the men are cleaning their guns or rehearsing their drill,—beside others, smoking in silence their very scanty supply of the beloved tobacco,—beside others, telling stories and shouting with laughter over the broadest mimicry, in which they excel, and in which the officers come in for a full share. The everlasting "shout" is always within hearing, with its mixture of piety and polka, and its castanet-like clapping of the hands. Then there are quieter prayer-meetings, with pious invocations and slow psalms, "deaconed out" from memory by the leader, two lines at a time, in a sort of wailing chant. Elsewhere, there are *conversazioni* around fires, with a woman for queen of the circle,—her Nubian face, gay head-

1. A novel by "Edmund Kirk" (pseudonym of James Roberts Gilmore, 1822–1903), published in New York in 1862. [*Editor*]
2. The Caliph of Bagdad in the legends of the *Arabian Nights*. [*Editor*]

dress, gilt necklace, and white teeth, all resplendent in the glowing light. Sometimes the woman is spelling slow monosyllables out of a primer, a feat which always commands all ears,—they rightly recognizing a mighty spell, equal to the overthrowing of monarchs, in the magic assonance of *cat, hat, pat, bat,* and the rest of it. Elsewhere, it is some solitary old cook, some aged Uncle Tiff, with enormous spectacles, who is perusing a hymn-book by the light of a pine splinter, in his deserted cooking booth of palmetto leaves. By another fire there is an actual dance, red-legged soldiers doing right-and-left, and "now-lead-de-lady-ober," to the music of a violin which is rather artistically played, and which may have guided the steps, in other days, of Barnwells and Hugers. And yonder is a stump-orator perched on his barrel, pouring out his exhortations to fidelity in war and in religion. To-night for the first time I have heard an harangue in a different strain, quite saucy, sceptical, and defiant, appealing to them in a sort of French materialistic style, and claiming some personal experience of warfare. "You don't know notin' about it, boys. You tink you's brave enough; how you tink, if you stan' clar in de open field,—here you, and dar de Secesh? You's got to hab de right ting inside o' you. You must hab it 'served [preserved] in you, like dese yer sour plums dey 'serve in de barr'l; you's got to harden it down inside o' you, or it's notin'." Then he hit hard at the religionists: "When a man's got de sperit ob de Lord in him, it weakens him all out, can't hoe de corn." He had a great deal of broad sense in his speech; but presently some others began praying vociferously close by, as if to drown this free-thinker, when at last he exclaimed, "I mean to fight de war through, an' die a good sojer wid de last kick,— dat's *my* prayer!" and suddenly jumped off the barrel. I was quite interested at discovering this reverse side of the temperament, the devotional side preponderates so enormously, and the greatest scamps kneel and groan in their prayer-meetings with such entire zest. It shows that there is some individuality developed among them, and that they will not become too exclusively pietistic.

Their love of the spelling-book is perfectly inexhaustible,—they stumbling on by themselves, or the blind leading the blind, with the same pathetic patience which they carry into everything. The chaplain is getting up a schoolhouse, where he will soon teach them as regularly as he can. But the alphabet must always be incidental business in a camp. . . .

One can hardly imagine a body of men more disconsolate than a regiment suddenly transferred from an adventurous life in the enemy's country to the quiet of a sheltered camp, on safe and familiar ground. The men under my command were deeply dejected when, on a most appropriate day,—the First of April, 1863,—they found themselves unaccountably recalled from Florida, that region of delights which had seemed theirs by the right of conquest. My dusky soldiers, who based their whole walk and conversation strictly on the ancient Israelites, felt that the prophecies were all set at naught, and that they were on the wrong side of the Red Sea; indeed, they regarded even me as a sort of reversed Moses, whose Pisgah fronted in the wrong direction. Had they foreseen how the next occupation of the Promised Land was destined to result, they might have acquiesced with more of their wonted cheerfulness. As it was, we were very glad to receive, after a few days of discontented repose on the very ground where we had once been so happy, an order to go out on picket at Port Royal Ferry, with the understanding that we might remain there for some time.

This picket station was regarded as a sort of military picnic by the regiments stationed at Beaufort, South Carolina; it meant blackberries and oysters, wild roses and magnolias, flowery lanes instead of sandy barrens, and a sort of guerilla existence in place of the camp routine. To the colored soldiers expecially, with their love of country life, and their extensive personal acquaintance on the plantations, it seemed quite like a Christmas festival. Besides, they would be in sight of the enemy, and who knew but there might, by the blessing of Providence, be a raid or a skirmish? If they could not remain on the St. John's River, it was something to dwell on the Coosaw. In the end they enjoyed it as much as they expected, and though we "went out" several times subsequently, until it became an old story, the enjoyment never waned. And as even the march from the camp to the picket lines was something that could not possibly have been the same for any white regiment in the service, it is worth while to begin at the beginning and describe it.

A regiment ordered on picket was expected to have reveille at daybreak, and to be in line for departure by sunrise. This delighted our men, who always took a childlike pleasure in being out of bed at any unreasonable hour; and by the time I had emerged, the tents were nearly all struck, and the great wagons were lumbering into camp to receive them, with whatever else was to be transported. The first rays of the sun must fall upon the line of these wagons, moving away across the wide parade-ground, followed by the column of men, who would soon outstrip them. But on the occasion which I especially describe the sun was shrouded, and, when once upon the sandy plain, neither camp nor town nor river could be seen in the dimness; and when I rode forward and looked back there was only visible the long, moving, shadowy column, seeming rather awful in its snakelike advance. There was a swaying of flags and multitudinous weapons that might have been camels' necks for all one could see, and the whole thing might have been a caravan upon the desert. Soon we debouched upon the "Shell Road," the wagon-train drew on one side into the fog, and by the time the sun appeared the music ceased, the men took the "route step," and the fun began.

The "route step" is an abandonment of all military strictness, and nothing is required of the men but to keep four abreast, and not lag behind. They are not required to keep step, though, with the rhythmical ear of our soldiers, they almost always instinctively did so; talking and singing are allowed, and of this privilege, at least, they eagerly availed themselves. On this day they were at the top of exhilaration. There was one broad grin from one end of the column to the other; it might soon have been a caravan of elephants instead of camels, for the ivory and the blackness; the chatter and the laughter almost drowned the tramp of feet and the clatter of equipments. At cross-roads and plantation gates the colored people thronged to see us pass; every one found a friend and a greeting. "How you do, aunty?" "Huddy (how d' ye), Budder Benjamin?" "How you find yourself dis mornin', Tittawisa (Sister Louisa)?" Such salutations rang out to everybody, known or unknown. In return, venerable, kerchiefed matrons courtesied laboriously to every one, with an unfailing "Bress de Lord, budder." Grave little boys, blacker than ink, shook hands with our laughing and utterly unmanageable drummers, who greeted them with this sure word of prophecy, "Dem's de drummers for de nex' war!" Pretty mulatto girls ogled and coquetted, and made eyes, as Thackeray would say, at half the young fellows in the battalion. Meantime the singing was brisk along the whole column, and when I sometimes reined up to see them pass, the chant of each company, entering my ear, drove out from the other ear the strain of the preceding. Such an odd mixture of things, military and missionary, as the successive waves of song drifted by! First, "John Brown," of course; then, "What make old Satan for follow me so?" then, "Marching Along"; then, "Hold your light on Canaan's shore"; then, "When this cruel war is over" (a new favorite, sung by a few); yielding presently to a grand burst of the favorite marching song among them all, and one at which every step instinctively quickened, so light and jubilant its rhythm,—

> "All true children gwine in de wilderness,
>   Gwine in de wilderness, gwine in de wilderness,
>   True believers gwine in de wilderness,
>   To take away de sins ob de world,"—

ending in a "Hoigh!" after each verse,—a sort of Irish yell. For all the songs, but especially for their own wild hymns, they constantly improvised simple verses, with the same odd mingling,—the little facts of to-day's march being interwoven with the depths of theological gloom, and the same jubilant chorus annexed to all; thus,—

> "We're gwine to de Ferry,
>   De bell done ringing;
> Gwine to de landing,
>   De bell done ringing;
> Trust, believer,
>   O, de bell done ringing;
> Satan 's behind me,
>   De bell done ringing;
> 'T is a misty morning,
>   De bell done ringing;
> O de road am sandy,
>   De bell done ringing;
> Hell been open,
>   De bell done ringing";—

and so on indefinitely.

The little drum-corps kept in advance; a jolly crew, their drums slung on their backs, and the drum-sticks perhaps balanced on their heads. With them went the officers' servant-boys, more uproarious still, always ready to lend their shrill treble to any song. At the head of the whole force there walked, by some self-imposed pre-eminence, a respectable elderly female, one of the company laundresses, whose vigorous stride we never could quite overtake, and who had an enormous bundle balanced on her head, while she waved in her hand, like a sword, a long-handled tin dipper. Such a picturesque medley of fun, war, and music I believe no white regiment in the service could have shown; and yet there was no straggling, and a single tap of the drum would at any moment bring order out of this seeming chaos. So we marched our seven miles out upon the smooth and shaded road,—beneath jasmine clusters, and great pine-cones dropping, and great bunches of mistletoe still in bloom among the branches. Arrived at the station, the scene soon became busy and more confused; wagons were being unloaded, tents pitched, water brought, wood cut, fires made, while the "field and staff" could take possession of the abandoned quarters of their predecessors, and we could look round in the lovely summer morning to "survey our empire and behold our home." . . .

Negro Spirituals

The war brought to some of us, besides its direct experiences, many a strange fulfilment of dreams of other days. For instance, the present writer had been a faithful student of the Scottish ballads, and had always envied Sir Walter [Scott] the delight of tracing them out amid their own heather, and of writing them down piecemeal from the lips of aged crones. It was a strange enjoyment, therefore, to be suddenly brought into the midst of a kindred world of unwritten songs, as simple and indigenous as the Border Minstrelsy, more uniformly plaintive, almost always more quaint, and often as essentially poetic.

This interest was rather increased by the fact that I had for many years heard of this class of songs under the name of "Negro Spirituals," and had even heard some of them sung by friends from South Carolina. I could now gather on their own soil these strange plants, which I had before seen as in museums alone. True, the individual songs rarely coincided; there was a line here, a chorus there,—just enough to fix the class, but this was unmistakable. It was not strange that they differed, for the range seemed almost endless, and South Carolina, Georgia, and Florida seemed to have nothing but the generic character in common, until all were mingled in the united stock of camp-melodies.

Often in the starlit evening I have returned from some lonely ride by the swift river, or on the plover-haunted barrens, and, entering the camp, have silently approached some glimmering fire, round which the dusky figures moved in the rhythmical barbaric dance the negroes call a "shout," chanting, often harshly, but always in the most perfect time, some monotonous refrain. Writing down in the darkness, as I best could,—perhaps with my hand in the safe covert of my pocket,—the words of the song, I have afterwards carried it to my tent, like some captured bird or insect, and then, after examination, put it by. Or, summoning one of the men at some period of leisure,—Corporal Robert Sutton, for instance, whose iron memory held all the details of a song as if it were a ford or a forest,—I have completed the new specimen by supplying the absent parts. The music I could only retain by ear, and though the more common strains were repeated often enough to fix their impression, there were others that occurred only once or twice.

The words will be here given, as nearly as possible, in the original dialect; and if the spelling seems sometimes inconsistent, or the misspelling insufficient, it is because I could get no nearer. I wished to avoid what seems to me the only error of Lowell's "Biglow Papers" in respect to dialect,—the occasional use of an extreme misspelling, which merely confuses the eye, without taking us any closer to the peculiarity of sound.

The favorite song in camp was the following,—sung with no accompaniment but the measured clapping of hands and the clatter of many feet. It was sung perhaps twice as often as any other. This was partly due to the fact that it properly consisted of a chorus alone, with which the verses of other songs might be combined at random.

I. HOLD YOUR LIGHT

"Hold your light, Brudder Robert,—
    Hold your light,
Hold your light on Canaan's shore.

"What make ole Satan for follow me so?
Satan ain't got notin' for do wid me.
    Hold your light,
    Hold your light,
Hold your light on Canaan's shore."

This would be sung for half an hour at a time, perhaps each person present being named in turn. It seemed the simplest primitive type of "spiritual." The next in popularity was almost as elementary, and, like this, named successively each one of the circle. It was, however, much more resounding and convivial in its music.

II. BOUND TO GO

"Jordan River, I'm bound to go,
    Bound to go, bound to go,—
Jordan River, I'm bound to go,
    And bid 'em fare ye well.

"My Brudder Robert, I'm bound to go,
    Bound to go," &c.

"My Sister Lucy, I'm bound to go,
    Bound to go," &c.

Sometimes it was "tink 'em" (think them) "fare ye well." The *ye* was so detached that I thought at first it was "very" or "vary well."

Another picturesque song, which seemed immensely popular, was at first very bewildering to me. I could not make out the first words of the chorus, and called it the "Romandàr," being reminded of some Romaic song which I had formerly heard. That association quite fell in with the Orientalism of the new tent-life.

III. ROOM IN THERE

"O, my mudder is gone! my mudder is gone!
My mudder is gone into heaven, my Lord!
    I can't stay behind!
Dere's room in dar, room in dar,
Room in dar, in de heaven, my Lord!
    I can't stay behind!
Can't stay behind, my dear,
    I can't stay behind!

"O, my fader is gone!" &c.

"O, de angels are gone!" &c.

"O, I'se been on de road! I 'se been on de road!
I 'se been on de road into heaven, my Lord!
I can't stay behind!
O, room in dar, room in dar,
Room in dar, in de heaven, my Lord!
I can't stay behind!"

By this time every man within hearing, from oldest to youngest, would be wriggling and shuffling, as if through some magic piper's bewitchment; for even those who at first affected contemptuous indifference would be drawn into the vortex erelong.

Next to these in popularity ranked a class of songs belonging emphatically to the Church Militant, and available for camp purposes with very little strain upon their symbolism. This, for instance, had a true companion-in-arms heartiness about it, not impaired by the feminine invocation at the end.

IV. HAIL MARY

"One more valiant soldier here,
One more valiant soldier here,
One more valiant soldier here,
To help me bear de cross.
O hail, Mary, hail!
Hail, Mary, hail!
Hail, Mary, hail!
To help me bear de cross."

I fancied that the original reading might have been "soul," instead of "soldier,"—with some other syllable inserted to fill out the metre,—and that the "Hail, Mary," might denote a Roman Catholic origin, as I had several men from St. Augustine who held in a dim way to that faith. It was a very ringing song, though not so grandly jubilant as the next, which was really impressive as the singers pealed it out, when marching or rowing or embarking.

V. MY ARMY CROSS OVER

"My army cross over,
My army cross over,
O, Pharaoh's army drownded!
My army cross over.

"We'll cross de mighty river,
My army cross over;
We'll cross de river Jordan,

> My army cross over;
> We'll cross de danger water,
>   My army cross over;
> We'll cross de mighty Myo,
>   My army cross over.   (*Thrice.*)
>   O, Pharaoh's army drownded!
>   My army cross over."

I could get no explanation of the "mighty Myo," except that one of the old men thought it meant the river of death. Perhaps it is an African word. In the Cameroon dialect, "Mawa" signifies "to die."

The next also has a military ring about it, and the first line is well matched by the music. The rest is conglomerate, and one or two lines show a more Northern origin. "Done" is a Virginia shibboleth, quite distinct from the "been" which replaces it in South Carolina. Yet one of their best choruses, without any fixed words, was, "De bell done ringing," for which, in proper South Carolina dialect, would have been substituted, "De bell been a-ring." This refrain may have gone South with our army.

VI. RIDE IN, KIND SAVIOUR

> "Ride in, kind Saviour!
>   No man can hinder me.
> O, Jesus is a mighty man!
>   No man, &c.
> We're marching through Virginny fields.
>   No man, &c.
> O, Satan is a busy man,
>   No man, &c.
> And he has his sword and shield,
>   No man, &c.
> O, old Secesh done come and gone!
>   No man can hinder me."

Sometimes they substituted "hinder *we*," which was more spicy to the ear, and more in keeping with the usual head-over-heels arrangement of their pronouns.

Almost all their songs were thoroughly religious in their tone, however quaint their expression, and were in a minor key, both as to words and music. The attitude is always the same, and, as a commentary on the life of the race, is infinitely pathetic. Nothing but patience for this life,—nothing but triumph in the next. Sometimes the present predominates, sometimes the future; but the combination is always implied. In the following, for instance, we hear simply the patience.

VII. This World Almost Done

"Brudder, keep your lamp trimmin' and a-burnin',
Keep your lamp trimmin' and a-burnin',
Keep your lamp trimmin' and a-burnin',
    For dis world most done.
So keep your lamp, &c.
    Dis world most done."

But in the next, the final reward of patience is proclaimed as plaintively.

VIII. I Want to Go Home

"Dere 's no rain to wet you,
    O, yes, I want to go home.
Dere 's no sun to burn you,
    O, yes, I want to go home;
O, push along, believers,
    O, yes, &c.
Dere's no hard trials,
    O, yes, &c.
Dere 's no whips a-crackin',
    O, yes, &c.
My brudder on de wayside,
    O, yes, &c.
O, push along, my brudder,
    O, yes, &c.
Where dere 's no stomy weather,
    O, yes, &c.
Dere 's no tribulation,
    O, yes, &c.

This next was a boat-song, and timed well with the tug of the oar.

IX. The Coming Day

"I want to go to Canaan,
I want to go to Canaan,
I want to go to Canaan,
    To meet 'em at de comin' day.
O, remember, let me go to Canaan, (*Thrice.*)
    To meet 'em, &c.
O, brudder, let me go to Canaan, (*Thrice.*)
    To meet 'em, &c.
My brudder, you—oh!—remember, (*Thrice.*)
    To meet 'em at de comin' day."

The following begins with a startling affirmation, yet the last line quite outdoes the first. This, too, was a capital boat-song.

X. ONE MORE RIVER

"O, Jordan bank was a great old bank,
    Dere ain't but one more river to cross.
We have some valiant soldier here,
    Dere ain't, &c.
O, Jordan stream will never run dry,
    Dere ain't, &c.
Dere's a hill on my leff, and he catch on my right,
    Dere ain't but one more river to cross."

I could get no explanation of this last riddle, except, "Dat mean, if you go on de leff, go to 'struction, and if you go on de right, go to God, for sure."

In others, more of spiritual conflict is implied, as in this next.

XI. THE DYING LAMB POETRY

"I wants to go where Moses trod,
    O de dying Lamb!
For Moses gone to de promised land,
    O de dying Lamb!
To drink from springs dat never run dry,
    O, &c.
Cry O my Lord!
    O, &c.
Before I'll stay in hell one day,
    O, &c.
I'm in hopes to pray my sins away,
    O, &c.
Cry O my Lord!
    O, &c.
Brudder Moses promised for be dar too,
    O, &c.
To drink from streams dat never run dry,
    O de dying Lamb!"

In the next, the conflict is at its height, and the lurid imagery of the Apocalypse is brought to bear. This book, with the books of Moses, constituted their Bible; all that lay between, even the narratives of the life of Jesus, they hardly cared to read or to hear.

XII. DOWN IN THE VALLEY

"We 'll run and never tire,
We 'll run and never tire,
We 'll run and never tire,
    Jesus set poor sinners free.
Way down in de valley,

> Who will rise and go with me?
> You 've heern talk of Jesus,
>   Who set poor sinners free.

> "De lightin' and de flashin'
>   De lightin' and de flashin',
>   De lightin' and de flashin',
>   Jesus set poor sinners free.
> I can't stand the fire.   (*Thrice.*)
>   Jesus set poor sinners free,
> De green trees a-flamin'.   (*Thrice.*)
>   Jesus set poor sinners free,
>   Way down in de valley,
>   Who will rise and go with me?
>   You've heern talk of Jesus
>   Who set poor sinners free."

"De valley" and "de lonesome valley" were familiar words in their religious experience. To descend into that region implied the same process with the "anxious-seat" of the camp-meeting. When a young girl was supposed to enter it, she bound a handkerchief by a peculiar knot over her head, and made it a point of honor not to change a single garment till the day of her baptism, so that she was sure of being in physical readiness for the cleansing rite, whatever her spiritual mood might be. More than once, in noticing a damsel thus mystically kerchiefed, I have asked some dusky attendant its meaning, and have received the unfailing answer,—framed with their usual indifference to the genders of pronouns,—"He in de lonesome valley, sa."

The next gives the same dramatic conflict, while its detached and impersonal refrain gives it strikingly the character of the Scotch and Scandinavian ballads.

XIII. CRY HOLY

> "Cry holy, holy!
>   Look at de people dat is born of God.
> And I run down de valley, and I run down to pray,
>   Says, look at de people dat is born of God.
> When I get dar, Cappen Satan was dar,
>   Says, look at, &c.
> Says, young man, young man, dere 's no use for pray,
>   Says, look at, &c.
> For Jesus is dead, and God gone away,
>   Says, look at, &c.
> And I made him out a liar, and I went my way,
>   Says, look at, &c.
>   Sing holy, holy!

"O, Mary was a woman, and he had a one Son,
    Says, look at, &c.
And de Jews and de Romans had him hung,
    Says, look at, &c.
      Cry holy, holy!

"And I tell you, sinner, you had better had pray,
    Says, look at, &c.
For hell is a dark and dismal place,
    Says, look at, &c.
And I tell you, sinner, and I wouldn't go dar!
    Says, look at, &c.
      Cry holy, holy!"

Here is an infinitely quaint description of the length of the heavenly road;—

XIV. O'er the Crossing

"Yonder 's my old mudder,
    Been a-waggin' at de hill so long.
It's about time she'll cross over;
    Get home bimeby.
Keep prayin', I do believe
    We're a long time waggin' o'er de crossin'.
Keep prayin', I do believe
    We'll get home to heaven bimeby.

"Hear dat mournful thunder
    Roll from door to door,
Calling home God's children;
    Get home bimeby.
Little chil'en, I do believe
    We're a long time, &c.
Little chil'en, I do believe
    We'll get home, &c.

"See dat forked lightnin'
    Flash from tree to tree,
Callin' home God's chil'en;
    Get home bimeby.
True believer, I do believe
    We're a long time, &c.
O brudders, I do believe,
    We'll get home to heaven bimeby."

One of the most singular pictures of future joys, and with a fine flavor of hospitality about it, was this:—

XV. Walk 'em Easy

"O, walk 'em easy round de heaven,
Walk 'em easy round de heaven,
Walk 'em easy round de heaven,
    Dat all de people may join de band.
Walk 'em easy round de heaven.   (*Thrice.*)
    O, shout glory till 'em join dat band!"

The chorus was usually the greater part of the song, and often came in paradoxically, thus:—

XVI. O Yes, Lord

"O, must I be like de foolish mans?
    O yes, Lord!
Will build de house on de sandy hill.
    O yes, Lord!
I 'll build my house on Zion hill,
    O yes, Lord!
No wind nor rain can blow me down,
    O yes, Lord!"

The next is very graceful and lyrical, and with more variety of rhythm than usual:—

XVII. Bow Low, Mary

"Bow low, Mary, bow low, Martha,
    For Jesus come and lock de door,
    And carry de keys away.
Sail, sail, over yonder,
And view de promised land.
    For Jesus come, &c.
Weep, O Mary, bow low, Martha,
    For Jesus come, &c.
Sail, sail, my true believer;
Sail, sail, over yonder;
Mary, bow low, Martha, bow low,
    For Jesus come and lock de door
    And carry de keys away."

But of all the "spirituals" that which surprised me the most, I think,—perhaps because it was that in which external nature furnished the images most directly,—was this. With all my experience of their ideal ways of speech, I was startled when first I came on such a flower of poetry in that dark soil.

XVIII. I Know Moon-Rise

"I know moon-rise, I know star-rise,
    Lay dis body down.

I walk in de moonlight, I walk in de starlight,
    To lay dis body down.
I 'll walk in de graveyard, I 'll walk through de graveyard,
    To lay dis body down.
I 'll lie in de grave and stretch out my arms;
    Lay dis body down.
I go to de judgment in de evenin' of de day,
    When I lay dis body down;
And my soul and your soul will meet in de day
    When I lay dis body down."

"I'll lie in de grave and stretch out my arms." Never, it seems to me, since man first lived and suffered, was his infinite longing for peace uttered more plaintively than in that line.

The next is one of the wildest and most striking of the whole series: there is a mystical effect and a passionate striving throughout the whole. The Scriptural struggle between Jacob and the angel, which is only dimly expressed in the words, seems all uttered in the music. I think it impressed my imagination more powerfully than any other of these songs.

XIX. Wrestling Jacob

"O wrestlin' Jacob, Jacob, day 's a-breakin';
    I will not let thee go!
O wrestlin' Jacob, Jacob, day 's a-breakin';
    He will not let me go!
O, I hold my brudder wid a tremblin' hand;
    I would not let him go!
I hold my sister wid a tremblin' hand;
    I would not let her go!

"O, Jacob do hang from a tremblin' limb,
    He would not let him go!
O, Jacob do hang from a tremblin' limb;
    De Lord will bless my soul.
O wrestlin' Jacob, Jacob," &c.

Of "occasional hymns," properly so called, I noticed but one, a funeral hymn for an infant, which is sung plaintively over and over, without variety of words.

XX. The Baby Gone Home

"De little baby gone home,
De little baby gone home,
De little baby gone along,
    For to climb up Jacob's ladder.
And I wish I 'd been dar,

> I wish I 'd been dar,
> I wish I 'd been dar, my Lord,
>> For to climb up Jacob's ladder."

Still simpler is this, which is yet quite sweet and touching.

XXI. JESUS WITH US

> "He have been wid us, Jesus,
>> He still wid us, Jesus,
> He will be wid us, Jesus,
>> Be wid us to the end."

The next seemed to be a favorite about Christmas time, when meditations on "de rollin' year" were frequent among them.

XXII. LORD, REMEMBER ME

> "O do, Lord, remember me!
>> O do, Lord, remember me!
> O, do remember me, until de year roll round!
>> Do, Lord, remember me!

> "If you want to die like Jesus died,
>> Lay in de grave,
> You would fold your arms and close your eyes
>> And die wid a free good will.

> "For Death is a simple ting,
>> And he go from door to door,
> And he knock down some, and he cripple up some,
>> And he leave some here to pray.

> "O do, Lord, remember me!
>> O do, Lord, remember me!
> My old fader 's gone till de year roll round;
>> Do, Lord, remember me!"

The next was sung in such an operatic and rollicking way that it was quite hard to fancy it a religious performance, which, however, it was. I heard it but once.

XXIII. EARLY IN THE MORNING

> "I meet little Rosa early in de mornin',
>> O Jerusalem! early in de mornin';
> And I ax her, How you do, my darter?
>> O Jerusalem! early in de mornin'.

> "I meet my mudder early in de mornin',
>> O Jerusalem! &c.
> And I ax her, How you do, my mudder?
>> O Jerusalem! &c.

"I meet Brudder Robert early in de mornin',
     O Jerusalem! &c.
And I ax him, How you do, my sonny?
     O Jerusalem! &c.

"I meet Tittawisa early in de mornin',
     O Jerusalem! &c.
And I ax her, How you do, my darter?
     O Jerusalem!" &c.

"Tittawisa" means "Sister Louisa." In songs of this class the name of every person present successively appears.

Their best marching song, and one which was invaluable to lift their feet along, as they expressed it, was the following. There was a kind of spring and *lilt* to it, quite indescribable by words.

XXIV. GO IN THE WILDERNESS

"Jesus call you.   Go in de wilderness,
     Go in de wilderness, go in de wilderness,
Jesus call you.   Go in de wilderness
     To wait upon de Lord.
Go wait upon de Lord,
Go wait upon de Lord,
Go wait upon de Lord, my God,
     He take away de sins of de world.

"Jesus a-waitin'.   Go in de wilderness,
     Go, &c.
All dem chil'en go in de wilderness
     To wait upon de Lord."

The next was one of those which I had heard in boyish days, brought North from Charleston. But the chorus alone was identical; the words were mainly different, and those here given are quaint enough.

XXV. BLOW YOUR TRUMPET, GABRIEL

"O, blow your trumpet, Gabriel,
     Blow your trumpet louder;
And I want dat trumpet to blow me home
     To my new Jerusalem.

"De prettiest ting dat ever I done
Was to serve de Lord when I was young.
     So blow your trumpet, Gabriel, &c.

"O, Satan is a liar, and he conjure too,
And if you don't mind, he 'll conjure you.
     So blow your trumpet, Gabriel, &c.

> "O, I was lost in de wilderness.
> King Jesus hand me de candle down.
> So blow your trumpet, Gabriel," &c.

The following contains one of those odd transformations of proper names with which their Scriptural citations were often enriched. It rivals their text, "Paul may plant, and may polish wid water," which I have elsewhere quoted, and in which the sainted Apollos would hardly have recognized himself.

XXVI. In the Morning

> "In de mornin',
> In de mornin',
> Chil'en? Yes, my Lord!
>> Don't you hear de trumpet sound?
> If I had a-died when I was young,
> I never would had de race for run.
>> Don't you hear de trumpet sound?
>
> "O Sam and Peter was fishin' in de sea,
> And dey drop de net and follow my Lord.
>> Don't you hear de trumpet sound?
>
> "Dere 's a silver spade for to dig my grave
> And a golden chain for to let me down.
>> Don't you hear de trumpet sound?
> In de mornin',
> In de mornin',
> Chil'en? Yes, my Lord!
>> Don't you hear de trumpet sound?"

These golden and silver fancies remind one of the King of Spain's daughter in "Mother Goose," and the golden apple, and the silver pear, which was doubtless themselves but the vestiges of some simple early composition like this. The next has a humbler and more domestic style of fancy.

XXVII. Fare Ye Well

> "My true believers, fare ye well,
> Fare ye well, fare ye well,
> Fare ye well, by de grace of God,
>> For I'm going home.
>
> "Massa Jesus give me a little broom
> For to sweep my heart clean,
> And I will try, by de grace of God,
>> To win my way home."

Among the songs not available for marching, but requiring the concentrated enthusiasm of the camp, was 'The Ship of Zion," of

which they had three wholly distinct versions, all quite exuberant
and tumultuous.

XXVIII. THE SHIP OF ZION

"Come along, come along,
 And let us go home,
O, glory, hallelujah?
Dis de ole ship o' Zion,
 Halleloo! Halleloo!
Dis de ole ship o' Zion,
 Hallelujah!

"She has landed many a tousand,
She can land as many more.
 O, glory, hallelujah! &c.

"Do you tink she will be able
For to take us all home?
 O, glory, hallelujah! &c.

You can tell 'm I 'm a comin',
 Halleloo! Halleloo!
You can tell 'em I 'm a comin',
 Hallelujah!
Come along, come along," &c.

XXIX. THE SHIP OF ZION (*Second version*)

"Dis de good ole ship o' Zion,
Dis de good ole ship o' Zion,
Dis de good ole ship o' Zion,
 And she 's makin' for de Promise Land.
She hab angels for de sailors, (*Thrice.*)
 And she 's, &c.
And how you know dey's angels? (*Thrice.*)
 And she 's, &c.
Good Lord, shall I be one? (*Thrice.*)
 And she 's, &c.

"Dat ship is out a-sailin', sailin', sailin',
 And she 's, &c.
She 's a-sailin' mighty steady, steady, steady,
 And she 's, &c.
She 'll neither reel nor totter, totter, totter,
 And she 's, &c.
She's a-sailin' away cold Jordan, Jordan, Jordan,
 And she 's, &c.
King Jesus is de captain, captain, captain,
 And she 's makin' for de Promise Land."

XXX. The Ship of Zion (*Third version*)

"De Gospel ship is sailin',
　　Hosann—sann.
O, Jesus is de captain,
　　Hosann—sann.
De angels are de sailors,
　　Hosann—sann.
O, is your bundle ready?
　　Hosann—sann.
O, have you got your ticket?
　　Hosann—sann."

This abbreviated chorus is given with unspeakable unction.

The three just given are modifications of an old camp-meeting melody; and the same may be true of the three following, although I cannot find them in the Methodist hymn-books. Each, however, has its characteristic modifications, which make it well worth giving. In the second verse of this next, for instance, "Saviour" evidently has become "soldier."

XXXI. Sweet Music

"Sweet music in heaven,
　　Just beginning for to roll.
Don't you love God?
　　Glory, hallelujah!

"Yes, late I heard my soldier say,
Come, heavy soul, I am de way.
　　Don't you love God?
　　Glory, hallelujah!

"I 'll go and tell to sinners round
What a kind Saviour I have found.
　　Don't you love God?
　　Glory, hallelujah!

"My grief my burden long has been,
Because I was not cease from sin.
　　Don't you love God?
　　Glory, hellelujah!"

XXXII. Good News

"O, good news! O, good news!
De angels brought de tidings down,
　　Just comin from de trone.

"As grief from out my soul shall fly,
　　Just comin' from de trone;

I 'll shout salvation when I die,
    Good news, O, good news!
Just comin' from de trone.

"Lord, I want to go to heaven when I die,
    Good news, O, good news! &c.

"De white folks call us a noisy crew,
    Good news, O, good news!
But dis I know, we are happy too,
    Just comin' from de trone."

XXXIII. THE HEAVENLY ROAD

"You may talk of my name as much as you please,
    And carry my name abroad,
But I really do believe I 'm a child of God
    As I walk in de heavenly road.
O, won't you go wid me? (*Thrice.*)
    For to keep our garments clean.

"O Satan is a mighty busy ole man,
    And roll rocks in my way;
But Jesus is my bosom friend,
    And roll 'em out of de way.
O, won't you go wid me? (*Thrice.*)
    For to keep our garments clean.

"Come, my brudder, if you never did pray,
    I hope you may pray to-night;
For I really believe I 'm a child of God
    As I walk in de heavenly road.
O, won't you," &c.

Some of the songs had played an historic part during the war. For singing the next, for instance, the negroes had been put in jail in Georgetown, S. C., at the outbreak of the Rebellion. "We'll soon be free" was too dangerous an assertion; and though the chant was an old one, it was no doubt sung with redoubled emphasis during the new events. "De Lord will call us home," was evidently thought to be a symbolical verse; for, as a little drummer-boy explained to me, showing all his white teeth as he sat in the moonlight by the door of my tent, "Dey tink *de Lord* mean for say *de Yankees*."

XXXIV. WE'LL SOON BE FREE

"We 'll soon be free,
We 'll soon be free,
We 'll soon be free,
    When de Lord will call us home.
My brudder, how long,

My brudder, how long,
My brudder, how long,
  'Fore we done sufferin' here?
It won't be long *(Thrice.)*
  'Fore de Lord will call us home.
We'll walk de miry road *(Thrice.)*
  Where pleasure never dies.
We'll walk de golden street *(Thrice.)*
  Where pleasure never dies.
My brudder, how long *(Thrice.)*
  'Fore we done sufferin' here?
We'll soon be free *(Thrice.)*
  When Jesus sets me free.
We'll fight for liberty *(Thrice.)*
  When de Lord will call us home."

The suspicion in this case was unfounded, but they had another song to which the Rebellion had actually given rise. This was composed by nobody knew whom,—though it was the most recent, doubtless, of all these "spirituals,"—and had been sung in secret to avoid detection. It is certainly plaintive enough. The peck of corn and pint of salt were slavery's rations.

XXXV. Many Thousand Go

"No more peck o' corn for me,
  No more, no more,—
No more peck o' corn for me,
  Many tousand go.

"No more driver's lash for me, *(Twice.)*
  No more, &c.

"No more pint o' salt for me, *(Twice.)*
  No more, &c.

"No more hundred lash for me, *(Twice.)*
  No more, &c.

"No more mistress' call for me,
  No more, no more,—
No more mistress' call for me,
  Many tousand go."

Even of this last composition, however, we have only the approximate date and know nothing of the mode of composition. Allan Ramsay says of the Scotch songs, that, no matter who made them, they were soon attributed to the minister of the parish whence they sprang. And I always wondered about these, whether they had always a conscious and definite origin in some leading mind, or whether they grew by gradual accretion, in an almost unconscious way. On this point I could get no information, though I asked many questions, until at last, one day when I was being rowed across from Beaufort to Ladies' Island, I found myself, with delight, on the actual trail of a song. One of the oarsmen, a brisk young fellow, not a soldier, on being asked for his theory of the matter, dropped out a coy confession. "Some good speritals," he said, "are start jess out o' curiosity. I been a-raise a sing, myself, once."

My dream was fulfilled, and I had traced out, not the poem alone, but the poet. I implored him to proceed.

"Once we boys," he said, "went for tote some rice and de nigger-driver he keep a-callin' on us; and I say, 'O, de ole nigger-driver!' Den anudder said, 'Fust ting my mammy tole me was, notin' so bad as nigger-driver.' Den I made a sing, just puttin' a word, and den anudder word."

Then he began singing, and the men, after listening a moment, joined in the chorus, as if it were an old acquaintance, though they evidently had never heard it before. I saw how easily a new "sing" took root among them.

XXXVI. The Driver

"O, de ole nigger-driver!
    O, gwine away!
Fust ting my mammy tell me,
    O, gwine away!
Tell me 'bout de nigger-driver,
    O, gwine away!
Nigger-driver second devil,
    O, gwine away!
Best ting for do he driver,
    O, gwine away!
Knock he down and spoil he labor,
    O, gwine away!"

It will be observed that, although this song is quite secular in its character, yet its author called it a "spiritual." I heard but two songs among them, at any time, to which they would not, perhaps, have given this generic name. One of these consisted simply in the endless repetition—after the manner of certain college songs—of the mysterious line,—

"Rain fall and wet Becky Lawton."

But who Becky Lawton was, and why she should or should not be wet, and whether the dryness was a reward or a penalty, none could say. I got the impression that, in either case, the event was posthumous, and that there was some tradition of grass not growing over the grave of a sinner; but even this was vague, and all else vaguer.

The other song I heard but once, on a morning when a squad of men came in from picket duty, and chanted it in the most rousing way. It had been a stormy and comfortless night, and the picket station was very exposed. It still rained in the morning when I strolled to the edge of the camp, looking out for the men, and wondering how they had stood it. Presently they came striding along the road, at a great pace, with their shining rubber blankets worn as cloaks around them, the rain streaming from these and from their equally shining faces, which were almost all upon the broad grin, as they pealed out this remarkable ditty:—

HANGMAN JOHNNY

"O, dey call me Hangman Johnny!
O, ho! O, ho!
But I never hang nobody,
O, hang, boys, hang!
O, dey call me Hangman Johnny!
O, ho! O, ho!
But we'll all hang togedder,
O, hang, boys, hang!"

My presence apparently checked the performance of another verse, beginning, "De buckra 'list for money," apparently in reference to the controversy about the pay-question, then just beginning, and to the more mercenary aims they attributed to the white soldiers. But "Hangman Johnny" remained always a myth as inscrutable as "Becky Lawton."

As they learned all their songs by ear, they often strayed into wholly new versions, which sometimes became popular, and entirely banished the others. This was amusingly the case, for instance, with one phrase in the popular camp-song of "Marching Along," which was entirely new to them until our quartermaster taught it to them, at my request. The words, "Gird on the armor," were to them a stumbling-block, and no wonder, until some ingenious ear substituted, "Guide on de army," which was at once accepted, and became universal.

"We'll guide on de army, and be marching along"

is now the established version on the Sea Islands.

These quaint religious songs were to the men more than a source of relaxation; they were a stimulus to courage and a tie to heaven. I never overheard in camp a profane or vulgar song. With the trifling exceptions given, all had a religious motive, while the most secular melody could not have been more exciting. A few youths from Savannah, who were comparatively men of the world, had learned some of the "Ethiopian Minstrel" ditties, imported from the North. These took no hold upon the mass; and, on the other hand, they sang reluctantly, even on Sunday, the long and short metres of the hymnbooks, always gladly yielding to the more potent excitement of their own "spirituals." By these they could sing themselves, as had their fathers before them, out of the contemplation of their own low estate, into the sublime scenery of the Apocalypse. I remember that this minor-keyed pathos used to seem to me almost too sad to dwell upon, while slavery seemed destined to last for generations; but now that their patience has had its perfect work, history cannot afford to lose this portion of its record. There is no parallel instance of an oppressed race thus sustained by the religious sentiment alone. These songs are but the vocal expression of the simplicity of their faith and the sublimity of their long resignation.

25. W. E. B. DuBois

⋙ Born in Massachusetts and equipped with a superior education, William Edward Burghardt DuBois (1868–1963) developed into one of the most articulate and militant leaders of black Americans. He began speaking in public and publishing articles even during his college days at Fisk University, and after receiving the Ph.D. degree from Harvard University in 1895 and studying further in Berlin, he set himself a program of writing a series of scientifically researched studies on the Negro. The first of these appeared in 1899, *The Philadelphia Negro: A Social Study*. Later works included investigations into the subjects of the Negro church, schools, and occupations. In 1905 DuBois organized the Niagara Movement, composed of militant young black intellectuals; in 1909 they joined with other blacks and whites to become the National Association for the Advancement of Colored People. Although DuBois followed several careers during his long, productive life and published prolifically in many genres, he is probably best remembered by most Americans for his collection of essays entitled *The Souls of Black Folk* (Chicago, 1903). In his preface to this book, DuBois wrote, "I have sought to sketch, in vague, uncertain outline, the spiritual world in which ten thousand Americans live and strive." The last essay is devoted to a discussion of Negro folksongs, entitled *Of the Sorrow Songs*. ⋘

From *The Souls of Black Folk* [1903] †

They that walked in darkness sang songs in the olden days— Sorrow Songs—for they were weary at heart. And so before each thought that I have written in this book I have set a phrase, a haunting echo of these weird old songs in which the soul of the black slave spoke to men. Ever since I was a child these songs have stirred me strangely. They came out of the South unknown to me, one by one, and yet at once I knew then as of me and of mine. Then in after years when I came to Nashville I saw the great temple builded of these songs towering over the pale city. To me Jubilee Hall seemed ever made of the songs themselves, and its bricks were red with the

† Text: The original edition (Chicago, 1903), pp. 378–87.

blood and dust of toil. Out of them rose for me morning, noon, and night, bursts of wonderful melody, full of the voices of my brothers and sisters, full of the voices of the past.

Little of beauty has America given the world save the rude grandeur God himself stamped on her bosom; the human spirit in this new world has expressed itself in vigor and ingenuity rather than in beauty. And so by fateful chance the Negro folk-song—the rhythmic cry of the slave—stands to-day not simply as the sole American music, but as the most beautiful expression of human experience, born this side the seas. It has been neglected, it has been, and is, half despised, and above all it has been persistently mistaken and misunderstood; but notwithstanding, it still remains as the singular spiritual heritage of the nation and the greatest gift of the Negro people.

Away back in the thirties the melody of these slave songs stirred the nation, but the songs were soon half forgotten. Some, like "Near the lake where drooped the willow," passed into current airs and their source was forgotten; others were caricatured on the "minstrel" stage and their memory died away. Then in war-time came the singular Port Royal experiment after the capture of Hilton Head, and perhaps for the first time the North met the Southern slave face to face and heart to heart with no third witness. The Sea Islands of the Carolinas, where they met, were filled with a black folk of primitive type, touched and moulded less by the world about them than any others outside the Black Belt. Their appearance was uncouth, their language funny, but their hearts were human and their singing stirred men with a mighty power. Thomas Wentworth Higginson hastened to tell of these songs, and Miss McKim and others urged upon the world their rare beauty. But the world listened only half credulously until the Fisk Jubilee Singers sang the slave songs so deeply into the world's heart that it can never wholly forget them again.

There was once a blacksmith's son born in Cadiz, New York, who in the changes of time taught school in Ohio and helped defend Cincinnati from Kirby Smith. Then he fought at Chancellorsville and Gettysburg and finally served in the Freedman's Bureau at Nashville. Here he formed a Sunday-school class of black children in 1866, and sang with them and taught them to sing. And then they taught him to sing, and when once the glory of the Jubilee songs passed into the soul of George L. White, he knew his life-work was to let those Negroes sing to the world as they had sung to him. So in 1871 the pilgrimage of the Fisk Jubilee Singers began. North to Cincinnati they rode,—four half-clothed black boys and five girl-women, —led by a man with a cause and a purpose. They stopped at Wilberforce, the oldest of Negro schools, where a black bishop blessed them.

Then they went, fighting cold and starvation, shut out of hotels, and cheerfully sneered at, ever northward; and ever the magic of their song kept thrilling hearts, while a burst of applause in the Congregational Council at Oberlin revealed them to the world. They came to New York and Henry Ward Beecher dared to welcome them, even though the metropolitan dailies sneered at his "Nigger Minstrels." So their songs conquered till they sang across the land and across the sea, before Queen and Kaiser, in Scotland and Ireland, Holland and Switzerland. Seven years they sang, and brought back a hundred and fifty thousand dollars to found Fisk University.

Since their day they have been imitated—sometimes well, by the singers of Hampton and Atlanta, sometimes ill, by straggling quartettes. Caricature has sought again to spoil the quaint beauty of the music, and has filled the air with many debased melodies which vulgar ears scarce know from the real. But the true Negro folk-song still lives in the hearts of those who have heard them truly sung and in the hearts of the Negro people.

What are these songs, and what do they mean? I know little of music and can say nothing in technical phrase, but I know something of men, and knowing them, I know that these songs are the articulate message of the slave to the world. They tell us in these eager days that life was joyous to the black slave, careless and happy. I can easily believe this of some, of many. But not all the past South, though it rose from the dead, can gainsay the heart-touching witness of these songs. They are the music of an unhappy people, of the children of disappointment; they tell of death and suffering and unvoiced longing toward a truer world, of misty wanderings and hidden ways.

The songs are indeed the siftings of centuries; the music is far more ancient than the words, and in it we can trace here and there signs of development. My grandfather's grandmother was seized by an evil Dutch trader two centuries ago; and coming to the valleys of the Hudson and Housatonic, black, little, and lithe, she shivered and shrank in the harsh north winds, looked longingly at the hills, and often crooned a heathen melody to the child between her knees, thus:

Do ba-na co-ba, ge-ne me, ge-ne me! Do ba-na co-ba, ge-ne me, ge-ne me! Ben d' nu-li, nu-li, nu-li, nu-li, ben d' le.

* The rhythms of measures 1 and 3 are reproduced exactly as notated in the source.

The child sang it to his children and they to their children's children, and so two hundred years it has travelled down to us and we sing it to our children, knowing as little as our fathers what its words may mean, but knowing well the meaning of its music.

This was primitive African music; it may be seen in larger form in the strange chant which heralds "The Coming of John":

> "You may bury me in the East,
> You may bury me in the West,
> But I'll hear the trumpet sound in that morning,"

—the voice of exile.

Ten master songs, more or less, one may pluck from this forest of melody—songs of undoubted Negro origin and wide popular currency, and songs peculiarly characteristic of the slave. One of these I have just mentioned. Another whose strains begin this book is "Nobody knows the trouble I've seen." When, struck with a sudden poverty, the United States refused to fulfill its promises of land to the freedmen, a brigadier-general went down to the Sea Islands to carry the news. An old woman on the outskirts of the throng began singing this song; all the mass joined with her, swaying. And the soldier wept.

The third song is the cradle-song of death which all men know,—"Swing low, sweet chariot,"—whose bars begin the life story of "Alexander Crummell." Then there is the song of many waters, "Roll, Jordan, roll," a mighty chorus with minor cadences. There were many songs of the fugitive like that which opens "The Wings of Atlanta," and the more familiar "Been a-listening." The seventh is the song of the End and the Beginning—"My Lord, what a mourning! when the stars begin to fall"; a strain of this is placed before "The Dawn of Freedom." The song of groping—"My way's cloudy"—begins "The Meaning of Progress"; the ninth is the song of this chapter—"Wrestlin' Jacob, the day is a-breaking,"—a pæan of hopeful strife. The last master song is the song of songs—"Steal away"—sprung from "The Faith of the Fathers."

There are many others of the Negro folk-songs as striking and characteristic as these, as, for instance, the three strains in the third, eighth, and ninth chapters; and others I am sure could easily make a selection on more scientific principles. There are, too, songs that seem to be a step removed from the more primitive types: there is the maze-like medley, "Bright sparkles," one phrase of which heads "The Black Belt"; the Easter carol, "Dust, dust and ashes"; the dirge, "My mother's took her flight and gone home"; and that burst of melody hovering over "The Passing of the First-Born"—"I hope my mother will be there in that beautiful world on high."

These represent a third step in the development of the slave song, of which "You may bury me in the East" is the first, and songs like "March on" (chapter six) and "Steal away" are the second. The first is African music, the second Afro-American, while the third is a blending of Negro music with the music heard in the foster land. The result is still distinctively Negro and the method of blending original, but the elements are both Negro and Caucasian. One might go further and find a fourth step in this development, where the songs of white America have been distinctively influenced by the slave songs or have incorporated whole phrases of Negro melody, as "Swanee River" and "Old Black Joe." Side by side, too, with the growth has gone the debasements and imitations—the Negro "minstrel" songs, many of the "gospel" hymns, and some of the contemporary "coon" songs,—a mass of music in which the novice may easily lose himself and never find the real Negro melodies.

In these songs, as I have said, the slave spoke to the world. Such a message is naturally veiled and half articulate. Words and music have lost each other and new and cant phrases of a dimly understood theology have displaced the older sentiment. Once in a while we catch a strange word of an unknown tongue, as the "Mighty Myo," which figures as a river of death; more often slight words or mere doggerel are joined to music of singular sweetness. Purely secular songs are few in number, partly because many of them were turned into hymns by a change of words, partly because the frolics were seldom heard by the stranger, and the music less often caught. Of nearly all the songs, however, the music is distinctly sorrowful. The ten master songs I have mentioned tell in word and music of trouble and exile, of strife and hiding; they grope toward some unseen power and sigh for rest in the End.

The words that are left to us are not without interest, and, cleared of evident dross, they conceal much of real poetry and meaning beneath conventional theology and unmeaning rhapsody. Like all primitive folk, the slave stood near to Nature's heart. Life was a "rough and rolling sea" like the brown Atlantic of the Sea Islands; the "Wilderness" was the home of God, and the "lonesome valley" led to the way of life. 'Winter'll soon be over," was the picture of life and death to a tropical imagination. The sudden wild thunderstorms of the South awed and impressed the Negroes,—at times the rumbling seemed to them "mournful," at times imperious:

> "My Lord calls me,
> He calls me by the thunder,
> The trumpet sounds it in my soul."

The monotonous toil and exposure is painted in many words.

One sees the ploughmen in the hot, moist furrow, singing:

> "Dere's no rain to wet you,
> Dere's no sun to burn you,
> Oh, push along, believer,
> I want to go home."

The bowed and bent old man cries, with thrice-repeated wail:

> "O Lord, keep me from sinking down,"

and he rebukes the devil of doubt who can whisper:

> "Jesus is dead and God's gone away."

Yet the soul-hunger is there, the restlessness of the savage, the wail of the wanderer, and the plaint is put in one little phrase:

My   soul   wants some - thing that's   new,   thats new

Over the inner thoughts of the slaves and their relations one with another the shadow of fear ever hung, so that we get but glimpses here and there, and also with them, eloquent omissions and silences. Mother and child are sung, but seldom father; fugitive and weary wanderer call for pity and affection, but there is little of wooing and wedding; the rocks and the mountains are well known, but home is unknown. Strange blending of love and helplessness signs through the refrain:

> "Yonder 's my ole mudder,
> Been waggin' at de hill so long;
> 'Bout time she cross over,
> Git home bime-by."

Elsewhere comes the cry of the "motherless" and the "Farewell, farewell, my only child."

Love-songs are scarce and fall into two categories—the frivolous and light, and the sad. Of deep successful love there is ominous silence, and in one of the oldest of these songs there is a depth of history and meaning:

Poor   Ro - sy,   poor   gal;   Poor   Ro - sy,   poor   gal;

Ro - sy break my   poor   heart,   Heav'n shall-a   be   my   home.

A black woman said of the song, "It can't be sung without a full heart
and a troubled sperrit." The same voice sings here that sings in the
German folk-song:

> "Jetz Geh i' an's brunele, trink' aber net." [1]

Of death the Negro showed little fear, but talked of it familiarly
and even fondly as simply a crossing of the waters, perhaps—who
knows?—back to his ancient forests again. Later days transfigured
his fatalism, and amid the dust and dirt the toiler sang:

> "Dust, dust and ashes, fly over my grave,
> But the Lord shall bear my spirit home."

The things evidently borrowed from the surrounding world under-
go characteristic change when they enter the mouth of the slave.
Especially is this true of Bible phrases. "Weep, O captive daughter of
Zion," is quaintly turned into "Zion, weep-a-low," and the wheels of
Ezekiel are turned every way in the mystic dreaming of the slave,
till he says:

> "There's a little wheel a-turnin' in-a-my heart."

As in olden time, the words of these hymns were improvised
by some leading minstrel of the religious band. The circumstances of
the gathering, however, the rhythm of the songs, and the limitations
of allowable thought, confined the poetry for the most part to single
or double lines, and they seldom are expanded to quatrains or longer
tales, although there are some few examples of sustained efforts,
chiefly paraphrases of the Bible. Three short series of verses have
always attracted me,—the one that heads this chapter, of one line of
which Thomas Wentworth Higginson has fittingly said, "Never, it
seems to me, since man first lived and suffered was his infinite
longing for peace uttered more plaintively." The second and third
are descriptions of the Last Judgment,—the one a late improvisation,
with some traces of outside influence:

> "Oh, the stars in the elements are falling,
> And the moon drips away into blood,
> And the ransomed of the Lord are returning unto God,
> Blessed be the name of the Lord."

And the other earlier and homelier picture from the low coast lands:

> "Michael, haul the boat ashore,
> Then you'll hear the horn they blow,
> Then you'll hear the trumpet sound,
> Trumpet sound the world around,

1. "Now I go to the fountain, but I don't drink." [*Editor*]

Trumpet sound for rich and poor,
Trumpet sound the Jubilee,
Trumpet sound for you and me."

Through all the sorrow of the Sorrow Songs there breathes a hope—
a faith in the ultimate justice of things. The minor cadences of
despair change often to triumph and calm confidence. Sometimes it
is faith in life, sometimes a faith in death, sometimes assurance of
boundless justice in some fair world beyond. But whichever it is,
the meaning is always clear: that sometime, somewhere, men will
judge men by their souls and not by their skins. Is such a hope
justified? Do the Sorrow Songs sing true?

The silently growing assumption of this age is that the probation
of races is past, and that the backward races of to-day are of proven
inefficiency and not worth the saving. Such an assumption is the
arrogance of peoples irreverent toward Time and ignorant of the
deeds of men. A thousand years ago such an assumption, easily possible, would have made it difficult for the Teuton to prove his right
to life. Two thousand years ago such dogmatism, readily welcome,
would have scouted the idea of blond races ever leading civilization.
So woefully unorganized is sociological knowledge that the meaning
of progress, the meaning of "swift" and "slow" in human doing, and
the limits of human perfectability, are veiled, unanswered sphinxes
on the shores of science. Why should Æschylus have sung two thousand years before Shakespeare was born? Why has civilization flourished in Europe, and flickered, flamed, and died in Africa? So long
as the world stands meekly dumb before such questions, shall this
nation proclaim its ignorance and unhallowed prejudices by denying
freedom of opportunity to those who brought the Sorrow Songs to
the Seats of the Mighty?

Your country? How came it yours? Before the Pilgrims landed we
were here. Here we have brought our three gifts and mingled them
with yours: a gift of story and song—soft, stirring melody in an ill-
harmonized and unmelodious land; the gift of sweat and brawn to
beat back the wilderness, conquer the soil, and lay the foundations
of this vast economic empire two hundred years earlier than your
weak hands could have done it; the third, a gift of the Spirit. Around
us the history of the land has centred for thrice a hundred years; out
of the nation's heart we have called all that was best to throttle and
subdue all that was worst; fire and blood, prayer and sacrifice, have
billowed over this people, and they have found peace only in the
altars of the God of Right. Nor has our gift of the Spirit been merely
passive. Actively we have woven ourselves with the very warp and
woof of this nation,—we fought their battles, shared their sorrow,
mingled our blood with theirs, and generation after generation have

pleaded with a headstrong, careless people to despise not Justice, Mercy, and Truth, lest the nation be smitten with a curse. Our song, our toil, our cheer, and warning have been given to this nation in blood-brotherhood. Are not these gifts worth the giving? Is not this work and striving? Would America have been America without her Negro people?

Even so is the hope that sang in the songs of my fathers well sung. If somewhere in this whirl and chaos of things there dwells Eternal Good, pitiful yet masterful, then anon in His good time America shall rend the Veil and the prisoned shall go free. Free, free as the sunshine trickling down the morning into these high windows of mine, free as yonder fresh young voices welling up to me from the caverns of brick and mortar below—swelling with song, instinct with life, tremulous treble and darkening bass, My children, my little children, are singing to the sunshine, and thus they sing:

> Let us cheer the weary traveler
> Cheer the weary traveler,
> Let us cheer the weary traveler
> Along the heavenly way.

And the traveler girds himself, and sets his face toward the Morning, and goes his way.

VIII. The Music of
a Free People

26. William Christopher Handy

➤➤ Born in Florence, Alabama, William Christopher Handy (1873–1958) became the most celebrated black musician of his time. He began to follow a musical career while in his early teens, working as a singer, bandsman, choral director, arranger, and trumpeter before becoming the bandmaster in a minstrel company, Mahara's Minstrels, at the age of twenty-three. In 1900, Handy went to Alabama's Agricultural and Mechanical College for Negroes to take charge of the music program there. After two years he left to resume his career as a bandleader and settled in Memphis, Tennessee. In later years Handy joined with businessman Harry Pace to establish a music publishing company, which moved to New York in 1918. After the partnership was dissolved in the 1920s, Handy continued the company as a family business. It was a political campaign in 1909 that marked the turning point in Handy's life. His band was engaged to work for one of the candidates, and he wrote a special song for use in the campaign, entitled *Mr. Crump*. In this song Handy tried to catch the wry, earthy mood of the folksongs he had heard sung by Negro roustabouts, honky-tonk singers, and other wandering music-makers, and he incorporated the unusual three-line, twelve-bar structure of such songs into his piece. The song became so popular that Handy published it, changing its title to *Memphis Blues*. More than any other person, Handy was responsible for popularizing the blues. His publication of numerous examples of the form, including that perennial favorite, the *St. Louis Blues* (1914), helped to win for him the deserved title of "Father of the Blues." ◄◄

The Heart of the Blues [1940] †

Blues is one of the oldest forms of music in the world. It is folk music of the purest type. It represents the full racial expression of the Negro, and its distinguishing characteristics are throwbacks to

† Text: *Etude Music Magazine*, March, 1940, pp. 152, 193–94. Reprinted by permission of Theodore Presser Company.

Africa. When I was a boy in my native Alabama, the doors of our schoolhouse were thrown open when spring came, and, along with the fresh breezes and the smell of earth and growing things, there drifted in a single fragment of song, intoned by a ploughman at work. The fragment consisted solely of the words, "Aye-oo, Aye-oo, Ah wouldn't live in Cairo."

Even as a child, I thought about this. Why did the man sing as he did? Why would he not live in Cairo? Why did he repeat this fragment over and over? What did it mean to him? What lay behind those curious turns of tonality and rhythm? Thinking about things like that has been most of my life's work, with the result that I have evolved certain conclusions about the music of my race—music which has developed as the modern blues. Let us consider this development.

In its origin, modern blues music is the expression of the emotional life of a race. In the south of long ago, whenever a new man appeared for work in any of the laborers' gangs, he would be asked if he could sing. If he could, he got the job. The singing of these working men set the rhythm for the work, the pounding of hammers, the swinging of scythes; and the one who sang most lustily soon became strawboss. One man set the tune, and sang whatever sentiments lay closest to his heart. He would sing about steamboats, fast trains, "contrairy" mules, cruel overseers. If he had no home, he sang about that; if he found a home next day, he sang about needing money or being lonesome for his gal. But whatever he sang was personal, and then the others in the gang took up the melody, each fitting it with personal words of his own. If fifty men worked on the gang, the song had fifty verses, and the singing lasted all day through, easing the work, driving rhythm into it. By word of mouth, the songs of these humble, untrained musicians traveled from place to place, wherever the roving workers went, exactly as folksongs always have traveled, all over the world, as expressions of national soul life.

The Doleful Ditty

The son of a governor of Kentucky met his death as the result of an unfortunate love affair; and, within twenty-four hours, all the Negroes of the region were commenting on the tragedy in a song known as *Careless Love*. As the news traveled, the song traveled with it, and presently the tune of *Careless Love* was used to fit the words of any tragedy. These much used songs (*Frankie and Johnnie*; *John Henry*; and so on) became traditions. There were no theaters or movies in those days, and the humble working men satisfied their hunger for action and emotional release by elaborating these ballads of human life. None was written down; the singers themselves kept the songs alive, unconsciously stamping them with the hallmark of their race.

That is the origin of the blues. The characteristics of this form have always existed; they are distinctly Negro; and they are always the same. There are four distinctive structural elements that characterize blues. First, the stanza is built of three lines instead of four, yielding a strain of twelve measures instead of the conventional sixteen. Originally, these three lines were repetitive. The singers wanted their songs to last as long as possible, easing them through a day's hard toil; hence they dwelt on their emotions, repeated them, spun them out. In the ballad *Joe Jacobs*, the mere facts of the story could be reduced to four lines: Joe Jacobs killed poor Carrie while she was ironing, gave himself up, and went to prison. The Negro workman developed a full stanza from each fact.

> You know Joe Jacobs,
> Yes, I mean Joe Jacobs,
> I mean Joe Jacobs,
>   Lawdy man!

> He killed poor Carrie,
> Killed poor Carrie,
> Yes, killed poor Carrie,
>   etc.

Thus the verse form sets the first distinguishing trait of blues. The second important characteristic is the curious, groping tonality, so clearly a throwback to Africa. We hear this "blue note" as a scooping, swooping, slurring tone. I have approximated it, for example, in *East St. Louis*, as well as in *Beale Street Blues*.

The slurring chromatics are, at best, an approximation of several principles:

1. Of a tonality found exclusively in the Negro voice.
2. Of the quarter tone scale of primitive Africa.
3. Of a deep-rooted racial groping for instinctive harmonies.

No modern voice or instrument can really reproduce the intervals of the primitive pentatonic scale; yet it remains the very heart of the blues. Its effect is rendered by chromatic slurs from one note to the next, holding the second note without releasing the harmonics of the first.

So far, there is nothing in the nature of folk themes or distinctive tonalities to indicate that the development of Negro music would lie along the lines of jazz. But Negro music is marked by other elements as well. The first of these is a marked, insistent syncopation. The second is the novel element of "filling of breaks." Take, for instance, the opening line of *Joe Turner:* "Tell me Joe Turner's come an' go-o-one."

Were a white man singing this, he would respect the rests in "go-o-one" and hold the note. The Negro becomes impatient of silences, and fills in the rest-spaces with impromptu embellishments of his own. He slips in an "Oh, Lawdy!", or an "Oh, Baby!" before the next regular beat is due. These natural improvisations are the foundations of jazz. As the old folk airs came to be written down, the composers filled in the rests, or "breaks," with the most elaborate embellishments of which they were capable. Then orchestras took them up and added new improvisations for each of the various instruments. Then more sophisticated arrangers put in still more elaborate curlicues. The grandson of the old gang worker who put in a simple "Oh, Lawdy," fills in with virtuosity on the saxophone; but both are expressing the identical racial instinct in a typically racial way.

A STYLE DEVELOPS

Just as the syncopations and fill-ins have become more elaborate, the form of the three-line stanza has undergone changes. The third line is no longer a repetition; it has taken on the color of an explanation. In my *St. Louis Blues,* the line "hate to see de evenin' sun go down" is repeated once, but the third line tells why, "Cause ma baby, he done lef' dis town." Later, too, the simple, natural twelve-measure strain became elaborated into the conventional chorus. So the blues developed into jazz.

I have been called the "Father of the Blues," and I am proud of the title. My old *Memphis Blues* was the first of the blues songs; and the success of the filled-in breaks was established the first time the orchestra played it, when the chorus had to be repeated time after time so that the saxophone, the drum, the violin, all the instruments, could have a share in improvising novel turns. My purpose, however, was not the creation of "hot" numbers. That they have developed so is due to the inherent characteristics of the music itself. My purpose was to capture in fixed form the highly distinctive music of my race. Everything I have written has its roots deep in the folk life of the South.

Although my *St. Louis Blues* is the more popular, I think *Beale Street* has the more interesting history. As I was walking down Beale Street one night, my attention was caught by the sound of a piano. The insistent Negro rhythms were broken first by a tinkle in the treble, then by a rumble in the bass; then they came together again. I entered the cheap café and found a colored man at the piano, dog tired. He told me he had to play from seven at night until seven in the morning, and rested himself by playing with alternate hands. He told me of his life, and it seemed to me that this poor, tired, happy-go-lucky musician represented his race. I set it down in notes, keeping faith with all that made the background of that poor piano thumper. If my songs have value, it is not that of dance numbers alone. I have tried to write history, to crystallize a form for the colored workman's personal music, just as the spirituals give form to his religious emotions. (Incidentally, you will find the same racial traits in the spirituals—the repetitive words, the groping blues tonalities, the syncopated rhythms, the impromptu fillings in—elaborated along religious rather than secular lines.) For that reason, I cannot admire the sophisticated, made to order, commercial blues, which mutilate the simple Negro elements by dressing them up. I have the feeling that real blues can be written only by a Negro, who keeps his roots in the life of his race.

THE JAZZ-SWING PROBLEM

I am often asked what differentiates swing from jazz, and I can best answer the query by telling a story. Long ago, I wrote *Yellow Dog Rag*. It sold mildly well, and after a while I forgot about it. When the popular taste for blues asserted itself I took out that old number and changed its name to *Yellow Dog Blues*. Other than the name, I altered nothing. Within an incredibly short time I had earned seventy-five hundred dollars in royalties from *Yellow Dog Blues*—which, as *Yellow Dog Rag*, had not sold well at all. That set me thinking. If a mere change in name could account for this sudden success, then it was just "new fashion" that caused its popularity. That is my answer to the swing question.

Swing is not a new musical form: it is merely a dressing up of jazz. It is artificial and often meretricious, emphasizing the "jittery" aspects of jazz improvisations, without the expressive depth that belongs to genuine blues. I suspect that it will pass in time, to make way for other "new fashions." But the blues, like the spirituals, will endure as long as the race does, because it is a genuine expression of folk traits. It may be born in Tin Pan Alley, but it is never conceived there. It is popular music in its truest sense, springing as it does from the soul of a people. For that reason, blues may well be regarded as "real music," and it should be performed in a musical way. It is helpful to remember that the fun and the gaiety of the blues state but half their meaning. The other half gives them their name; they express the pain as well as the joyous hopefulness of an essentially simple race.

Let me illustrate the psychology of the blues. Imagine a Negro who owes his rent and has been able to scrape but half of it together the night before it is due. He knows he will be evicted in the morning, because half the amount is not good enough; so he takes what he has and buys a good dinner and a good time, half hoping that something may turn up overnight to save him, yet half fearing the worst, all the while. And he sings of what he does to give himself courage. That is the spirit behind the blues—a joyousness calculated to drown out underlying apprehension. The formula for the blues is easy enough to state. Blues psychology, blues notes, repetitive lines, syncopated rhythms, filled-in breaks; but I shall always believe that the real blues must come from the heart and the pen of the Negro race itself. Blues belong to the Negro, as the mazurka belongs to the Poles. Whatever the future of the blues is to be, I am proud of being the first to collect their elements in orderly documentation, and to give this form of the music of my race a typical expression.

From *Father of the Blues* [1941] †

Our teacher's hobby was vocal music. Instead of the usual prayers and scripture readings of the morning devotional period, he spent the first half hour of each day in singing and in giving us musical instruction. This was, needless to say, the part of my school life that I enjoyed most.

This teacher was Y. A. Wallace, and he had come to Florence from Fisk University, where he had been a member of the first graduating class. Curiously enough, Professor Wallace had no interest in the spirituals. Though the famous Fisk Jubilee Singers toured the world in his day and created a lasting esteem for these songs, he made no attempt to instruct us in this remarkable folk music. This, however, was just one item in a great catalogue of Professor Wallace's eccentricities. . . .

My introduction to the rudiments of music was largely gained during the eleven years I spent under this quaint instructor in the Florence District School for Negroes. I began in the soprano singing section, progressed to alto and then shuttled back and forth between the tenor and bass as my voice cut up and played pranks.

There was no piano or organ in our school, just as there were few

† Text: The original edition (New York, 1941), pp. 12–18, 34–37, 69–70, 274–77. Reprinted with permission of The Macmillan Company from *Father of the Blues* by W. C. Handy. Copyright 1941 by W. C. Handy, renewed 1969 by Irma L. Handy, W. C. Handy, Jr., Katharine Handy Lewis, and Wyer Owens Handy.

instruments in the homes of the pupils. We were required to hold our books in our left hand and beat time with our right. Professor Wallace sounded his A pitch pipe or tuning fork, and we understood the tone to be *la*. If C happened to be the starting key, we made the step and a half in our minds and then sang out the key note in concert. We would then sound the notes for our respective parts, perhaps *do* for the basses, *mi* for the altos, and *sol* and *do* for the sopranos and tenor, depending of course on the first note of the sopranos. Before attempting to sing the words of any song, we were required to work out our parts by singing over and over the proper *sol-fa* syllables. In this way we learned to sing in all keys, measures and movements. We learned all the songs in *Gospel Hymns,* one to six. Each year we bought new instruction books and advanced to a point where we could sing excerpts from the works of Wagner, Bizet, Verdi and other masters—all without instrumental accompaniment.

When I was no more than ten, I could catalogue almost any sound that came to my ears, using the tonic *sol-fa* system. I knew the whistle of each of the river boats on the Tennessee. One whistle, I remember, sounded like a combination of *do* and *sol* in the musical scale. Another seemed to combine *do* and *mi*. By the same means I could tell what the birds in the orchards and woodlands were singing. Even the bellow of the bull became in my mind a musical note, and in later years I recorded this memory in the *Hooking Cow Blues.*

As a child I had not heard of the Pipes of Pan, but pastoral melody was nevertheless a very real thing to me. Whenever I heard the song of a bird and the answering call of its mate, I could visualize the notes in the scale. Robins carried a warm alto theme. Bobolinks sang contrapuntal melodies. Mocking birds trilled cadenzas. Altogether, as I fancied, they belonged to a great outdoor choir.

There was a French horn concealed in the breast of the blue jay. The tappings of the woodpecker were to me the reverberations of a snare drum. The bullfrog supplied an effective bass. In the raucous call of the distant crow I would hear the jazz motif. The purple night would awaken a million crickets with their obbligatos of mournful sound, also the katydids, and down the lonely road the hooves of the galloping horses beat in syncopation. I knew the gait of horses by the rhythm of their hooves. As I grew older I added the saxophonic wailing of the moo-cows and the clarinets of the moody whippoorwills. All built up within my consciousness a natural symphony. This was the primitive prelude to the mature melodies now recognized as the blues. Nature was my kindergarten.

We Handy's Hill kids made rhythm by scraping a twenty penny nail across the teeth of the jawbone of a horse that had died in the woods near by. By drawing a broom handle across our first finger lying on a table we imitated the bass. We sang through fine-tooth combs. With the thumb of the right hand interlocked with the little finger of the left, we placed the thumb of the left hand under our chin and made rhythmic sounds by rattling our teeth. We would put the thumb of our right hand on our goozle or Adam's apple, yelling at the time:

> Went down the river
> Couldn't get across
> Paid five dollars for an old gray horse.

Sometimes we were fortunate enough to have a French harp on which we played the fox and the hounds imitated the railroad trains— harmonica masterpieces. For drums we wore out our mother's tin pans and milk pails, singing:

> Cornstalk fiddle and shoestring bow
> Broke in the middle, jumped up Joe.

Toward the end of my school days Jim Turner came to town. Jim was from Memphis. He had recently been in love with a girl who had done him bad and broken his heart. Love, as everyone should know, is a strange disease. Jim Turner tried to cure his on whisky. Then, when this didn't work, he staggered to the M. & C. depot and made his way to the ticket cage. Putting down a handful of greenbacks, he asked for a hundred dollars' worth of tickets.

"Where do you want to go?" the agent asked.

"Anywheres," Jim Turner said. "Just anywheres."

The agent sold him a ticket to Florence, and our proud little town entertained a genius unawares. That sad-eyed boy, stabbed to his heart by the scorn of a haughty yellow gal, was perhaps the best violin player Florence ever knew. Fortunately his lovesickness and his drinking did him no harm musically. The drunker Jim Turner was, the better he played.

But Jim brought more than just a fiddle and a broken heart to Florence. He brought a glimpse of another world. He organized an orchestra and taught dancing. Those were the days of the quadrille, the lancers, the polka, the schottische, the mazurka, the york, the two-step, the gavotte, the minuet and the varsovienne. The waltz was popular, as was also the rye waltz, a combination of three-four and two-four tempos. Jim Turner knew them all. He talked about Beale Street in Memphis, where life was a song from dawn to dawn. He described darktown dandies and high-brown belles. He recalled the glitter and finery of their latest fashions. Finally, he planted in my heart a seed of discontent, a yearning for Beale Street and the gay universe that it typified.

Meanwhile, without letting my father or Professor Wallace into the secret, I obtained a cornet and commenced to study the instrument. It came about accidentally. A circus became stranded in our town, and its capable white bandmaster was reduced to teaching a colored band in a barber shop. I formed the habit of stopping at the barber shop on the way home from school and peeping through the windows to study the blackboard chart which he had made to illustrate the fingering of the various instruments. At school I would practice fingering on my desk during classes. In this way I mastered the scales and developed speed. This came to the attention of one of the band members, Will Bates, and he persuaded me to buy his old rotary-valve cornet, an instrument with the valves on the side instead of in the vertical position of more modern cornets. The valves were worked by an attachment with catgut strings. It was an odd contraption, to say the least, but since the price was only one dollar and seventy-five cents, payable in installments, we made a deal. At that, however, it took forty years to clear the account, for on meeting Bates again at the end of that time I found that I had neglected a balance which, with interest, had reached the sum of seventy-five cents.

I continued to play with the Florence band until my father and school teacher caught up with me. By then, of course, it was too late to do much about it. The climax came when Jim Turner got an engagement to play at a land sale at Russellville, Alabama. They needed an alto player, so I skipped school and joined them. At that performance I made the acquaintance of a barefoot boy who was following the band, Charles E. Toney, who was to become one of the first Negro judges elected in New York City, and for whose election my family worked although I had been taught since Cleveland against Blaine never to vote Democrat. For the day's work at Russellville I received eight dollars, which seemed big indeed against the three dollars a week that I was accustomed to receiving for hard labor, and I imagined that my father would have a change of heart when I put it in his hand. But the tainted wages impressed him not at all. He refused to forgive me, and my teacher finished up the job by applying the hickory the next day when I returned to school.

There was no holding me now. I attended dances against their wishes, and I sang with a quartet that often serenaded the moon until the wee hours. Shortly afterwards, when Bill Felton, a minstrel man and a singing banjo player, came to Florence and organized a home town minstrel show, I joined up as first tenor for his quartet. I was fifteen at the time and my colleagues told me I looked pretty funny stepping along with the "walking gents" in my father's Prince Albert. We had seen the famous Georgia Minstrels in Florence, and we knew how to make the pivot turns. We were all acquainted with Billy Kersands, the man who could "make a mule laugh," and we remembered his trick of proving on the stage that his enormous mouth would accommodate a cup and saucer. We had seen Sam Lucas and Tom McIntosh walking at the head of the parade in high silk hats and long-tailed coats. We had an idea of how the thing should be done, but I suppose our trouble was lack of experience.

Our minstrels took to the road. In one of the quartet songs I had a solo part which contained the prophetic words, "Take me back home again; let me see it once more." Sooner than I had hoped, this request was granted. After playing a few towns in Tennessee and northern Alabama, the show got stranded in Jasper. Before skipping town, the manager called me aside and took pity on me because of my youth. He gave me train fare back to Florence, but cautioned me not to tell the others that he had jumped the outfit. Instead of taking his advice, however, I divided with the other boys and decided to take my chances with them.

We rode the train till our money ran out. The conductor dropped us near a lonely water tank. From that point we counted the cross-ties back to Florence, stopping periodically to sing or play for buttermilk and biscuits. The home town boys never forgot this trip. They maintained for years that I never sang so well as when we were stranded along the railroad tracks.

This was my baptism. I have been a trouper ever since. . . .

Encyclopedists and historians of the American stage have slighted the old Negro minstrels while making much of the burnt cork artists who imitated them. But Negroes were the originators of this form of entertainment, and companies of them continued to perform as long as the vogue lasted. Mahara's outfit, like the Georgia Minstrels, the McCabe and Young Minstrels, and the Hicks and Sawyer Colored Minstrels, was the genuine article, a real Negro minstrel show. Our show, like most of the others of its type, was under white management.

Life began at 11:45 A.M. in a minstrel company. At that time the manager of the parade blew his whistle in the theatre, ordering "all out." The order of things would be varied slightly if the train reached the city late. In such a case we would dress in our private Pullman car and commence the parade from the railroad tracks. Either way we were sure to find a swarm of long-legged boys on hand, begging for a chance to carry the banners advertising the show —the same young rabble, perhaps, that invariably swept down upon the circus with the offer to water the elephants in return for free tickets.

The parade itself was headed by the managers in their four-horse carriages. Doffing silk hats and smiling their jeweled smiles, they acknowledged with easy dignity the small flutter of polite applause their high-stepping horses provoked. After them came the carriage in which the stars rode. The "walking gents" followed, that exciting company which included comedians, singers and acrobats. They in turn were followed by the drum major—not an ordinary drum major beating time for a band, mind you, but a performer out of the books, an artist with the baton. His twirling stick suggested a bicycle wheel revolving in the sun. Occasionally he would give it a toss and then recover the glistening affair with the same flawless skill. The drum major in a minstrel show was a character to conjure with; not infrequently he stole the parade. Our company had two such virtuosi; in addition to twirling their batons, they added the new wrinkle of tossing them back and forth to each other as they marched.

Finally, distributed at intervals from one end of the parade to the other, there were the boys with the banners. Each banner described one outstanding feature of the colossal spectacle.

The band played marches as this procession paraded the principal streets of a town. Curiously, we made few concessions to low-brow taste in our selection of music. We used the heaviest works of W. P. Chambers, C. W. Dalbey and C. L. Barnhouse; even the stiff composition *Alvin Joslin* by Pettee was not beyond us. It was only when we were lip-weary that we eased off on the light, swingy marches of R. B. Hall and John Philip Sousa.

The procession circled on the public square, and the band played a program of classical overtures plus a medley of popular airs for the throngs that assembled there in the open. *Brudder Gardner's Picnic* (a selection containing the gems of Stephen C. Foster) was always in order. Special features like trombone, piccolo or clarinet solos were interspersed among our numbers. Usually too we included a comic act such as a trick bicyclist made up as a tramp or an interlude by the lanky D. C. Scott, a "natural-born reacher," in his slapstick get-up. And here, finally, was the place for the oratorical gifts of the re- markable George L. Moxley whose business it was to sell the show to the natives.

Another parade with music brought us back to the theatre. For the remainder of the afternoon our time was our own—and did we flirt—but at seven-thirty we played a program of classical music in front of the opera house. In all probability, we would pull the "Musi- cians' Strike" out of our bag of tricks. During this well-rehearsed feature each musician would, when his turn came, pretend to quarrel

with someone else and quit the band in a huff. When, to the dismay
of the innocent yokels, the band had dwindled to almost nothing, a
policeman who had been "fixed" and planted at a convenient spot
would come up and ask questions. This would lead to a fight between
some of the remaining musicians, and the officer would promptly
arrest them.

The crowd could be depended on to express its disappointment in
strong language. "Just like niggers," they'd groan. "They break up
everything with a fight. Damn it all, they'd break up Heaven." During
these recriminations we would spring the old hokum. The band,
having reassembled around the corner, would cut loose with one of
the most sizzling tunes of the day, perhaps *Creole Belles, Georgia
Camp Meeting,* or *A Hot Time In the Old Town Tonight,* and presently the ticket seller would go to work. Our hokum hooked them.

Inside the opera house the curtain rose on a conventional orchestra
of fourteen players sitting high on an elevated platform. Before the
orchestra sat the two brilliant semi-circles of performers. The first
was occupied by the featured soloists; the second, by singers and
others later to take part in the olio. Immediately upon the rise of
the curtain this entire group burst into song. And what singing it
was! Anyone who ever followed the old minstrel shows of the last
century will bear witness to the quality of the ensemble singing of
these amazingly well-trained groups.

Old-timers will remember as well what followed. Following the
curtain music, the interlocutor entered togged in blue silk and lace à
la knickerbocker and introduced the comedians. A thrill that the
present generation may never know waited only for this individual's
trite but magical words: "Ladies and Gentlemen, we've come out
tonight to give you a pleasing entertainment. With bones on the
right and tambourines on the left we'll proceed with the overture.
Gentlemen, be seated!" That gave the end men their cue, and they
promptly joined the grand ensemble, beating tambourines and rattling bones while they made faces, pantomimed and otherwise laid
the spectators in the aisles with their tomfoolery.

It is interesting to recall that our sopranos and altos in the minstrel chorus were men, but that was no handicap with men like Dicky
Lewis and William Burton in our company. They could hit top C
like women. Our tenors and bassos were equally capable. Sloan Ed-
wards, the big basso, had no trouble getting down to double B
flat. Any of our top tenors, when they were soaring, could bring a
mist to the eyes.

That was as it should have been. Tenor singers in those days
had peculiar responsibilities. Everyone knew that there were those
who came to a minstrel show to cry as well as to laugh. Ladies of

that mauve decade were likely to follow the plot of a song with much the same sentimental interest that their daughters show in the development of a movie theme nowadays. The tenors were required to tell the stories that jerked the tears. For this purpose they had at their disposal such songs as *She May Have Seen Better Days* or *Just Tell Them That You Saw Me*. If he failed to do this, he was simply not first string by minstrel standards and could expect to be replaced by a better man. . . .

Right here, perhaps, I should ring down the curtain on Mahara's Minstrels. My association with them had made of me a professional musician and a bandmaster. It had taken me from Cuba to California, from Canada to Mexico. It had shown me almost every river and mountain, every city and state that my geography book had taught me to name. It had thrown me into contact with a wistful but aspiring generation of dusky singers and musicians. It had taught me a way of life that I still consider the only one for me. Finally it had brought me back, after trying days, into the good graces of such home folks as my father and the old school teacher. The time had been well spent.

If I could bring back those times just once, however, I think I could set up an all-star show that even the generation of today couldn't deny. This is how I'd do it.

I'd bring the company to blasé Broadway. The first drums would rumble at noon as I led my forty-five men down the Great White Way. Their heads high, their feet nimble, I'd pour them into Times Square playing *Bill Bailey Won't You Please Come Home*. We would stop before the Winter Garden, and my concert would begin—no, not with *St. Louis Blues*—with Sousa's *Stars and Stripes Forever*.

That evening, in the second part, as nine trumpets bleated the trebles and seven trombones rumbled the glissandos of *Cotton Blossoms* I would secretly challenge all comers to beat the effects. I'd give a pretty to the ear that could forget them. Presently I would bring George Moxley before a loud-speaker with the simple instruction to get them told. Behind us, as the superb Moxley strutted his stuff, the lobby of the theatre would be lit up with W. A.'s diamonds. Frank Mahara would occupy the ticket cage. Looka here, looka here!

Inside, as the last seat was snapped down in the balcony and the S.R.O. sign was being put in place, my curtain would begin to rise. It would disclose a pyramid of sixty men, "Sixty, count 'em!" With Moxley, the interlocutor, seated in the center and Billy Young, George Tichenor, Gordon Collins, Lew Hall, all-time end men, premiering on the flanks, you'd feel a strange enchantment creeping over you. The show would be definitely on.

From the circle you'd hear songs that should never have been forgotten: *Night Bird's Cooing, Song That Reached My Heart, That Is Love, Across the Bridge He Goes, Little Empty Stockings on a Christmas Night, Bye Bye, Baby, Bye Bye, Gwine Back to Dixie, When the Robins Nest Again, Six Feet of Earth, Her Own Boy, Jack, Mottoes on the Wall, Picture 84, In the Baggage Coach Ahead,* and *My Dad's the Engineer.*

In the olio I would use modern blackouts to snap up such sketches as *Book Agent, You'll Like the Place, Clam Seller,* and *The Laudophone.* Then when the show was over I would let the curtain descend as Julius Glenn, Will Garland, Simon Epps and the handsome basso Jack Johnson, against the soft humming of sixty men, were singing Pensuti's *Goodnight, Beloved, Goodnight.* . . .

ASCAP celebrated its Silver Jubilee at Carnegie Hall in New York City, during the week of October 1, 1939. It was the greatest program of all-American music ever staged—and free to the public. Each night the program was of a different character.

It opened Sunday evening with excerpts from outstanding musical comedies. Monday evening had a program of Negro music from symphony to swing. Tuesday evening was devoted to various military bands; Wednesday—folk and heart songs; Thursday—symphonic works; Friday—American symphonic jazz, melody and swing, purveyed by Paul Whiteman, Glenn Miller, Benny Goodman, and Fred Waring with his orchestra and choir. The demand for seats was so great that in order to accommodate the overflow the bandsmen repeated their respective performances immediately following at the 71st Regiment Armory. The Saturday matinee performance was devoted to compositions of children's music, for an audience mainly made up of young people. On Saturday evening, the second concert was devoted to symphonic works.

The entire festival was produced under the personal direction of Gene Buck, assisted by Deems Taylor, Frank Black, John J. O'Connor, W. C. Handy, George W. Meyer, Abram Chasins, Roy Harris, and Fred Ahlert, with R. H. Burnside as stage manager.

I should like to go into the details of the composers who took part and how the audience thrilled at hearing their works played and sung by the authors and composers themselves. These programs were repeated in San Francisco at the Golden Gate International Exposition on Treasure Island and at the New York World's Fair, "The World of Tomorrow," a month later. So to avoid repetition we pass along to the all-Negro program from symphony to swing that took place on the evening of October 2, 1939.

The committee thought it fitting and proper that this night be set apart to show the creative and interpretative gifts of the Negro. Another committee consisting of J. Rosamond Johnson, Harry T. Burleigh and myself was designated to arrange matters. The actual labor fell upon the capable shoulders of Charles L. Cooke, Joe Jordan and my secretary, Pearl Carn.

ASCAP empowered me to engage the most outstanding concert artists, and the Negro Symphony, whatever the cost. The program proved a real success due to the cooperation of the choirs of the Abyssinian Baptist Church, Wen Talbot, Donald Heywood and Juanita Hall, plus renditions by Jessie Zachary, Clyde Barrie, the Southernaires, Minto Cato and my daughter, Katherine Lewis. The program opened with the three hundred and fifty voices of the combined choirs, accompanied by the seventy-five piece orchestra under the baton of Joe Jordan, in *Lift Every Voice and Sing*. Then followed excerpts from three symphonies conducted in turn by their respective composers, James P. Johnson, *From Harlem*; Charles L. Cooke, *Sketches of the Deep South*; and William G. Still, *[Afro-]American Symphony*.

The second half of the program opened with a minstrel first part, consisting of members of the Crescendo Club, of which J. C. Johnson is president. Henry Troy acted as the interlocutor, with Tom Fletcher and Laurence Deas as end men. Plantation melodies ranging from the earliest minstrel days to songs from the various musical productions of Williams and Walker, Cole and Johnson, Sissle and Blake and others were rendered. Each member of the club, being a song writer, presented in turn his own famous compositions, many of which had ushered in various dance crazes: *Pas-a-ma-la, Ballin' the Jack, Shimmie, Charleston*, etc. Maceo Pinkard and Clarence Williams were ably assisted in their respective songs, *Mammy o' Mine* and *Baby, Won't You Please Come Home?* by their vocalist wives, Edna Alexander and Eva Taylor.

The minstrel grand finale was Cramer and Layton's *'Way Down Yonder in New Orleans*, thrillingly sung by the entire company, followed by a wild orgy of blues, jazz, jitterbug and jive, now called swing, in which the following bands participated: Cab Calloway, Noble Sissle, Louis Armstrong and Claude Hopkins. Although they were unable to be there in person, Duke Ellington, Thomas "Fats" Waller, Andy Razaf, Benny Carter and Jimmie Lunceford were represented by the playing of some of their noted compositions. In this concert, as has been the case in all others in which I have had managerial interest, the Musicians' Union, Local 802, A. F. of M., gave wonderful cooperation through its secretary, William Feinberg.

27. WILL MARION COOK

>>> The end of the nineteenth century began a golden era for black musicians, particularly in the field of musical comedy. In 1866, the United States had given the world its first musical comedy, *The Black Crook* (with an all-white cast). During the summer of 1899, Will Marion Cook (1869–1944) presented the first Negro musical-comedy sketch, *Clorindy, the Origin of the Cakewalk*. With lyrics written by black poet Paul Laurence Dunbar, the work created a sensation at its opening on Broadway.

Cook was well equipped for his role as a pioneer composer of musical comedies. He had studied music at Oberlin and later took violin lessons from the renowned Joseph Joachim in Berlin. After several years abroad, Cook returned to the United States and matriculated at the National Conservatory of Music in New York, then headed by Antonín Dvořák. Bitter experiences in the concert world cut off Cook's career as a violinist, despite his talent and excellent preparation, and he turned to the world of musical comedy. After *Clorindy*, Cook became the "composer in chief" for a steady stream of musicals, most of which featured the celebrated vaudeville team of George Walker and Bert Williams. His later career included activity as a conductor of syncopated symphony orchestras and as a composer of art music. <<<

Clorindy, the Origin of the Cakewalk [1944] †

When Bert Williams and George Walker met in California, the Negro god of comedy and drama must have opened his thick lips and wide mouth and laughed loud, long, raucously! After failures around the country in medicine shows and cheap vaudeville houses, the team found themselves at French Lick Springs where Canary, George W. Lederer's partner, happened to catch their act. Immediately he put them on a train for New York and Lederer's Casino Theatre, where the famous producer introduced them between the acts of *The Gold*

---

† Text: *Theatre Arts,* September, 1947, pp. 61–65. Reprinted by permission of Mercer Cook.

Bug. They swamped New York and then went on to one of the longest runs that had ever been made at Koster and Bial's. That was where I came into the picture.

Since I had come to New York to learn to write good music, I met Williams and Walker and gave them my ideas on creating a story of how the cakewalk came about in Louisiana in the early Eighteen Eighties. *Clorindy, the Origin of the Cakewalk* was the result and though, when the time came, Williams and Walker were unable to play in it, it was for them that I wrote the show.

But all that came later. At our first meeting Williams and Walker made a few suggestions to me and then introduced me to their manager, Will McConnell, who lent me ten dollars to go back home to Washington. I was barred anyhow from the classes at the National Conservatory of Music because I wouldn't play my fiddle in the orchestra under Dvorak. I couldn't play; my fingers had grown too stiff. Dvorak didn't like me anyway; Harry T. Burleigh was his pet. Only John White, the harmony and counterpoint teacher, thought I had talent, and insisted that I attend his classes.

With McConnell's ten dollars I returned home with my tremendous idea. After a long siege of persuasion, I finally got Paul Laurence Dunbar to consent to write the *Clorindy* libretto (which was never used) and a few of the lyrics. We got together in the basement of my brother John's rented house on Sixth Street, just below Howard University, one night about eight o'clock. We had two dozen bottles of beer, a quart of whiskey, and we took my brother's porterhouse steak, cut it up with onions and red peppers and ate it raw. Without a piano or anything but the kitchen table, we finished all the songs, all the libretto and all but a few bars of the ensembles by four o'clock the next morning. By that time Paul and I were happy, so happy that we were ready to cry "Eureka!" only we couldn't make any noise at that hour so both of us sneaked off to bed, Paul to his house three blocks away and I to my room.

The following morning or rather later that morning, I was at John's piano trying to learn to play my most Negroid song, "Who Dat Say Chicken in Dis Crowd?" My mother, who was cooking my breakfast, came into the parlor, tears streaming from her eyes, and said:

"Oh, Will! Will! I've sent you all over the world to study and become a great musician, and you return such a nigger!" My mother was a graduate of Oberlin in the class of 1865 and thought that a Negro composer should write just like a white man. They all loved the Dunbar lyrics but weren't ready for Negro songs.

After the writing of *Clorindy* many days are to elapse before I get any kind of action. Williams and Walker come through Washington with the Hyde and Behman show, on their way to the coast. They listen to my music and, after praising it highly, again get McConnell to lend me ten dollars so that I may go to New York and play it for Isidore Witmark, the head of Witmark and Sons, then located in Thirty-seventh Street just beyond Broadway.

That weekend I go to New York. McConnell makes an appointment by telephone for me for Saturday afternoon at one o'clock, which was the Saturday closing hour. After keeping me waiting for two hours, the cooling-off process, Isidore Witmark comes into the large front professional office and curtly says, "Go ahead! What's you got?" I am not now and never have been a great pianist, and I could sing only a little bit, but for forty minutes I struggled to give this man some idea of the songs and ensembles. At last, starting for the door of his private office, he interrupted me long enough to say that he thought I must be crazy to believe that any Broadway audience would listen to Negroes singing Negro opera.

There I was, on a Saturday afternoon in New York, with only a few pennies in my pocket, and no place to eat or sleep. I started to walk to the Twenty-third Street ferry, hoping for some good luck and found it. An old pal of mine, Sol Johnson, was on the same boat, on his way to the Penn Depot in Jersey City, where he was a porter on the Washington train. As his train did not leave until night, I loafed about for a while. Later he locked me in a closed dining car, telling me to be quiet until we reached Washington.

And so I got back, hungry, mad with the world and heartbroken at such a failure. It took me some months to recover my spirit, and by this time my brother John, who worked at the pension office and was always good for a touch, became disgusted with the whole idea and wanted me to go to work at something that would at least take care of me. What was more tragic, he even refused to lend me any more money! Bill Higgins, secretary to Congressman White, one of the last colored congressmen from North Carolina, lent me ten dollars. Higgins had been a classmate of my brother at Howard University.

This time it's do or die. So I hunt up Sol Johnson again, and again he hides me on his train, but he charges me two dollars for the favor, since I seem to have become a regular passenger. A long, long struggle and much suffering is to ensue until George Archer, head usher at the Casino Roof Garden, says, "Why don't you go to see Ed Rice? His office is in the Standard Theatre Building at Sixth Avenue and Thirty-second Street. He runs the show up on George Lederer's Roof and needs an outstanding attraction."

For weeks, whenever I could get three or four of my prospective cast together or find a place to rehearse, I had been teaching them the *Clorindy* music. I taught them with or without a piano; sometimes just singing or trying to sing the different parts. But this was a genius aggregation, Negro talent that had made much of little. And besides, they believed in me.

As directed by George Archer, I went to see Ed Rice, and I saw him every day for a month. Regularly, after interviewing a room full of people, he would say to me (I was always the last): "Who are you, and what do you want?" On the thirty-first day—and by now I am so discouraged that this is my last try—I heard him tell a knockabout act: "Come up next Monday to rehearsal, do a show and, if you make good, I'll keep you on all the week."

I was desperate. My feet, with soles worn through, were burnt black by walking on the hot cobblestones of New York streets. I was hungry almost all the time, except when I could meet Harry Burleigh, who had recently become soloist in St. George's Church. He only made a small salary but always had enough to treat me to coffee and crullers at a little dairy called Cushman's, on the corner of Fifteenth Street and Third Avenue, or to a twenty-five-cent dinner at a German restaurant near Union Square.

On leaving Rice's office, I went at once to the Greasy Front, a Negro club run by Charlie Moore, with a restaurant in the basement managed by Mrs. Moore. There I was sure to find a few members of my ensemble. I told them a most wonderful and welcome story; we were booked at the Casino Roof! And I sent them to contact all the others. Everybody was notified to be at the Casino Roof Garden on Monday at eleven a.m. Only Ernest Hogan, my comedian, could not be reached because, unless he was working (and sometimes even then), he stayed up all night carousing. Consequently he slept all day. Just to play safe, I sent him a note in care of his landlady. "We were booked!" I exclaimed. That was probably the most beautiful lie I ever told.

Hogan, whose real name was Rube Crowders [*sic*], had become my comedian because Williams and Walker, for whom *Clorindy* had been written, had been delayed on the Coast by the terrific success of the Hyde and Behman show. I had come in contact with Hogan one day in the back room of the Greasy Front where I was playing "Who Dat Say Chicken?" for a couple of unimpressed comedians. Suddenly I heard a full-bellied laugh and a loud but musical voice: "That's great, son! Who are you? Come on and have a glass of beer."

As I went into the front room to join the man who had called me, Charlie Moore whispered: "That's Ernest Hogan, leading comic with Black Patti's Troubadours, and the man who wrote 'All Coons Look Alike to Me.' He's a great comedian and can do lots for you." That same night Hogan learned "Who Dat Say Chicken?" and my "Hottes' Coon in Dixie."

Back to *Clorindy*. On Monday morning, in answer to my call, every man and woman, boy and girl that I had taught to sing my music was at the Casino Roof. Strange to say, Hogan was the first one to show up.

Luckily for us, John Braham, the English conductor of the Casino orchestra, was a brick. And, still more luckily for us, Ed Rice did not appear at rehearsal that morning until very late. When Braham had finished with the smaller acts, he turned to me questioningly. There I sat, orchestra books in hand. In two minutes I told him how I had studied violin under Joachim, a bit of composition under Dvorak, harmony and mighty little counterpoint under John White. I explained that I had some new music, a Negro operetta. Right then he stopped me, turned to his orchestra men and said: "Gentlemen, a new composer!" He held out his hand for my orchestra parts. Again I got his ear and told him that my singers understood my direction, they understood my gestures and that I was afraid. . . . [*sic*] He again turned and announced: "Gentlemen, a new composer and a new conductor."

By this time my singers were grouped on the stage and I started the opening chorus, an orchestral and choral development of "Darktown Is Out Tonight." Remember, reader, I had twenty-six of the finest Negro voices in America, twenty-six happy, gifted Negroes, who saw maybe weeks of work and money before them. Remember, too, that they were singing a new style of music. Like a mighty anthem in rhythm, these voices rang out.

Rice must have heard the voices and the pulsing Darktown rhythm as he came up Broadway, but his only comment when he came was shouted to Braham: "No nigger can conduct my orchestra on Broadway!" And Braham—God bless him! and He must still be blessing him if there is a place for the great-hearted—simply said: "Ed, go back to your little cubby-hole"—Rice had a little pagoda at one end of the roof, where he "entertained" some of his pretty girls after the show at night—"Go back to your little cubby-hole and keep quiet! That boy's a genius and has something great!"

Well, we didn't get on that Monday night after all. It rained pitchforks until about nine o'clock and the Roof, which was uncovered, was in no condition to receive the high-class habitués. We were sent home about nine-thirty. A more disappointed bunch of people you've never seen. I was heartbroken. Another failure! Was I never to get going? Only Hogan was in good spirits. He had taken charge of things by now, and had spent the day staging the different numbers. Naturally, he had eliminated Dunbar's dialogue, for a lot of dialogue on an uncovered roof garden after eleven p.m. would have been impossible. Hogan also hurriedly gathered three or four sensational dancers. He seemed to know everybody. In short, it was just as well that we didn't go on that night, for Hogan really needed the extra time to whip the dancers into shape, especially the cakewalk. After all, our subtitle was "The Origin of the Cakewalk" and we mustn't fall down on that part of the performance.

Our opening for Rice was postponed until the following Monday and by then all was ready. About 11:45 Mr. Price, Rice's manager, made the simple announcement that the Negro operetta, *Clorindy, the Origin of the Cakewalk*, would now be produced for the first time on any stage. Immediately I struck up the introduction and opening chorus. When I entered the orchestra pit, there were only about fifty people on the Roof. When we finished the opening chorus, the house was packed to suffocation. What had happened was that the show downstairs in the Casino Theatre was just letting out. The big audience heard those heavenly Negro voices and took to the elevators. At the finish of the opening chorus, the applause and cheering were so tumultuous that I simply stood there transfixed, my hand in the air, unable to move until Hogan rushed down to the footlights and shouted: "What's the matter, son? Let's go!"

So I started his strut song, which began and ended with an ensemble, "Hottes' Coon." This was hardly Dunbar's finest lyric, but the chorus, the dances and the inimitable Ernest Hogan made that Broadway audience think it was. The rest of the performance kept them at the same pitch, especially "Who Dat Say Chicken in Dis Crowd?" This number (which Rice had thought too slow) had to be repeated ten times before Hogan could leave the stage, and there were encores galore when Belle Davis sang "Jump Back, Honey, Jump Back!"

The Darktown finale was of complicated rhythm and bold harmonies, and very taxing on the voice. My chorus sang like Russians, dancing meanwhile like Negroes, and cakewalking like angels, black angels! When the last note was sounded, the audience stood and cheered for at least ten minutes. This was the finale which Witmark had said no one would listen to. It was pandemonium, but never was pandemonium dearer to my heart as I stood there sweating in Charles W. Anderson's old full dress coat (Charlie weighed 200 pounds; I, 126), Harry T. Burleigh's vest (Harry was very short; I, quite tall) and my own out-at-the-seat and frayed-at-the-cuffs light street pants, and the same feet-mostly-on-the-ground shoes. These, with a clean shirt and tie (thank heaven), completed my evening clothes.

But did that audience take offense at my rags and lack of conducting polish? Not so you could notice it! We went on at 11:45 and finished at 12:45. Boy, oh boy! Maybe, when the pearly gates open wide and a multitude of hosts march in, shouting, laughing, singing, emoting, there will be a happiness which slightly resembles that of *Clorindy's* twenty-six participants. I was so delirious that I drank a glass of water, thought it wine and got gloriously drunk. Negroes were at last on Broadway, and there to stay. Gone was the uff-dah of the minstrel! Gone the Massa Linkum stuff! We were artists and we were going a long, long way. We had the world on a string tied to a runnin' red-geared wagon on a down-hill pull. Nothing could stop us, and nothing did for a decade.

28. JAMES REESE EUROPE

>>> At the beginning of the twentieth century the headquarters of black artistic talent in New York City was the Marshall Hotel on West Fifty-third Street. Here were to be found the celebrated actors, musicians, poets, writers, and sportsmen of the period. One of the most talented of the musicians was James Reese Europe (1881–1919), who had come to New York from Washington, D.C., where he spent his childhood (he was born in Mobile, Alabama). Europe plunged into the musical activities of the city, performing with syncopated orchestras, working with musical-comedy companies, composing, and traveling with the professional dance team of Vernon and Irene Castle. In 1910, Europe organized the Clef Club, one of the first large black musicians' unions in the nation. In 1912, a Clef Club Symphony Orchestra under the direction of Jim Europe took its infectious rhythms and unorthodox instrumentation to Carnegie Hall for a gala concert that astounded the white critics and public, who had not yet become acquainted with the sound of syncopated music or "jazz."

When the United States entered World War I, Jim Europe was charged with organizing a Negro band that would measure up to his Clef Club groups. Europe's 369th Infantry Band took jazz abroad and made a lasting impression. It was inevitable that the press should have called upon Europe to explain the new music labeled jazz. <<<

A Negro Explains "Jazz" [1919] †

The latest international word seems to be "jazz." It is used almost exclusively in British papers to describe the kind of music and dancing—particularly dancing—imported from America, thereby arousing discussions, in which bishops do not disdain to participate, to fill all the papers. While society once "ragged," they now "jazz." In this country, tho we have been tolerably familiar with the word for two years or more, we still try to pursue its mysterious origins. Lieut.

† Text: *Literary Digest*, April 26, 1919, pp. 28–29.

James Reese Europe, late of the Machine-Gun Battalion of the 15th Regiment, tells Mr. Grenville Vernon, of the New York *Tribune*, that the word comes from Mr. Razz, who led a band in New Orleans some fifteen years ago and whose fame is perpetuated in a somewhat modified form. Besides the information we supply here, another statement about Mr. Razz's band from a New Orleans paper may be seen on page 47, to which the reader is referred. Lieutenant Europe says:

"I believe that the term 'jazz' originated with a band of four pieces which was found about fifteen years ago in New Orleans, and which was known as 'Razz's Band.' This band was of truly extraordinary composition. It consisted of a barytone horn, a trombone, a cornet, and an instrument made out of the chinaberry-tree. This instrument is something like a clarinet, and is made by the Southern negroes themselves. Strange to say, it can be used only while the sap is in the wood, and after a few weeks' use has to be thrown away. It produces a beautiful sound and is worthy of inclusion in any band or orchestra. I myself intend to employ it soon in my band. The four musicians of Razz's Band had no idea at all of what they were playing; they improvised as they went along, but such was their innate sense of rhythm that they produced something which was very taking. From the small cafés of New Orleans they graduated to the St. Charles Hotel, and after a time to the Winter Garden, in New York, where they appeared, however, only a few days, the individual musicians being grabbed up by various orchestras in the city. Somehow in the passage of time Razz's Band got changed into 'Jazz's Band,' and from this corruption arose the term 'jazz.'

"The negro loves anything that is peculiar in music, and this 'jazzing' appeals to him strongly. It is accomplished in several ways. With the brass instruments we put in mutes and make a whirling motion with the tongue, at the same time blowing full pressure. With wind instruments we pinch the mouthpiece and blow hard. This produces the peculiar sound which you all know. To us it is not discordant, as we play the music as it is written, only that we accent strongly in this manner the notes which originally would be without accent. It is natural for us to do this; it is, indeed, a racial musical characteristic. I have to call a daily rehearsal of my band to prevent the musicians from adding to their music more than I wish them to. Whenever possible they all embroider their parts in order to produce new, peculiar sounds. Some of these effects are excellent and some are not, and I have to be continually on the lookout to cut out the results of my musicians' originality."

The news from Paris is so filled with weightier matters and the French Papers are so much less loquacious than our Anglo-Saxon ones on the lighter sides of life that, until the Lieutenant speaks, we haven't heard of the impression jazz has made on the French:

"I recall one incident in particular. From last February to last August I had been in the trenches, in command of my machine-gun squad. I had been through the terrific general attack in Champagne when General Gouraud annihilated the enemy by his strategy and finally put an end to their hopes of victory, and I had been through many a smaller engagement. I can tell you that music was one of the things furthest from my mind when one day, just before the Allied Conference in Paris, on August 18, Colonel Hayward came to me and said:

" 'Lieutenant Europe, I want you to go back to your band and give a single concert in Paris.'

"I protested, telling him that I hadn't led the band since February, but he insisted. Well, I went back to my band, and with it I went to Paris. What was to be our only concert was in the Théâtre des Champs-Elysées. Before we had played two numbers the audience went wild. We had conquered Paris. General Bliss and French high officers who had heard us insisted that we should stay in Paris, and there we stayed for eight weeks. Everywhere we gave a concert it was a riot, but the supreme moment came in the Tuileries Gardens when we gave a concert in conjunction with the greatest bands in the world—the British Grenadiers' Band, the band of the Garde Républicain [*sic*], and the Royal Italian Band. My band, of course, could not compare with any of these, yet the crowd, and it was such a crowd as I never saw anywhere else in the world, deserted them for us. We played to 50,000 people at least, and, had we wished it, we might be playing yet.

"After the concert was over the leader of the band of the Garde Républicain came over and asked me for the score of one of the jazz compositions we had played. He said he wanted his band to play it. I gave it to him, and the next day he again came to see me. He explained that he couldn't seem to get the effects I got, and asked me to go to a rehearsal. I went with him. The great band played the composition superbly—but he was right: the jazz effects were missing. I took an instrument and showed him how it could be done, and he told me that his own musicians felt sure that my band had used special instruments. Indeed, some of them, afterward attending one of my rehearsals, did not believe what I had said until after they had examined the instruments used by my men."

It is the feeling of this musician, who, indeed, before the war supplied most of the music in New York dancing circles, that a higher plane in music may be attained by negroes if they stick to their own form. He concludes:

"I have come back from France more firmly convinced than ever that negroes should write negro music. We have our own racial feeling and if we try to copy whites we will make bad copies. I noticed that the Morocco negro bands played music which had an affinity to ours. One piece, 'In Zanzibar,' I took for my band, and tho white audiences seem to find it too discordant, I found it most sympathetic. We won France by playing music which was ours and not a pale imitation of others, and if we are to develop in America we must develop along our own lines. Our musicians do their best work when using negro material. Will Marion Cook, William Tires [Tyers], even Harry Burleigh and Coleridge-Taylor are [only] truly themselves in the music which expresses their race. Mr. Tires, for instance, writes charming waltzes, but the best of these have in them negro influences. The music of our race springs from the soul, and this is true to-day with no other race, except possibly the Russians and it is because of this that I and all my musicians have come to love Russian music. Indeed, as far as I am concerned, it is the only music I care for outside of Negro."

The Lieutenant then tells how he formed his band.

"When war broke out I enlisted as a private in Colonel Hayward's regiment, and I had just passed my officer's examination when the Colonel asked me to form a band. I told him that it would be impossible, as the Negro musicians of New York were paid too well to have them give up their jobs to go to war. However, Colonel Hayward raised $10,000 and told me to get the musicians wherever I could get them. The reed-players I got in Porto Rico [*sic*], the rest from all over the country. I had only one New York Negro in the band—my solo cornetist. These are the men who now compose the band, and they are all fighters as well as musicians, for all have seen service in the trenches."

29. ARTHUR LITTLE

⇛ In 1917 a white colonel, William Haywood, was invited to organize a regiment of black infantrymen for the National Guard of New York. The result was the 15th Infantry of New York (later called the 369th). Arthur Little was assigned as the captain of Company F on April 13, 1917. He kept a diary throughout his war years in which he recorded his experiences with the black soldiers under his command. According to Little's statement, his book *From Harlem to the Rhine* (1936) was "written between June 1919 and August 1920 from notes in my war diary." Little's regiment included two of the nation's most talented musicians, Sergeant Noble Sissle, the regimental drum major, and Lieutenant James Reese Europe, the band's organizer and director. ⇚

From *From Harlem to the Rhine* [1936] †

On Sunday morning May 13th, we started for Peekskill. Our 2nd Battalion left the Brooklyn armory at about half past eight. We travelled by elevated railroad train across the Brooklyn Bridge and up Third Avenue. At Forty-Second Street we detrained, and marched to Park Avenue where we formed in line between Forty-Fifth and Fiftieth Streets. There we waited to be joined by the 1st and 3rd Battalions, the Machine Gun Company and the Band, which had to come down from the Harlem armory at 132nd Street and Seventh Avenue. There was delay and confusion.

At about half past twelve, midday, we marched up Fifth Avenue. The march was made in the simplest of formations. Many of our men had had no drilling at all; none had had much drilling. We took no more chances of disaster, by passing from one formation to another, than were absolutely unavoidable. Our men, however, were natural born marchers and cadence observers. With a band playing,

† Text: The original edition (New York, 1936), pp. 9–11, 14, 56–63, 95, 126–41.

or with spectators cheering, they just couldn't be held from keeping step. That bright, sunny, Sunday morning we had both—the playing band and the cheering spectators. The churches had just concluded their services; and the crowds, inspired by sermons of patriotic appeal, were strolling along New York's wonderful promenade avenue as our picturesque organization swung up the line, to the brass toned expression of *Onward Christian Soldiers.*

As I heard those roars of applause, trying to drown out Jim Europe's bandsmen at the head of the column, I forgot all about the mis-fit and incomplete uniforms hidden through the ranks of my company, I forgot all about the ignorance and other weaknesses of our command, I forgot that we were merely going to a state training camp for drill and for rifle practice, forgot that we were, as some newspaper cynic had said, merely a glorified organization of *Mulligan Guards,* and I felt, as I am sure twelve hundred other men of that column felt that morning, that *we were* Christian and American soldiers marching on to war.

At Fifty-Seventh Street we turned West, and made our way by the most favorable route to the New York Central freight yards running along the river front. At about Sixtieth Street we found our special trains waiting. But here, also, we found waiting a wonderful band of ladies, armed with baskets and pots, filled with sandwiches and steaming coffee and packages of chocolate and cigarettes. We had had very early and very sketchy breakfasts. No train ration had been provided. Our first meal at Peekskill was (as we were later to discover) to be served between ten thirty that evening and midnight. If it had not been for those angels in Red Cross Canteen Service uniform, the first day in the field of the 15th Heavy Foot would have developed some pretty bad cases of faintness. We hadn't learned as much about roughing it up to that time as we learned later.

It was during the march up Fifth Avenue, that morning, that Major Dayton's horse won his name. The horse was restive, and, upon the slippery pavement, difficult to control. So a couple of orderlies laid quieting hands upon the bridle and marched, one upon either side of the horse's head. Our men, ever ready to see a joke or to make one, and being well versed in the language of the Bible and the hymnal, promptly named Major Dayton's horse "*Kindly Light.*" The Major, being blessed with a sense of humor of that delightful quality that admits of appreciation of a joke even when upon oneself, was the first to accept the name for his steed, and for months one of the favorite stories the regiment told to visitors was the story of how the Major rode in safety up the Avenue at the head of his Battalion, with two of his faithful attendants detailed to "*Lead Kindly Light.*"

Arrived, at about three o'clock in the afternoon, at the great camping plain upon a bluff overlooking the Hudson River two miles north of the city of Peekskill, we worked, under conditions of confusion and imperfect organization, all through the afternoon and evening, making camp. Only a small percentage of our men had ever made a military camp. Most of our officers had had experience as enlisted men but not as officers. There is considerable difference between driving a peg, digging a hole, or pulling on a rope when told to do so and planning for seventy-five or eighty men to drive pegs, dig holes and pull on ropes, all at the same time, and in such a manner as to create a village of tentage and drains along lines of symmetry. . . .

Our first evening parade presented some most astonishing features. It was functioned upon the evening of our second day at Peekskill. The field and staff officers paraded on foot. Probably no greater proportion of all officers than twenty percent had ever before commanded troops in a ceremony; and of that experienced twenty percent group most of us were far from up to date. The band labored and brought forth noise. At times it brought forty forty-two noises; and between times, when the forty-two musicians stopped playing, the imprecations of Jim Europe could be heard from one end of the field to the other, striving by fantastic forms of speech to prevent his musicians from acquiring the malady known as swelled head. . . .

THE SPARTANBURG, SOUTH CAROLINA CAMP

The talk which some of us overheard through that crowd, during the early stages of the concert, was by no means reassuring. At first it seemed, almost, as if an error of judgment had been made in forcing the colored regiment into prominence at so early an hour after our arrival. But there must be something in the time-honored line about music and its charms; for, gradually, the crowd grew larger, but the noises of the crowd grew less and less, until finally, in that great public square of converging city streets, silence reigned. Lieutenant Europe conducted, as was his custom, with but a few seconds between numbers, and the program appeared to be short. When the final piece had been played and the forty or fifty bandsmen had filed out of the stand in perfect order with the "Hep—Hep—Hep—" of the sergeants as the only sound from their ranks, the flower of Spartanburg's citizenry looked at each other foolishly, and one could be heard to say:—"Is that all?" while another would say:—"When do they play again?"

That evening, a committee of business men found Colonel Hayward, before he got started back to camp, and invited him to have a little chat in a private room of the hotel. I attended the meeting with the Colonel. According to my recollection, Major Morris and Captain Hinton were also present. The sense of the informal meeting was that the interview of Mayor Floyd as expressed in the daily newspapers did not represent the true spirit of the conservative or responsible citizenship of Spartanburg. The gentlemen present at that meeting appeared to deplore the expressions of the Mayor. They were quite frank in criticizing the War Department for forcing such a delicate situation as had developed by ordering a colored regiment to a Southern state; but they offered us full cooperation in striving to prevent the delicate situation from becoming an indelicate one. They agreed that we had made a good start. They invited all of the officers of the regiment to consider themselves honorary members of the Country Club. They requested the Colonel let the Band play for dancing at the club dance the following week, for which services they desired to make up a purse. . . .

The conservative element of Spartanburg, the element represented by the peace-promoting group of business men, to whom reference has been made, worked constructively for the betterment of conditions. While they tried to make things pleasant for our officers, at their clubs, they arranged entertainments for the men as well. These entertainments, for the most part, took the form of dances, to which the best class of the civilian colored population was invited. The well-to-do colored citizens also made a point of inviting our men to join their family parties at church, on Sundays, and to enjoy with them afterwards, Sunday dinners of home cooking. The business men's self-appointed committee encouraged and helped to steer these developments, and went to a lot of trouble to arrange for smooth-running transportation facilities. In all of these affairs full consideration was given to the Southern tradition. The conservative and constructure elements of both sides were striving to make the best of a difficult situation.

A social atmosphere of great promise was developing at Spartanburg. We feared that our regiment would be forced to spend the winter at Camp Wadsworth, and we prepared to make the best of it. Already, the families of a number of officers of other organizations were settled in town; and both officers and men of our regiment spent much of such spare time as they had, in house hunting.

Every afternoon at *Retreat*, our Band would play a short concert in front of Regimental Headquarters, immediately following the playing of the National Anthem. Many of the ladies, and officers of other organizations, whom we had met at Division Headquarters, would drop in to hear Europe's Band. General and Mrs. Phillips honored us several times upon such occasions. . . .

At Sea

Sunday, December 23rd, was like a beautiful Spring day, at sea.

We had religious services on deck. There was no chaplain on board, so the Colonel conducted the services. He did it well, too. The Band played *Onward Christian Soldiers, Nearer My God To Thee, Rock of Ages, Holy, Holy, Holy,* and *Come Ye Disconsolate.* The men all sang—officers, too.

Everybody was very serious. We were in the so-called "danger zone"; and the church service seemed to emphasize the gravity of our mission. . . .

The Band Tours France
February 12—March 20, 1918

Upon February 10, 1918, the special order quoted below was received at our camp:

LINE OF COMMUNICATIONS

BASE COMMANDER, BASE SECTION NO. 1

FRANCE

Special Orders }   February 10, 1918.
No. 41　　　 }

EXTRACT

*　　*　　*　　*　　*　　*　　*　　*

3. Pursuant to telegraphic instructions, Headquarters, L. of C., dated February 1-4-26, 1918, the Band, 15th N. Y. Infantry, and detachment Hqrs. Co., that organization, consisting of two officers and fifty-six men, with necessary cooking utensils and eighteen days rations, (under command of Captain A. W. Little, Adjutant, 15th N. Y. Inf.), will proceed from this Base to Aix-les-Bains, so as to arrive at that station not later than February 15, 1918, reporting upon arrival thereat to the Provost Marshal for duty in connection with the opening of the Rest Station at that point. This detachment will remain at the above mentioned station until March 2, 1918, on which date it will return to its proper station, at these Headquarters.

The Quartermaster Corps will furnish the necessary transportation and travel rations and coffee money for eight days for the journey to and return from Aix-les-Bains.

The travel directed is necessary in the military service.

By command of Brigadier General Walsh.

ORRIN H. WOLFE

Copies to: Adjutant General.

C. O. L. of C.

DQM (3)

FIN (2)

RTO

C. O. 15th N. Y. Inf.

Capt. Little.

Line of Communications (L. of C) was, at that time, the name of the department of the service subsequently known as Service of Supply (S. O. S.).

I was provided with two 3rd class coaches for the men, one car for freight and baggage, and 1st class reservations for Lieutenant Europe and myself. We took with us about eight tons of rations.

At about 1 o'clock in the afternoon of February 12th, 1918 (Lincoln's Birthday, and exactly one year before the return of our regiment in triumph to New York), Lieutenant Sattler reported to me that my cars were completely packed and ready to be moved, that two trucks were waiting for the men outside of the company quarters, and that we should entrain at 3:45 P.M.

Our first stopping point was Nantes. The run was but a short one—about an hour and a half.

At Nantes, our cars were detached from the train and held in the station, over night. The men detrained, and marched to some French barracks, where they were quartered and messed as guests of the U. S. Military Police detachment of Nantes. The officers and men of this command were most cordial in their hospitality.

The Band was scheduled for a concert at the Opera House, at nine o'clock in the evening. The concert was in honor of Lincoln's Birthday, but for the benefit (financially) of a French charitable institution.

The Opera House faced a plaza of about two hundred yards square, bounded by handsome buildings. This entire plaza was crowded with an audience which maintained silence during the playing of a number —and then made up for lost time, by wild applause. With the French, a shrill whistle, or "cat call," is the supreme effort of applause. The thoughtful French manager had explained this to our men. He had been informed, so he said, that in America such sounds are indulged in to denote disapproval; and he desired no incident to mar "the happiness of the evening of this beautiful day."

I elbowed my way through the crowd, and reached the Opera House in time to hear a couple of pieces. Then, the band went inside, to the back stage, to prepare for the formal appearance; and the doors were opened to the public for general admission. Subscribers for boxes and orchestra seats had been admitted by side doors during the playing of the advance concert. Most of the audience seated in these reserved sections were in evening dress. The galleries were crowded, and all standing room was occupied. I doubt if any first night or special performance at the Metropolitan Opera House in New York ever had, relatively, a more brilliant audience.

The French people knew no color line. All they seemed to want to know, that night, was that a great national holiday of their ally was being celebrated—and that made the celebration one of their own. The spirit of emotional enthusiasm had got into the blood of our men; and they played as I had never heard them play before.

Upon the morning of February 13th, 1918, our detachment resumed its journey, leaving Nantes at 9:27 A.M. with our cars attached to a regular train, with destination—Tours.

At about half past twelve our train stopped at Angers. There we had lunch. The Band played in a public square, near the station, for a quarter of an hour. At about two o'clock we resumed our journey.

Tours was reached at about six o'clock in the evening.

No advance agent had arranged for us in Tours. After some delay, orders were given to attach our cars to the south bound express, leaving Tours at 3:18 A.M. In the meantime, I had been fortunate enough to find at the station another hospitable military police officer; and the men, under command of Lieut. Europe, had been piled into trucks, and carried off to barracks, for a hot supper.

The railroad business attended to, I strolled off to find the office of the Provost Marshal. As I presented my orders, to be stamped, the A. P. M. (I can't recall his name; but I believe he was Lieutenant Colonel) looked up and smiled. "So you've got a band with you! Can they play?"

"They can, sir. Also, they would like to—if you can arrange a couple of concerts for us," I answered.

"Fine! Any suggestions as to where or when?"

"Yes, sir. I should like to go out to the Commanding General's place and give him a surprise serenade, if you know some staff officer out there with nerve enough to help me stage it. After that, I'd like to play a formal indoor concert, in the biggest theatre you can get for us at this late hour."

"All right, I believe I can fix you up both ways," said the Assistant

Provost Marshal. He was a regular fellow—that A. P. M.!

He started a clerk telephoning a series of calls, while we waited, and our conversation was resumed.

"Have you got a good band?"

"Pretty good," I said. "It's the only one I've heard over here; but I believe it's the best in the army."

"Well, I dunno," the colonel came back, "I dunno about that. Some of our young officers here came back from St. Nazaire a couple of weeks ago, and they've been talking ever since about some colored band they heard down there. They say that's the real thing in bands— about double the size of the regulation article, and wonderful to listen to. The leader, I believe, is a chap by name of Europe—Jim Europe, who used to play dance music in New York for Mr. and Mrs. Vernon Castle, when they were all the rage. Ever hear that band?"

"That's the band I've got out at your barracks, right now," I answered.

"Wel, I'll be damned!"

Presently, Mr. Europe came in to tell me that the men were waiting outside, in trucks, ready to go to the house of the Commanding General.

We found Major General Kernan quartered in a beautiful little chateau on top of a steep hill upon the outskirts of the city. The serenade was a surprise and a success. After a number of pieces had been played, the General requested some of his favorite Southern melodies; and then, he said he would like to make a little talk to the men.

General Kernan complimented the man of the Band upon their music, and he thanked them for the pleasure they had given him. He prophesied that the tour would be a great success from the viewpoint of the entertainment to be given to American soldiers on leave. But he appealed to the men to remember that their duty throughout the tour was not merely to consist of playing music for the entertainment of the crowd. He explained that where we were going, no American soldiers had as yet been; that, according to the impression left by us upon the minds of the French population of the great territory through which we were to pass, so would rest the reputation of American soldiers in general. He told the men that France recognized no color line. He begged the men not to be the cause of the establishment, in the minds of French people, of a color line. He told the men that they were upon a mission of great importance; that they were not merely musicians and soldiers of the American Army but that they were representatives of the American nation. The eyes of France would be upon them; and through the eyes of

France, the eyes of the world.

Major General Kernan, in his manner of appeal to our men, proved himself a master student of human nature. The men of our regiment, when appealed to in that way, never failed to respond in satisfactory manner.

The men of the Band and Headquarters detachment made a splendid record all through their tour. They left behind them enviable reputations—everywhere.

The cause of the colored race suffered in no particular on account of their representation through the peaceful territory of France by the men of the 15th Heavy Foot.

The American Army in general had no cause for complaint in its representation by the men of my command.

After playing for Major General Kernan, at Tours, that night of the thirteenth of February, the Band returned to the city, and played before a large and appreciative audience in the rooms of the Red Cross Club.

After the concert, the men were taken to barracks for a few hours' sleep.

Shortly before half-past three upon the morning of the fourteenth of February, our train left Tours.

From Tours we visited Saincaize, Moulins, Bessay, La Ferte, Varennes and Créchy. Our tour also included St. Etienne, Lyon, Culoz and St. Germain des Fossés. We arrived at Aix-les-Bains on Feb. 15, 1918.

Our first official duty at Aix-les-Bains consisted of participation in a parade, as a part of the formal ceremonies in the opening of the Leave Area.

The first troop train, filled with American soldiers booked for seven days of rest and recreation, arrived at about noon. The city was *en fête*. The Mayor made a speech of welcome, in French. The Chairman of the Citizens Committee seconded the motion, in English. The Assistant Provost Marshal declaimed a few well chosen threats. Mr. Franklin S. Edmonds, the head of the Y. M. C. A. for that area, told the boys that he and his assistants loved them. A French band of school boys played the Star Spangled Banner (at least their leader told us that that was what it was). Our band responded with the Marseillaise. Then, the head of the committee waved his hand and the parade started.

I have never been able to figure out exactly why I happened to be picked upon to lead that parade, when there were so many persons present of such superior eminence. But, as Tennyson told us, a soldier's lot is not to reason why. I had my orders. I led the parade.

A couple of French detectives served as guides. Their conception of duty seemed to be to march as close to me as possible; and, I regret to report that, upon a number of occasions—owing to the fact that our Regulations provide that a soldier's eyes shall be "straight to the front,"—I stepped on the guides. Outside of that, everything went all right.

The Band played splendidly and without ceasing, the citizens cheered, the officials rode with dignity in their carriages, and bowed with graciousness. The Sun shone. The three thousand soldier boys (*permissionaires*) marched with the snap of Americans—and wondered when that "rest and recreation" was to begin.

Our original orders for Aix were for two weeks. Upon February 26th, telegraphic orders from the Commanding General, S.O.S., were received providing for an extension of our service in the Leave Area for an additional fortnight.

So, the Band had a full month at Aix-les-Bains, and a total of about nine days on the road.

While at Aix, the Band rehearsed every morning in the Casino theatre. Every afternoon, it played a concert—Tuesdays and Fridays in the Park, and upon the other days in the general assembly hall of the Casino. Every evening it played a big concert in the Casino Theatre as a part of the professional vaudeville show, put on under the direction of Mr. Winthrop Ames, and including among its personnel Mr. E. H. Sothern.

Not long after this there was a considerable discussion running in the newspapers at home having to do with an accusation against the American command of unfair treatment of negro troops. The following clipping came to us. It was written as a contribution to the discussion mentioned. It is a matter of no small satisfaction to be able to present it here.

N. Y. Herald, Monday, April 17, 1918

To the Editor of the Herald:

It is good to see the Herald and the Telegram declaring that sinister state- ments that our colored troops are abused by their officers are false. Of course they are vilely false.

I had the pleasure in company with Mr. and Mrs. Winthrop Ames, about six weeks ago, of being the guest of the Colonel and officers of the Old Fif- teenth New York Infantry in France.

Our mission, concerning the entertainment of the American troops, led us to the post of this regiment. We passed half a day there and were enter- tained by the remarkable band of the regiment, conducted by the celebrated Mr. Europe. Colonel Hayward talked with great enthusiasm of his men and of certain prizes he had established for cleanliness and for perfection in equipment and behavior. He especially was proud of his regiment's record for health and gave his soldiers great credit for their discipline. His officers stood by and echoed his enthusiasm. We talked with the men, who were equally proud of their colonel and his aids. There was no question of the genuine affection and regard these colored soldiers had for their officers. Later the quite remarkable band of this regiment was permitted to take part in the opening ceremonies of the rest camp at Aix-les-Bains. Here Captain Arthur Little, who was in charge of the fifty musicians, and the men themselves were quartered in our hotel. We saw them constantly, and it was easy to observe Capt. Little's pride in his band and their affection for him.

Colonel Hayward raised among his own friends $10,000 to provide instruments for his regimental band. It was the bright particular success of the opening at the Aix-les-Bains season. I am sure that no one would resent the reports of ill treatment more vehemently than the colored soldiers who serve proudly under Colonel Hayward.

E. H. SOTHERN

New York City, April 13, 1917.

Upon a number of occasions, during intermissions at the park concerts, civilians would hand Mr. Europe a sheet of music, and request that the Band play the piece at the next concert. Such requests were invariably accompanied by a glimpse into a family's heart yearning. It might be a song written by a daughter who had died. It might be a valse composed by the firstborn son of the family now serving at the front. Europe's sympathy and courtesy went out to all alike. No such request was ever refused. One morning, I noticed that Mr. Europe's eyes had the appearance of great fatigue. I inquired if he was unwell. He said that he was quite well, but that he had been up most of the night, arranging the orchestration for one of those amateur musical compositions. As Europe expressed it, he had written three million notes, representing over twenty different instrumental scores. Of course the three million estimate was an exaggeration; but in Europe's Band no more than two men ever played the same score. His arrangements were always marvels of effective harmony. No one instrument was ever offensively distinguishable.

The Band played several formal and several other informal concerts at Chambéry, the fascinating old cathedral city a few kilometers from Aix.

I once figured up roughly that my black babies and I travelled, during that tour, almost 2000 miles in France; and the Band furnished music in more than twenty-five cities or towns. . . .

We also received many bouquets of flowers, and many verbal

bouquets, some oral and some printed.

The official resolutions of the Y.M.C.A., issued in the form of a printed card for mailing, I quote as follows:—

Y. M. C. A.—A. E. F.

SAVOIE LEAVE AREA

MARCH, 17, 1918

An Expression of Appreciation

The Secretary and Workers of the Y.M.C.A. in the Savoie Leave Area wish to express to Capt. Little, Lieut. Europe and the Members of the 15th New York Infantry Band, their heartfelt appreciation of the service rendered by them to the American Soldiers on leave at Aix-les-Bains and Chambéry during the past month.

The music of the Band has been easily the most important single element in the programme provided for the amusement and refreshment of the men sent here from the camps and trenches.

The Band has responded in the most cordial manner to every request. In the evenings their music and minstrel show have added greatly to the vaudeville, and their special programmes have been enthusiastically received. In the afternoons their concerts in the Casino or in the Park have given great pleasure, not only to our own boys but also to the citizens of Aix, and this has aided greatly in cementing the friendly relations between the two nationalities.

The willing co-operation and courtesy of all the individual Members of the Band have endeared them to the staff, and their stay here will always be remembered by us with the keenest pleasure.

FRANKLIN S. EDMONDS
Secretary

Far too many interesting, inspiring and sentimental incidents occurred during our tour to permit mentioning many. But some cannot be neglected.

At Chambéry, for example, the band gave a concert at the Orphan Asylum.

How those children did enjoy the music!

One little fat faced kiddie made me homesick. He was fascinated by the gestures of Lieutenant Europe, in conducting; and, standing behind Jim, he followed every movement in imitation. The crowd laughed, and Europe turned to catch the little fellow in the act.

And then followed one of those delightful incidents of inspiration by a big hearted man.

With a crash of brass wind and cymbals, Jim brought to a close the piece which he was playing. Then he walked over to the little fellow, placed the baton in his hand, led him out in front of the band, gave instructions to his men for the playing of a piece of simple time, walked over to the side lines to stand beside me—and the little French orphan led the Band.

The crowd just went crazy!

I couldn't help thinking of the words of Major General Kernan, as he started our men upon their mission—that they were representatives of the American nation—that the eyes of France would be upon them; and through the eyes of France, the eyes of the world.

As I watched the faces of the crowd, while that little French boy led the *orchestre militaire Américaine*, I knew that in so far as the eyes of France might be centered upon the spirit of America, through the representation of Jim Europe and his colored band, that the *entente cordiale* between our two countries was safe.

Upon March 14th telegraphic orders were received for us to proceed upon completion of our tour of duty at Aix to Connantre, Department of the Marne, to rejoin our regiment.

Upon the evening of March 16th, 1918, at the conclusion of the usual vaudeville entertainment in the Casino Theatre, Gerry Reynolds, the Y man in charge of entertainment features, a man of remarkable personality, and an indefatigable worker, stepped out on the stage to make a speech—to bid good bye to the Band, and to thank them for their services.

Mr. Reynolds said:—

"Ladies and gentlemen of Aix-les-Bains—men of the Army: It is my sad duty to announce that we have listened to our last concert by the Band of the 15th New York Infantry. Orders have been received for them to rejoin their regiment. Tomorrow, these men, who for a month have given us so much pleasure, proceed to the front lines, to serve in the trenches against——"

Cheers interrupted the speaker. The audience of that theatre rose *en masse*. Men and boys yelled and whistled. Women cried. The civilian orchestra played; but no sound of music could be heard. Flags, hanging from the balcony, as decorations, were torn loose and waved.

Gerry Reynolds never finished that speech.

On the stage, the colored soldiers who had been spat upon in Spartanburg, rose and bowed—and grinned. . . .

March 17th was a busy day for us. We were scheduled to leave at 7:58 in the evening; but our cars were spotted for us during the forenoon; and Supply Sergeant Holliday and Mess Sergeant Granville Malichi and their details had their hands full in packing and trucking and loading.

Our meals, during the trip South, had been too irregular for comfort; so, for the return trip, we decided to rig up a kitchen in one end of our baggage car. Our rations were fairly well used up, so we had plenty of room. We set up a field range in a clay-filled packing case, as we had learned to do in America. I had bought the cooks and kitchen police men white jackets, aprons, and caps, such as are worn by chefs; and when the people of Aix crowded in under the station shed to see us off at train time they saw the cheery sight of a cooking supper about ready to be served—a neat kitchen on wheels—and four immaculately dressed "chef cooks," who would have been a credit to the Pullmans.

It was Park concert day; and the Band played during the afternoon. I had calls to make, and callers to receive, and packing to superintend. The hours slipped away.

At six o'clock I went to my room to harness up in marching order. M. Leder, proprietor of the de l'Europe, met me as I entered the hotel. He begged that I join him in a bottle of champagne.

M. Leder had been a delightful and generous host. His son was a Blue Devil, and a prisoner of war in Germany. My son had driven ambulances for the Blue Devils. There was a little bond between us. Frequently, we had dined together. We were friends.

The champagne was delicious. M. Leder's cordiality was inspiriting. I tore myself away, to hurry to the hotel where the men were quartered.

The streets were already crowded with civilians, waiting to see us march by. I had about a third of a mile to walk, from my hotel to that of the men. Scores of demonstrative French civilians rushed out and delayed me—to shake hands with the men and women, to kiss the cheeks of the babies held up to me.

I reached the Hotel Exertier, to find the band assembled and waiting, with hundreds of men, women, and children crowded about them. Mr. Europe was in front, beside 1st Sergeant Thompson, the Drum-Major. As I approached, they both saluted, as though to report formation.

"Are you all ready?" I shouted to make myself heard above the din.

"Yes, Sir."

"Then we'll start right along," I said. And I moved out to take my post.

"My God, Captain," Europe protested. "You'll break that landlady's heart if you do. She's been waiting for you the last hour, with a bottle of champagne."

"Jim, it can't be done. I've just finished one with Leder, and the afternoon was a busy one before that."

But the landlady and her sister cut short the argument by rushing out and drawing my arms through theirs. Mr. Europe followed, and the bottle was divided between four—for which I was truly thankful.

Some more babies were kissed; and the parade to the station started.

The Chief of Police had reported, and placed himself and a squad of men at our service to clear the way. The school cadet corps band had been reported by the dignified old master at their head—as an escort of honor.

Three times we were stopped in our march to listen to speeches; and twice I had to respond. The third speech was made by the Assistant Provost Marshal, in front of his headquarters.

He praised the men generously for good behavior and splendid service; which was a source of delight to me, as he had been none too friendly in his manner towards us at the time of our arrival, a month before.

I thanked Major Alcorn.

He asked me if there was anything he could do for us.

I asked him to speak of us in his official report, as he had just spoken to us in his farewell.

He promised to do so, and later mailed me a copy of his report, which I am proud to publish:

HEADQUARTERS ASSISTANT PROVOST MARSHAL
Aix-les-Bains

Mar. 17, 1918.

From: William F. Alcorn, Major 102nd Inf. A.P.M.
To: Colonel E. D. Isbell, P. M. Tours.
Subject: Report.

1. Pursuant to telegraphic instructions I have ordered the Band and Headquarters detachment 15th New York Regiment under the Command of Captain A. W. Little and 1st Lieutenant James R. Europe as Officers to proceed to Connantre Department of Marne, and they are leaving to-day March 17th at 9:56.

2. The Band has been in this leave area since Feby. 16th and while here have provided a great deal of amusement to the men on leave and have assisted greatly in making their vacation a pleasant one, the conduct of the men of the Band has been of the very highest order and their work deserves high commendations.

3. Would request that a Band be kept here at all times.

WILLIAM F. ALCORN
Major 102nd Inf. A.P.M.

Throughout the line of march to the station, the police failed utterly to keep the street clear. I marched, of course alone, at the head of my command; but I was so closely surrounded by civilians that the greatest care had to be exercised to avoid stepping upon them. Between me and my orderlies, five paces to the rear, marched a solid phalanx of civilians from curb to curb; and the distance between the orderlies and the Band, fifteen paces, furnished marching space for no less than from four hundred to five hundred old men, women, and children. Of young men, there were none in France outside of the army.

When we arrived at the railroad station, a lane had to be forced, to admit of our getting through to where the trains were to be boarded. And when the train rolled (or rather crept) in, a guard of police and railroad attendants had to precede it, to clear the tracks to avoid wholesale carnage. During the delay attendant upon attaching our cars to the train, the Band played its farewell; the crowd cheered without ceasing; women and chidren wept. When, at last, the call *"En voiture"* passed down the line, the cheeks of the few remaining unkissed babies of that town were presented to me for attention; and, joy and glory be; as the train commenced to move, two ladies of high caste dressed in mourning black, stepped upon the running board of the car as I leaned out of my window—and made my farewell complete.

30. ETHEL WATERS

>>> Actress-singer Ethel Waters (b. 1900) began her long career as a singer in Baltimore about 1917. Hers was a "Cinderella" story. To be sure, she assisted her fairy godmother, "Lady Luck," by providing more than her share of hard work and persistence. As an entertainer Ethel Waters reached stardom during the Negro Renaissance of the 1920s. Sometime later she began her second career, acting, and again found herself receiving accolades from the press and the public. In her autobiography, *His Eye Is on the Sparrow* (with Charles Samuels, New York, 1950), Waters tells the story of how she climbed to the top and of the persons who helped her along, and in the process imparts much information about musical practices of the period. <<<

From *His Eye Is on the Sparrow* [1950] †

The first Negro woman singer to make a phonograph record was Mamie Smith. My first was made for the Cardinal Company and had "New York Glide" on one side, "At the New Jump Study Ball" on the other. You'll find Bojangles Robinson's favorite word—copesetic—in the "Jump Study Ball" lyrics. I'd heard it all over the South.

The same talent scout who dug me up for Cardinal worked for other record companies. After catching my act at Edmond's [a Harlem night spot] a second time, he asked if I would care to make some records for Black Swan, a new company just started by Harry H. Pace and W. C. Handy, the two grand old men of Negro music.

The Black Swan office was, I think, in the home of one of the owners. The day I went there I found Fletcher Henderson sitting behind a desk and looking very prissy and important. Fletcher had

† Text: The original edition (New York, 1950), pp. 141–42, 145–47, 173–75, 183–85, 215–17. From *His Eye Is on the Sparrow*, by Ethel Waters with Charles Samuels. Copyright 1950, 1951 by Ethel Waters and Charles Samuels. Reprinted by permission of Doubleday & Company, Inc.

come up from Georgia to study chemistry at one of the big New York colleges. But he was making side money doing arrangements and musical backgrounds for the company. He also made band records for them.

There was much discussion of whether I should sing popular or "cultural" numbers. They finally decided on popular, and I asked one hundred dollars for making the record. I was still getting only thirty-five dollars a week and tips, so one hundred dollars seemed quite a lump sum to me. Mr. Pace paid me the one hundred dollars, and that first Black Swan record I made had "Down Home Blues" on one side, "Oh, Daddy" on the other. It proved a great success and a best seller among both white and colored, and it got Black Swan out of the red. In those days you sang down into little horns just like the one you see in those ads of His Master's Voice. My second Black Swan record had "There'll Be Some Changes Made" on one side and "One Man Nan" on the other. Like all the other early records I made, these are now collector's items.

Pace and Handy then suggested that I go out on tour with Fletcher Henderson's band, which was called Fletcher Henderson's Black Swan Jazz Masters, with Fletcher as my accompanist. They said such a tour would sell a lot more of my records. They didn't call such trips personal-appearance tours in those days. I don't know what they called them; I guess they didn't call 'em anything. They just had 'em.

I didn't like to give up my steady thirty-five dollars a week and tips at Edmond's to go out of town, but the Black Swan people talked me into it.

Fletcher Henderson wasn't sure it would be dignified enough for him, a college student studying chemistry, to be the piano player for a girl who sang blues in a cellar. Remember those class distinctions in Harlem, which had its Park Avenue crowd, a middle class, and its Tenth Avenue. That was me, then, low-down Tenth Avenue.

Before he would go out Fletcher had his whole family come up from Georgia to look me over and see if it would be all right. They not only put their stamp of approval on me but they all fell in love with me at first sight. For advance man, Black Swan hired Lester A. Walton of the New York *World*. He was the first Negro reporter ever hired by a great white daily paper. Years later he became United States Minister to Liberia. . . .

I was learning a lot in Harlem about music and the men up there who played it best. All the licks you hear, now as then, originated with musicians like James P. Johnson. And I mean *all* of the hot licks that ever came out of Fats Waller and the rest of the hot piano boys. They are just faithful followers and protégés of that great man, Jimmy Johnson.

Men like him, Willie (The Lion) Smith, and Charlie Johnson could make you sing until your tonsils fell out. Because you wanted to sing. They stirred you into joy and wild ecstasy. They could make you cry. And you'd do anything and work until you dropped for such musicians.

The master of them all, though, was Lucky Roberts. Everybody calls him Pop, but reverently. He now runs a restaurant up on the hill in Harlem. I don't call it Sugar Hill. I don't use that kind of language. Any night you can go up to Pop Roberts' place and hear operatic arias sung magnificently by the great singers who are waiters and waitresses there.

Fine singers! People I know, people I admire, people I've worked with! But they are Negroes and have to wait on tables because they can't get any work in show business. They are colored. Period.

We had a jolly bunch of musicians in Fletcher Henderson's Jazz Masters. The trumpets were Joe Smith and Gus Aiken. Gus's brother Buddy and Lorenzo Brashear were the trombones, and a boy named Raymond Green was at the drums. Our clarinet was Garvin Bushell, who now has an eating place up in Harlem. He also plays the oboe in the New York Civic Opera Company, being the only Negro musician in that group.

We were stranded everywere on that trip, through we had a lot of fun. The boys all adopted me as their sister, but when they played badly I told them they sounded like Jenkins' Band. This was the famous kid band sent out by a Charleston orphanage. That band has developed some first-rate musicians, but as kids they didn't toot any dream symphonies. . . .

I kept having arguments with Fletcher Henderson about the way he was playing my accompaniments. Fletcher, though a fine arranger and a brilliant band leader, leans more to the classical side. On that tour Fletcher wouldn't give me what I call "the damn-it-to-hell bass," that chump-chump stuff like real jazz needs.

All 'during the tour I kept nagging at him. I said he *couldn't* play as I wanted him to. When we reached Chicago I got some piano rolls that Jimmy Johnson had made and pounded out each passage to Henderson. To prove to me he could do it, Fletch began to practice. He got so perfect, listening to James P. Johnson play on the player piano, that he could press down the keys as the roll played, never missing a note. Naturally, he began to be identified with that kind of music, which isn't his kind at all. . . .

I can't read music, never have. But I have almost absolute pitch. My music is all queer little things that come into my head. I feel these little trills and things deep inside of me, and I sing them that way. All queer little things that I hum. . . .

There was so much music day and night on that tour with the Jazz Masters that even Bubbles, my Pekinese dog, developed a sensitive ear for it. The last song on my program was "Down Home Blues." On hearing me finish that number Bubbles would know it was time for me to come off. He'd trot out of the dressing room and onto the stage, pawing at my dress to be picked up. . . .

I was booked into the Monogram in Chicago and another theater out there. I talked Pearl [1] into playing those dates with me. I also had in my act James O'Brien, a colored violinist whose playing could make your heart dance—or break.

I have already mentioned the Monogram. That was the theater where you had to dress way downstairs with the stoker and come up to the stage climbing slave-ship stairs. While working there I took sick from the migraine headaches I'd had off and on for years. The air was very bad down there where the stoker was.

Somebody told me that Earl Dancer was in town and one night he came to see me. He had a dream-crammed look in his eye.

"Remember us talking together a long while ago in Harlem, Ethel?" he asked. "Remember me telling you then that you oughta go on the white time?"

"Yes."

"Well, why don't you let me go now and see about getting you an audition in a white theater?"

"No white audience would understand my blues. I'd be a complete flop."

I'd sung the blues at those midnight performances given for whites—but that had been in the South, where the white people are hep to everything about the Negro, his blues, moods, and humor, particularly his humor. But, as I pointed out to Earl, that wasn't so with Northern whites.

This, by the way, is no longer true, since Northern whites have been educated to the blues. Today you can sing your blues to them just as to a Negro audience and go the full limit. I argued that I never exaggerated or overemphasized my characterizations. I said that most of the Negroes who were getting by on the white time were like caricatures of human beings and portrayed buffoons who were lazy and shiftless beyond belief.

1. Pearl Wright was a pianist, and Ethel Waters' accompanist. [*Editor*]

"And I ain't changing my style for nothing or nobody," I told him.

But Earl Dancer just wouldn't shut up. He kept picking at me, kept insisting that I would be a sensation on the big time.

"Have you ever seen Fanny Brice work?" he asked.

"No."

Then he told me how Irene Bordoni had brought the song, "My Man," to the United States and sung it in French. Brice did it in English, he went on, in the *Ziegfeld Follies*. "She did it almost as a satire, and the people who heard it called it the blues," he said. "That's only because they've never heard the real blues, the kind you sing, Ethel."

Well, the yapping went on, with me insisting white people would be puzzled by my blues, and also bored to death.

Earl argued, "You don't have to sing as you do for colored people, verse after verse after verse of the blues. You can break it up: sing some blues, then talk the story in the song, and end up with more blues. They'll love it. Why should an artist like you have to dress down in a dirty old coal cellar, Ethel? They'll never treat you like that on the Keith time. You won't get migraine headaches because the air is poisoned. You gotta give yourself a break."

When I consented to do a break-in date on the big time it was only to shut him up. I wanted to get rid of Earl's big talk and dreams. I was sure I'd flop even after he'd arranged for the tryout at, I think, the Kedzie Theatre there in Chicago.

With malice and impatience I looked forward to the joy of cussing him out for leading me into the humiliation of flopping in a white theater.

It was the first time I'd worked on the stage of a big-time vaudeville theater. We were getting only forty dollars for the three-day engagement, but any act was willing to take a nominal fee on a so-called break-in date, the whole object being to showcase your routine to the bookers.

Earl went on and did the "Where is that partner of mine?" patter. Then I appeared in my gingham apron and funny hat and sang "Georgia Blues." I did other songs, and Earl did his specialty number. There was applause when we finished, and I went upstairs to our dressing room.

Earl took one look at my unhappy face and asked, "What's wrong, Ethel? What's the matter?"

"What's the matter?" I cried. "You know we took the flop of our lives just now. Those people out front applauded us only because they wanted to be polite. Nobody stomped as they always do in colored theaters when I finish my act. Nobody screamed or jumped up and down. Nobody howled with joy. On account of you I have the first and worst flop of my whole life."

Earl said the people out front had been crazy about our act, but I told him I didn't want any more of his jive. I was sure I had failed in front of my first Northern white audience.

I was on the verge of tears. I was still bawling out Earl Dancer when the manager came back to see us. He was smiling with excitement and elation.

"We'll keep you on for a whole week," he said, "and pay you $350 for your act."

I didn't know what to say. I was even more speechless when the reviews came out. One critic called me "the ebony Nora Bayes." There was no mistaking what that meant. Nora Bayes was one of the most popular of the white vaudeville singers. She had elegance, dignity, class. She was the great lady of the two-a-day, so I liked being called "the ebony Nora Bayes."

Dozens of people in show business say they discovered me. This always irritates me. Edmond's piano player, Lou Henley, was the first one to get me to sing different types of songs. Earl Dancer pushed me into the white time.

Talent can be developed, but no one in show business discovers it. Only the public can do that. It was the public who discovered me every step of the way—from Jack's Rathskeller, through my season with the Hill Sisters, at Barney Gordon's and Edmond's, to Broadway and Hollywood. . . .

In 1924, while I was doing good for myself in vaudeville from coast to coast, Florence Mills had become the sensation of New York. She had done such big business at Sam Salvin's Plantation Club at Broadway and Fiftieth Street that the management wanted to keep open all summer.

But Florence insisted on touring, and Mr. Salvin started to look for a colored name to replace her. Earl Dancer, always a great one for getting about and talking to people, heard they'd tried out several girls, including Katherine Yarber [Caterina Jarboro], a choir singer who'd been in *Shuffle Along*.

"They're still auditioning," he told me. "Why don't you go down there?"

I shook my head. I felt that Broadway and all downtown belonged to Florence Mills. I also thought our singing styles were too similar for me to follow her at the Plantation. But Earl, who never got tired of nagging me, went on and on about it.

"It won't hurt you none, Ethel, just to go down there and talk to those people."

In the end I did go down, but only to shut him up. Florence Mills was vivacious, a cutie, and a whirlwind when it came to selling a song and dance. But she had a small voice. They had been using a choir around her to get volume, and then Florence would come in and sing the punch line. However, she was a public idol, and I didn't think that following her at the Plantation was going to be easy. But I went there for the tryout, and in those days I was as trim and shapely as Florence or anyone else.

Mr. Salvin, along with Harry Akst and Joe Young, who were writing the songs for that floor show, was there for my audition. They asked me to do a couple of my own numbers, and I started off with "Georgia Blues." I could see that Sam Salvin was tremendously impressed. After I finished my own songs Harry Akst and Joe Young asked if I'd try a new one they'd written. And they sang it themselves for me, doing it fast and corny.

"Is that the way you want me to sing it?" I asked.

Akst and Young looked at each other.

"Why not sing it your own way?" they said. "Take it home. Work it over, kid, then come back and let us hear your version."

Now I've always had a strict rule about this. I'll do any new number the way I'm asked to sing it. But once you say, "Do it your own way, kid," I sing it my way and won't try any other style that is second-guessed on me.

So that day I took that song home and worked on it with Pearl. "This is a nice little number, Pearl," I said.

That nice little number was "Dinah."

After I sang it in my style for Mr. Salvin and the boys who wrote it, I won the wooden apple: the uphill job of following Florence Mills at the Plantation—and this through the hot weather when most sane New Yorkers dash off to the beaches and mountains to get much-needed air-conditioning.

It was a fine night-club show, though, that Sam Salvin was putting together that summer of 1924 at the Plantation. He'd hired lots of first-rate creative talent. Leonard Harper and Bill Seabury did the staging, and Bill Vodery contributed his *Swing Mikado*, the original jazzed-up version of the Gilbert and Sullivan operetta.

Now this was fifteen years before Michael Todd got the critics' kudos and love and kisses for his *Hot Mikado* and the same idea. Mike Todd, who was hailed in 1939 as Broadway's brilliant boy-wonder producer for bringing in that show, must have been a tiny street gamin who was playing with his toy balloons back in 1924.

"Dinah," with your girl Ethel singing it in her own way, made history from Tin Pan Alley to Tokyo because it was the first international song hit ever to come out of an American night club. . . .

At the Plantation there were three of us in the same dressing room—Josephine Baker, Bessie Allison, who later married the manager of the Savoy Ballroom in Harlem, and me.

Josephine was in the chorus, but she stepped out of the line to do her specialty once during each show. Josephine was a mugger with a great comic sense, and she had a beautiful form. She could dance and she could clown joy into you. She could also play the trombone.

I'd met her while touring the South. She was like an orphan then and was with one of those Negro kid gypsy bands they have down there.

I worked through all that hot summer at the Plantation, but in late August or early September they closed me out because Florence was coming back. And Florence Mills came in on my smoke.

But, after all, it was her show and it had been built around her. So I had no beef. The world loves a winner, but you have to be a hell of a good loser, too, in show business. . . .

I had been away from the U.S.A. for eight long months. But not a single theater had closed up. No maddened mobs had threatened to lynch J. J. and Lee Shubert for keeping me out of sight and hearing distance.

So I lost no time getting vaudeville dates and making new records. Then Lew Leslie, who had never wanted me before, asked Goldie and Gumm if they could get me for his new edition of *Blackbirds*. Leslie had split up with Bill Robinson, his box-office ace in the hole, and Bojangles now had his own show, *Brown Buddies*. Adelaide Hall, Leslie's own star, was in Europe.

Leslie wanted me as his big name, and he had some good acts lined up: Flourney Miller [*sic*], formerly of Miller and Lyles; Buck and Bubbles, Jazzlips Richardson, Mantan Moreland, and Eubie Blake's Orchestra.

That show started off by almost being stranded in rehearsal. Leslie was splitting up quarters each day among the cast so they wouldn't have to walk home to Harlem.

Blackbirds opened at a Forty-second Street theater right next to the flea circus. Our show was a flop, and the fleas outdrew us at every performance. The depression came in and made our business worse. But it didn't dent the take of the flea circus at all. It reminded me of the old vaudeville joke about the flea circus that became so prosperous each flea was given his own private dog.

My best number in that show was "You're Lucky to Me," a take-off on Rudy Vallee, then the crooner who was getting sighs from all young girls who didn't have any fellows, also many who had fellows but weren't satisfied. I had recorded that song with "Memories of You" on the other side.

Rudy, who always was a darling, loved that take-off on him and he had me as guest star on his radio program. Another girl on that broadcast was Alice Faye. She had won a contest in Atlantic City and was going to Hollywood for her first screen tests. And in Hollywood she got starred and, eventually, Phil Harris.

The *Blackbirds* shuffled off to Philadelphia, where business was bad, and then to Newark, where the troupe was stranded. The back of my car almost broke down under the weight of all the entertainers I drove back to Harlem with me.

The depression was in full swing, but Lew Leslie told me he wanted to build a show around me—with a choir and a stage band. And he was going to call it *Rhapsody in Black.* . . .

Rhapsody in Black ran through the grimmest days of the depression, usually dragging in from $22,000 to $24,000. But no week was bad for me. Even when the show pulled a comparatively miserable $17,000, I made $2,400—my $700 plus $1,700, the ten per cent peeled off the top of the horrified Lew Leslie's bank roll.

When *Rhapsody in Black* finished its long, profitable run Leslie condensed the show for the big time and movie-presentation houses.

31. Imamu Amiri Baraka
(LeRoi Jones)

⇶ Author Imamu Amiri Baraka [LeRoi Jones] (b. 1934) was graduated from Howard University in 1954 and soon earned a reputation as one of the most articulate black voices of the time. Among the honors he has received are Whitney and Guggenheim fellowships and prizes for two of his stage works, *Dutchman* (1964) and *The Slave* (1966). His list of books includes two surveys of Negro music—*Blues People* (1963) and *Black Music* (1967)—a miscellaneous collection of newspaper and magazine articles, critical reviews, and liner notes for recordings. The following essay is from the latter book. ⇷

The Jazz Avant-Garde [1961] †

There is definitely an avant-garde in jazz today. A burgeoning group of young men who are beginning to utilize not only the most important ideas in "formal" contemporary music, but more important, young musicians who have started to utilize the most important ideas contained in that startling music called bebop. (Of course I realize that to some of my learned colleagues almost anything that came after 1940 is bebop, but that's not exactly what I meant.) And I think this last idea, the use of bop, is the most significant aspect of the particular avant-garde I'm referring to, since almost any so-called modern musicians can tell you all about Stravinsky, Schoenberg, Bartók, etc., or at least they think they can. I say *particular* avant-garde since I realize that there is also another so-called "new music," called by some of my more serious colleagues, *Third Stream*, which seeks to invest jazz with as much "classical" music as blatantly as possible. But for jazzmen now to have come to the beautiful and logical conclusion that bebop was perhaps the most legitimately

† Text: *Black Music* (New York, 1967), pp. 69–79. Used by permission of author.

complex, emotionally rich music to come out of this country, is, for me, a brilliant beginning for a "new" music.

Bebop is roots, now, just as much as blues is. "Classical" music is not. But "classical" music, and I mean now contemporary Euro-American "art" music, might seem to the black man isolated, trying to exist within white culture (arty or whatever), like it should be "milked" for as many *definitions* as possible, i.e., *solutions* to engineering problems the contemporary jazz musician's life is sure to raise. I mean, more simply, Ornette Coleman has had to live with the attitudes responsible for Anton Webern's music whether he knows that music or not. They were handed to him along with the whole history of formal Western music, and the musics that have come to characterize the Negro in the United States came to exist as they do today only through the acculturation of this entire history. And actually knowing that history, and trying to relate to it culturally, or those formal Euro-American musics, only adds to the *indoctrination*. But jazz and blues *are* Western musics; products of an Afro-American culture. But the definitions must be black no matter the geography for the highest meaning to black men. And in this sense European anything is irrelevant.

We are, all of us, *moderns*, whether we like it or not. Trumpet player Ruby Braff is *responsible*, finally, to the same ideas and attitudes that have shaped our world as Ornette Coleman. (Ideas are things that must drench everyone, whether directly or obliquely). The same history has elapsed in the world for both of them, and what has gone before has settled on both of them just as surely as if they were the same man. For Ornette Coleman, as it was for Charlie Parker *or* James Joyce, the relationship between their actual lives and their work seems direct. For Braff or for Charlie Parker and Bud Powell imitators or Senator Goldwater, the relationship, the meaning, of all the ideas that history has stacked so wearily in front of them, and some utilization in their own lives, is less direct. But if an atomic bomb is dropped on Manhattan, moldy figs will die as well as modernists, and just because some cornet player looks out his window and says, "what's going on" does not mean that he will not be in on things. He goes, too. (I am trying to explain "avant-garde." Men for whom history exists to be *utilized* in their lives, their art, to make something for themselves and not as an overpowering reminder that people and their ideas did live before us.) "How to play exactly what I feel," is what one of these musicians told me. How? (Which is a *technical* consideration.)

Before I go further, I want to explain *technical* so as not to be confused with people who think that Thelonius Monk is "a fine pianist, but limited technically." But by *technical*, I mean more specifically being able to use what important ideas are contained in the residue of history or in the now-swell of living. For instance, to be able to doubletime Liszt piano pieces might help one to become a musician, but it will not make a man aware of the fact that Monk was a greater composer than Liszt. And it is the consciousness, on whatever level, of facts, ideas, etc., like this that are *the* most important part of technique. Knowing how to play an instrument is the barest super-ficiality if one is thinking of becoming a musician. It is the ideas that one utilizes *instinctively* that determine the degree of profundity any artist reaches. To know, in some way, that it is better to pay attention to Duke Ellington than to Aaron Copland is part of it. (And it is exactly because someone like Oscar Peterson has instinctive profundity that technique *is* glibness. That he can play the piano rather handily just makes him easier to identify. There is no serious instinct working at all.)

To my mind, *technique* is inseparable from what is finally played as content. A *bad* solo, no matter how "well" it is played is still *bad*.

APHORISMS: 'Form can never be more than an extension of content." (Robert Creely) "Form is determined by the nature of matter. . . . Rightly viewed, order is nothing objective; it exists only relatively to the mind." (Psalidas) "No one who can finally be said to be a "mediocre' musician can be said to possess any *technique*." (Jones)

"Formal" music, for the jazz musician, should be *ideas*. Ideas that can make it easier for this modern jazz player to get at his roots. And as I have said, the strongest of these roots are blues and what was called bebop. They sit autonomous. Blues and bebop are *musics*. They are understandable, emotionally, as they sit: without the barest discussion of their origins. And the reason I think for this is that they *are* origins, themselves. Blues is a beginning. Bebop, a beginning. They define other varieties of music that come after them. If a man had not heard blues, there is no reason to assume that he would be even slightly interested in, say, Joe Oliver (except perhaps as a curio or from some obscure social conviction). Cannonball Adderley is *only* interesting because of bebop. And not because he plays bebop, but because he will occasionally repeat an idea that bop once represented as profound. An idea that we love, no matter what the subsequent disfigurement.

The *roots*, blues and bop, are emotion. The *technique*, the ideas, the way of handling the emotion. And this does not leave out the consideration that certainly there is pure intellect that can come out of the emotional experience and the rawest emotions that can proceed from the ideal apprehension of any hypothesis. The point is that such displacement must exist as instinct.

To go further towards a general delineation of the musicians I will cite later as part of a growing jazz avant-garde, I think first I should furnish at least two more definitions, or distinctions.

Using, or implementing an idea or concept is not necessarily imitation, and, of course, the converse is true; imitation is not necessarily use. I will say first that use is proper, as well as *basic*. Use means that some idea or system is employed, but in order to reach or understand quite separate and/or dissimilar systems. Imitation means simply reproduction (of a concept), for its own sake. Someone who sings exactly like Billie Holiday or someone who plays exactly like Charlie Parker (or as close as they can manage) *produces* nothing. Essentially, there is nothing added to the universe. It is as if these performers stood on a stage and did nothing at all. Ornette Coleman uses Parker only as a hypothesis; his (Coleman's) conclusions are quite separate and unique. Sonny Rollins has certainly listened quite a bit to Gene Ammons, but Rollins' conclusions are insistently his own, and are certainly more profound than Ammons'. A man who rides the IND [a subway line] to work doesn't necessarily have to think he's a subway. (And a man who thinks he's a subway is usually just crazy. It will not help him to get to work either.)

REEDS: *Ornette Coleman, Eric Dolphy*, Wayne Shorter, Oliver Nelson, Archie Shepp.
BRASS: *Don Cherry, Freddie Hubbard.*
PERCUSSION: *Billy Higgins, Ed Blackwell*, Dennis Charles (drums); Earl Griffith (vibraharp).
BASS: *Wilbur Ware, Charlie Haden*, Scott LaFaro, Buell Neidlinger, others.
PIANO: *Cecil Taylor.*
COMPOSITION: *Ornette Coleman, Eric Dolphy, Wayne Shorter*, Cecil Taylor.

These are most of the people this essay intends to hamper with the *nom de guerre* avant-garde. (There are a few others like Ken McIntyre whom I think, from the reports I've received, also belong in the group, but I've not yet had a chance to listen.) The names in italics are intended to serve as further delineation as far as the quality and quantity of these players' innovations. Hence, Ornette Coleman sits by himself in reeds, Dolphy in his groove and Shorter, Nelson and Shepp in theirs. (There are more bass players than anything else simply because the chief innovator on that instrument, Wilbur Ware, has been around longer and more people have had a chance to pick up.)

But actually, this naming of names is not meant as a strict categorizing of "styles." Each of these men has his *own* way of playing, but as a group they represent, at least to me, a definite line of departure.

Melodically and rhythmically each of these players use bebop extensively. Coleman's "Ramblin'" possesses a melodic line the spatial tensions of which seem firmly rooted in 1940's Gillespie-Parker composition and extemporization. The very jaggedness and abruptness of the melodic fabric itself suggest the boppers' seemingly endless need for deliberate and agitated rhythmical contrast, most of the melodies being almost extensions of the dominating rhythmical patterns. Whistle "Ramblin'," then any early Monk, e.g., "Four in One" or "Humph" or Bird's [1] "Cheryl" or "Confirmation," and the basic *physical* similarities of melodic lines should be immediately apparent. There seems to be an endless changing of direction; stops and starts; variations of impetus; a "jaggedness" that reaches out of the rhythmic bases of the music. (It seems to me that only Jackie McLean of the post-bop "traditionalists" has as much linear contrast and rhythmic modulation in his compositions and playing as the boppers, e.g., "Dr. Jackle," "Condition Blue," etc.) In fact, in bop and avant-garde compositions it seems as if the rhythmic portion of the music is inserted directly into the melodic portion. The melody of *Ramblin'* is almost a rhythmic pattern itself. It accents are almost identical to the rhythmic underpinnings of the music. The same was true in bop. The very name bebop comes from an onomatopoetic attempt to reproduce the new rhythms that had engendered this music, hence; *bebop*, and with that the rebop. (While it is true that "scat" singing came into use in the early days of jazz, "bopping," the kind of scat singing (scatting) that became popular during the 40's was more intent on reproducing rhythmic effects and as such making a melody out of them, e.g., *OoShubeeDobee Oo Oo* or *OoBopsh'bam-a-keukumop*, etc. But even in the incunabula of jazz and blues, something like the chants and field hollers were little more than highly rhythmical lyrics.)

One result of this "insertion" of rhythm into the melodic fabric of bop as well as the music of the avant-garde is the subsequent freedom allowed to instruments that are normally supposed to carry the entire rhythmic impetus of the music. Drum and bass lines are literally "sprung" . . . away from the simple, cloying 4/4 that

1. I.e. Charlie Parker's. [*Editor*]

characterized the musics that came immediately before and after bop. And while it is true that the post-boppers took their impetus from bop, I think the development of the *cool school* served to obscure the really valuable legacies of bop. Rhythmic diversity and freedom were the really valuable legacies. The cool tended to regularize the rhythms and make the melodic line smoother, less "jagged," relying more on "formal" variation of the line in the strict theme and variation sense. More and more emphasis was put on "charts" and written parts. Formal European music began to be canonized not only as a means but as some kind of *model*. The insistence of Brubeck, Shorty Rogers, Mulligan, John Lewis, that they could write fugues and rondoes or even improvise them was one instance. The almost legitimate harmonies that were used in cool or West Coast jazz reminded one of the part singing tradition of Europe. And groups like Shorty Rogers' Giants made a music that sounded like it came out of an organ grinder, the variations and improvisations as regular and static as a piano roll.

The "hard boppers" sought to revitalize jazz, but they did not go far enough. Somehow, they had lost sight of the important items to be gotten from bop and substituted largeness of timbre and the recent insistence on quasi-gospel influences for actual rhythmic diversity. The usual rhythms of the post-cool hard bopper of the 50's are amazingly static and smooth compared to the jazz of the 40's and the 60's. The rhythmic freedom of the 40's is lost in the 50's only to be rediscovered in the 60's. Because rhythm and melody complement each other so closely in the "new" music, both bass player and drummer also can play "melodically." They need no longer to be strictly concerned with thumping along, merely carrying the beat. The melody itself contains enough rhythmic accent to propel and stabilize the horizontal movement of the music, giving both direction and impetus. The rhythm instruments can then serve to elaborate on the melody itself. Wilbur Ware's playing is a perfect example of this. And so it is that drummers like Blackwell, Higgins and Charles can roam around the melody, giving accent here, inferring actual melody elsewhere. Elvin Jones, in his recent work with John Coltrane, also shows that he understands the difference between playing melody and "elegant" elaboration around a static rhythm.

So if the heavily accented melody springs the rhythm section, it also gives the other soloists more room to swing. The strict 4/4 is missing, and the horn men can even improvise on the melodic efforts of the rhythm section. This is one reason why in a group like Coleman's it seems as if they have gone back to the concept of collective improvisations. No one's role in the group is as *fixed* as it was in the "part singers" of the 50's. Everyone has a chance to play melody or rhythm. Cecil Taylor's left hand is used as much as a purely rhythmic insistence as it is for the melodic-harmonic placement of chords. The left hand constantly varies the rhythms his music is hinged on. Both Taylor and Coleman constantly utilize melodic variations based on rhythmic figures. Bebop proved that so called "changes," i.e., the repeated occurrence of certain chords basic to the melodic and harmonic structure of a tune, are almost arbitrary. That is, that they need not be *stated*, and that since certain chords infer certain improvisatory uses of them, why not improvise on what the chords infer rather than playing the inference itself.

The greater part of the avant-garde's contribution is melodic and rhythmic; only a few have made any notable moves harmonically, though Coleman and Dolphy tend to utilize certain ideas that are also in use in contemporary "European" music, notable, timbre as a harmonic principle. That is, where the actual sound of the horn, regardless of the note, contributes *unmeasured* harmonic diversity. (Also check out the hard blues singer, as a *first*. John Coltrane has done some marvelous work in harmonics as well.) Nelson, Shepp and Shorter also, to a lesser degree, utilize this concept, and even stranger, Shorter and Nelson have learned to utilize the so called "honking" sounds of the rhythm and blues bands to great effect. Nothing was wrong with honking in the first place, except that most of the R&B people who honked did little else.

It is also important that all of the reed players I have named are intrigued by the sound of the human voice. And it is my idea that jazz cannnot be removed too far from the voice, since the whole concept of Afro-American music is hinged on vocal references. Earlier, I mentioned my belief that bebop and blues are almost autonomous musics. To add some weight, or at least provide a measure of clarification, I'd add that not only are blues and bebop the two facets of Afro-American music that utilize the rhythmic potentials of the music most directly, but also they are the two musics in which the vocal traditions of African music are most apparent. Purely instrumental blues is still the closest western instruments can come to sounding like the human voice, and the horns of Charlie Parker, Sonny Rollins, John Coltrane and most of the reed players of the new avant-garde maintain this tradition as well. The timbres of these horns suggest the human voice much more than the "legitimate," i.e., white, instrumental sound of swing or the staid, relatively cool timbres that were in evidence post-bop.

I mention these general aspects of what I have termed the avant-

garde, i.e., their rhythmic and melodic concepts and the use of tim-
bral effects to evoke the vocal beginnings of jazz, but only to show
a line of demarcation. There are certainly a great many "new" features individual players possess that are not common to the group as
a whole, individual discoveries and/or idiosyncracies that give each
player his easily identifiable style. To name a few: the unusual harmonies that Wayne Shorter employs in his writing and his integra-
tion of Rollins' use of space and John Coltrane's disdain for it;
(Shorter's main trouble, it now seems, is The Jazz Messengers.)
Vibist Earl Griffith's lovely discovery that one can play the vibes
like Lester Young, instead of continuing to imitate Milt Jackson's
appropriation of Coleman Hawkins; Griffith's light, gauzy tone and
behind-the-beat placement of his line all point to Pres [2] and a fresh
approach to vibes. Charlie Haden's guitar player approach to the
bass, even going as far, sometimes, as *strumming* the big instrument;
Don Cherry's fantastic melodic sense (I think that Cherry is the
only *real* innovator on his instrument). Archie Shepp's refusal to
admit most of the time that there is a melody or Oliver Nelson's use
of R&B and so called "Mickey Mouse" timbres to beautiful effect.
All these are separate facets of this new music, an amassing of
talent and ideas that indicate a fresh road for jazz.

The first music Negroes made in this country had to be African;
its subsequent transmutation into what we know as blues and the
parallel development of jazz demonstrated the amazing flexibility of
the basic character of the music. But to move as far away from the
parent music as popular swing, or so-called West Coast jazz, or even
into the artificially exciting, comparatively staid regular rhythms of
hard-bop traditionalism demonstrates how the African elements of the
music can be rendered almost to neutrality. Blues was the initial
Afro-American music, and bebop the reemphasis of the non-western
tradition. And if the latter saved us from the vapid wastes of swing
singlehandedly, the new avant-garde (and John Coltrane) are saving
us from the comparatively vapid 50's. And they both utilized the
same general methods: getting the music back to its initial rhythmic
impetuses and away from the attempts at rhythmic regularity and
melodic predictability that the 30's and the 50's had laid on it.

2. I.e. Lester Young. [*Editor*]

32. MAHALIA JACKSON

>>> Gospel singer Mahalia Jackson (b. 1911), a native of New Orleans, won international recognition for her swinging, blues-style gospel hymns. Born into the same musical environment that produced such jazz figures as King Oliver, Jelly Roll Morton, and Louis Armstrong, Jackson absorbed the sounds of Negro music—particularly church music and the blues—from earliest childhood. Black jazzmen of New Orleans began to migrate to Chicago after World War I and produced there the music that made the period "a golden age of jazz." Mahalia Jackson, too, became a part of the migratory movement and in Chicago began the climb that took her to stardom in the field of gospel music. <<<

From *Movin' on Up* [1968] †

I say this out of my heart—a song must do something for me as well as for the people that hear it. I can't sing a song that doesn't have a message. If it doesn't have the strength it can't lift you. I just can't seem to get the sense of it.

It's been that way ever since I started singing and I guess I was singing almost as soon as I was walking and talking. I always had a big voice, even as a child, and I was raised with music all around me.

New Orleans was full of music when I was born and all the time I was growing up there. It was the time when they had all the brass bands. There was still music on the showboats on the Mississippi River and there were all the cabarets and cafes where musicians like Jelly Roll Morton and King Oliver were playing Ragtime music and jazz and the blues were being played all over.

Everybody was buying phonographs—the kind you wound up on

† Text: The original edition (New York, 1966), pp. 29–33, 56–57, 62–63, 180–85, 212. From the book *Movin' on Up*, by Mahalia Jackson with Evan McLeod Wylie. Copyright © 1966 by Mahalia Jackson and Evan M. Wylie. Published by Hawthorn Books, 70 Fifth Avenue, N.Y.

the side by hand—just the way people have television sets today—and everybody had records of all the Negro blues singers—Bessie Smith . . . Ma Rainey . . . Mamie Smith . . . all the rest.

The famous white singers like Caruso—you might hear them when you went by a white folks' house, but in a colored house you heard blues. You couldn't help but hear blues—all through the thin partitions of the houses—through the open windows—up and down the street in the colored neighborhoods—everybody played it real loud.

I saw lots of the famous New Orleans brass bands when I was growing up. They advertised the fish fries and the house-rent parties and played for the secret order lodge dances and funerals. When there was going to be a big fish fry or lodge dance they would fill a wagon up with a load of hay or they'd put some chairs in it. The brass band—some of them were five pieces—would climb up in that wagon and they would drive around town, stopping and playing at every street corner to drum up a crowd.

Everybody who possibly could would go that night to the fry or the lodge party. They would put sawdust down in the yard and string up lots of those pretty-colored Japanese lanterns and have eats on the inside and dancing on the outside. Those parties were the only social diversions Negroes had except for the church. No decent Negro —no churchgoing Negro, at least—would be caught dead down in Storyville where all the saloons and sportin' houses used to be.

They had the brass bands for the funerals—when a very popular man or a secret lodge man or a sportin' man died. They never had a band behind a minister or an unimportant man.

But people today are mixed up about the brass bands. They didn't play jazz at the funerals. The band would play as solemn as a choir or a big pipe organ—right out in front of the church where the funeral service was being held. Then they would march behind the hearse—all the way to the cemetery. They didn't play jazz on the way either—that's the bunk. After the family had left and the man was buried, then on the way back they would jazz it up. The musicians had been paid so they would play coming back from the cemetery, full of spirit—blow it out free of charge—and the folks along the way would have a good time. That's the way a funeral band really was.

I liked it and approved it. The Scripture says: "Rejoice at the outgoing." So why not have bands for funerals? . . .

Aunt Duke stood for so little play at home that I used to spend all my spare time at the Baptist church. If you helped scrub it out, they might let you ring the bell for the early-morning service. On Saturday nights they showed silent movies in the church community hall. There were services there every evening and in those days people thought as much of the evening prayer service as they did of the Sunday service so there was always lots going on for children to watch. Sinners who sat in the back would come forward to be prayed over by the preacher and be saved. On Baptism Sundays the women, all dressed in white, would lead the way out the door and across the street to the levee singing "Let's Go Down to the River Jordan," and the preacher would hold the services right down in the Missis- sippi, blessing the water and baptizing the congregation.

In those days, once you were baptized, you were looked after properly by the church. You were under the eye of the missionaries of the church, who kept track of whether you attended church and prayer meeting and led a Christian life. The churches of today have gotten away from this. They accept you on your word that you believe in the Lord and they don't see you again until the next Sun- day. Today they are not doing the job they should to help people keep the faith. There's bad in all of us and most of us can't save ourselves without help.

I loved best to sing in the congregation of our church—the Mount Moriah Baptist Church. All around me I could hear the foot-tapping and hand-clapping. That gave me bounce. I liked it much better than being up in the choir singing the anthem. I liked to sing the songs which testify to the glory of the Lord—those anthems are too dead and cold for me. As David said in the Bible—"Make a joyous noise unto the Lord!"—that's me.

I know now that a great influence in my life was the Sanctified or Holiness Churches we had in the South. I was always a Baptist, but there was a Sanctified Church right next door to our house in New Orleans.

Those people had no choir and no organ. They used the drum, the cymbal, the tambourine, and the steel triangle. Everybody in there sang and they clapped and stomped their feet and sang with their whole bodies. They had a beat, a powerful beat, a rhythm we held on to from slavery days, and their music was so strong and ex- pressive it used to bring the tears to my eyes.

I believe the blues and jazz and even the rock and roll stuff got their beat from the Sanctified Church. We Baptists sang sweet, and we had the long and short meter on beautiful songs like "Amazing Grace, How Sweet It Sounds," but when those Holiness people tore into "I'm So Glad Jesus Lifted Me Up!" they came out with real jubilation.

First you've got to get the rhythm until, through the music, you have the freedom to interpret it. Perhaps that's why white folks just never do clap in time with my music the right way. I tell them, "Honey, I know you're enjoying yourself but please don't clap along with me." . . .

Many of the young colored people lost their way during Depression times in Chicago. The times were so hard that it broke their spirits. And although I didn't realize it at the time, I know now that the Lord must have had his arms around me in those days and he protected me. God moves in mysterious ways—and in a mysterious way, the Depression became responsible for my whole career in gospel singing.

It came about because at the Greater Salem Baptist Church the Johnson boys had formed a little singing and entertainment group. There were the three brothers, Prince, Robert and Wilbur, a girl named Louise Barry, and myself.

Robert Johnson was only eighteen years old, but he was a spirited young man. He was like Sammy Davis, Jr.—just full of pep and energy all the time. He loved to sing and act. He was good at writing skits and directing them, and he had us putting on little plays for the church socials. One was called *Hellbound*; another was *From Earth to Glory* and another was *The Fatal Wedding*. He would play the husband and I would play the wife and the others would play old folks and young folks. We cut up and had wonderful times and everybody enjoyed watching us.

After a while we also formed a little singing group and Prince Johnson worked out our arrangements on the piano. He had his own style of playing and it seemed to suit us just right. We called ourselves the Johnson Gospel Singers. With Prince at the piano, we had a bounce that made us popular from the start.

We improved on the music and strayed from the score and gave our own way to each song. Looking back, I'd say that Prince really was the first gospel piano player in Chicago and we were really the first Negro gospel group in the city.[1]

At first we only sang for our church people, but then we began to get asked around. People who heard about us would come and invite us to sing at their church and then pass us along to another church in another part of the South Side.

The reason was that all over the South Side churches were struggling desperately to keep their doors open. All during the boom days of the twenties, colored people had been buying white people's churches and synagogues. They bought them with big mortgages, but

---

1. Actually, Thomas A. Dorsey was the first active gospel musician (pianist-composer and song leader) in Chicago. [*Editor*]

in those good times there was plenty of money to meet the notes. The Depression hadn't stopped the flow of money and the congregations couldn't meet their mortgages and pay for the coal to heat their churches and the electricity to light them. They passed the plate over and over again at the services, but people had so little that the churches began to try to raise a little bit of extra money with suppers and socials. . . .

I had met Professor [Thomas] A. Dorsey, the great writer of gospel songs—he is to gospel music what W. C. Handy is to the blues—and we used to travel together to the same church meetings and conventions.

A lot of folks don't know that gospel songs have not been handed down like spirituals. Most gospel songs have been composed and written by Negro musicians like Professor Dorsey.

Before he got saved by the Lord and went into the church, Professor Dorsey was a piano player for Ma Rainey, one of the first of the blues singers. His nickname in those days was "Georgia Tom" and everybody who went to the tent shows used to know him for the rocking, syncopated beat he had on his piano.

When he began to write gospel music he still had a happy beat in his songs. They're sung by thousands of people like myself who believe religion is a joy.

There are still some Negro churches that don't have gospel singers or choirs and only sing the old hymns and anthems, but among Baptists and the Methodists and the Sanctified church people you will always hear gospel music.

Professor Dorsey would have copies of his wonderful songs like "Precious Lord" and "Peace in the Valley" along with him when we traveled together and he would sell these for ten cents a piece to the folks who wanted to own them. Sometimes he would sell five thousand copies a day. But I was still what you call a "fish and bread" singer in those days. I was still singing for my supper as well as for the Lord.

The more gospel singing took hold in Chicago and around the country, the more some of the colored ministers objected to it. They were cold to it. They didn't like the hand-clapping and the stomping and they said we were bringing jazz into the church and it wasn't dignified. Once at church one of the preachers got up in the pulpit and spoke out against me.

I got right up, too. I told him I was born to sing gospel music. Nobody had to teach me. I was serving God. I told him that I had been reading the Bible every day most of my life and there was a

Psalm that said: "Oh, clap your hands, all ye people! Shout unto the Lord with the voice of a trumpet!" If it was undignified, it was what the Bible told me to do.

The European hymns they wanted me to sing are beautiful songs, but they're not Negro music. . . .

The Negroes' new fight for rights had come to a new focus down in the heart of the "Black Belt" in Albany, Georgia, where the colored people have never been granted their rights, including the right to vote. Two weeks before Christmas [1962], 737 colored people led by Dr. W. G. Anderson, a Negro doctor from Albany, and the Reverend [Martin Luther] King, marched together in downtown Albany. They held a meeting and prayed for the white people to please see the light and let them have their rights.

In that great Christmas congregation there were young people, old women in their seventies, working men, doctors, lawyers and housekeepers. They were all arrested and put in jail.

Martin Luther King, Jr., and Ralph Abernathy were convicted of leading the demonstration and went to jail. Later, Reverend King and nine other Negroes were jailed again when they prayed on the steps of the City Hall, but the Albany Movement only grew stronger.

The Negroes began letting the white people know their feelings by not going into the city's downtown stores, and the boycott emptied the streets of shoppers.

Once again it was in the churches that the colored people rallied for their cause. The white people oppressed them and threatened them, but the Negroes would swing into hymns like "We Are Climbing Jacob's Ladder" and "Pass Me Not, O Gentle Saviour" and the song that got famous during the student sit-ins—"We Shall Overcome."

It has meant so much to me that a great part of the brave fight for freedom down South now is coming from inside the church and from the hymns and gospel songs the people are singing.

The "Freedom Songs" began back during the Montgomery boycott when the Negroes began singing in the churches to keep up their courage. When the students began to go to jail during the sit-ins they began to make up new words to the spirituals and hymns and old gospel melodies that the Negroes had been singing in their churches for generations. Some got printed, some got put on records and some just got passed around.

Using songs as a way of expressing protest and gaining strength and hope runs way back deep in the American Negro's past. When the colored slaves on the plantations sang, "Steal away to Jesus, I ain't got long to stay here," they weren't talking just about Heaven; they were expressing their secret hope that they, too, would have their chance to escape up North to freedom. . . .

The soul of the Negro just naturally has so much rhythm and music in it that "testifying" to music in church and "getting happy" with singing has always been a way in which the Negro has sought to renew his strength.

Now all through the South the Negroes are singing. They sang while they were put in jail by the hundreds and sometimes the power of their music was so great that the white guards began singing right along with them.

They sing in churches and in mass meetings while deputies and sheriffs go around taking names and white gangs burn up their cars.

The big song of the movement that is now sung in the South by thousands of Negroes almost every night is "We Shall Overcome." . . .

The "Freedom Songs" have caught on because music speaks a language to individual souls that cannot always be expressed by the spoken word. There's something about music that is so penetrating that your soul gets the message. No matter what trouble comes to a person, music can help him face it. Some who didn't believe in God have found him through music.

Many colored people in the South have been kept down so hard that they have had little schooling. They can't handle a lot of reading, but as one preacher said, "The singing has drawn them together. Through the songs they have expressed years of suppressed hopes, suffering and even joy and love."

One young Negro leader said, "Without music there could have been no Albany Movement."

And Martin Luther King, Jr., said, "The Freedom Songs are giving people new courage, a radiant hope in the future in our most trying hours." . . .

Mahalia Jackson Galloway!

Once again I was moving on up into a new life with my hopes for happiness always a little higher. Along the new way I would rejoice with the Lord and sing my gospel music.

There are still some people who will try to tell you that gospel singing is a fad and that it will fade away. Don't you believe it!

Gospel music is nothing but singing of good tidings—spreading the good news. It will last as long as any music because it is sung straight from the human heart. Join with me sometime—whether you're white or colored—and you will feel it for yourself. Its future is brighter than a daisy.

33. HALL JOHNSON

→»» The Negro Renaissance of the 1920s brought about a deeper awareness of black culture on the part of all Americans, black and white. It was during this period that Hall Johnson (1888–1970) organized the first professional Negro choral group in history to win international distinction. To be sure, there had been touring Negro choruses and ensembles since the time of the Fisk Jubilee Singers and the Hampton Institute Singers in the nineteenth century, but with the exception of minstrel-troupe singers the groups had been amateurs.

Johnson's extensive training in music, which included graduate study at the University of Pennsylvania and Juilliard, had prepared him for a career as an instrumentalist. But although he played for many years in bands and orchestras, his real interest lay in choral music. Finally he turned his back on the orchestral world and organized a chorus.

The first Hall Johnson Choir made its debut at New York in 1926. Johnson's express purpose in gathering together the singers was to preserve the integrity of Negro spirituals as they had been performed during the slavery period. From that time on he singlemindedly devoted himself to his self-appointed task—that of acquainting the world with the beauty of Negro spirituals. His choruses over the years demonstrated how spirituals should be sung—on the concert stage, on Broadway in such musicals as *The Green Pastures* and *Run Little Chillun*, in Hollywood films, and at festivals, national and international. Johnson, in addition to his conducting activities, composed constantly, incorporating spiritual melodies or employing characteristic musical idioms of the spiritual in his works. «←

Notes on the Negro Spiritual [1965] [†]

The folk-song of the American Negro came to the United States with the first shipload of slaves from Africa. At that time the Ameri-

† Used by permission of the Hall Johnson Estate. Further reproduction of all or any portion of "Notes on the Negro Spiritual" by means of mimeographing, xeroxing, photocopying, or any other means of duplication, may not be performed without the written permission of the Hall Johnson Estate.

can settlers had only European music, mostly hymns and social songs of simple construction. They thought of music only for church worship and other special occasions. The Africans, however, came from a long tradition of functional music in daily use in lieu of the written word, songs filled with varied emotions to fit the most dramatic occasions: rituals for worship, birth, death, funeral, wedding, sowing and harvesting, journeying and war—to name a few. The musical instruments of the primitive African tribes were crude and undeveloped so that the songs were dependent on the voices of the singers. Only the drum, in manufacture and performance, left nothing to be desired.

All consideration of music as art is based upon the three elements: rhythm, melody and harmony. The English custom of music for the *ear* only, without any necessary accompaniment of physical motion, tended to develop in the English only the simple static rhythms; but it did give them a feeling for *melody* and *harmony* hitherto unknown to the African slaves. On the other hand, the African had a much more highly developed sense of *rhythm*—with his constant singing of all types of songs—all punctuated by the insistent beat of the omnipresent drum. Here was a wonderful opportunity to fuse the basic elements of rhythm, melody and harmony into a great American music. Only the Negro slaves, though quite unconsciously, profited by this opportunity. The American settlers had a country to build,—no time to think seriously about music. On the other hand, the slave had no life of his own *except* music,— the making of songs.

Now, no *slave* ever has any *rights:* personal, family, property, time, privacy, freedom of motion, freedom of opinion nor freedom of the physical body. That is the symbolism of the chains. But the only thing that cannot be chained is human thought *unexpressed.* So if you do not want your slave to *speak* freely you should also forbid him to sing,—even without words. The human voice in speech only *releases* the thought; in singing, the same voice gives it wings. But the American master permitted, even *encouraged* his slaves to sing. He got more work done—and, he enjoyed the singing.

So the slaves went on singing in their new home,—at first old homesick songs in their own language,—songs of their lost liberty. But, as the years passed, succeeding generations lost the old memories. The new country, new language, customs and occupations filled their life and gradually obliterated every image of the motherland. But still the slaves continued to sing—even in bondage, indeed, on account of their very chains.

For they found an entirely new subject to sing about. They soon heard the white man's religion, alleviating the woes of this world with the sure hope of eternal freedom in the next. Being unable to read or write, the slaves received these glad tidings at second hand. Every Sunday the coachmen, footmen and body servants sat in the slaves' galleries of the churches and attentively drank up the sermons, prayers, and hymns intended for their masters in the pews. Then the house servants, who worked all day in the "big house," heard, with the master's children, the old Bible stories of prophets, saints and heroes. These privileged ones, when the day's work was over, hurried to the slave quarters to share with the field hands the priceless treasures garnered in the churches, parlors and nurseries of their masters. These second-hand versions were certainly not models of orthodox scriptural prose,—but whatever they may have lacked in authenticity was more than compensated by vivid insight and dramatic fervor.

This new religion of the slaves was no Sunday religion. They needed it every day and every night. The gospel of Jesus, the Son of God, who had lived and died for men, even the lowliest, took hold of their imagination in a strange personal way, difficult to understand for the average Christian of the formal church. For them, He was not only King Jesus but also "Massa Jesus" and even "*my* Jesus." The American Negro slaves literally "embraced" Christianity and, with this powerful spiritual support, life took on new meaning, a new dimension. For now they *knew* with absolute, unshakeable faith, that somewhere, sometime—they would be FREE! And then the slaves began to sing—as they had never sung before.

In fact, the North American Negro slaves were completely satisfied with their new religion,—but not with the *music* that came with it. The songs in the master's church were good enough for the master. He only needed them on Sunday; the other days he had other business to occupy his mind. In a word, he was free,—and the comfortable, roomy hymns of his church services echoed the calm freedom that filled his soul. As for the slave,—he had never heard any music, on land or sea, that could describe his rapture at the very *name* of Jesus. And, after all, from time immemorial, hadn't he always made his own songs? So he opened his mouth and, from a heart bursting with love, faith and adoration, a new song poured forth—and kept pouring and pouring,—renewing his hope in a promised land of Freedom. The American Negro slaves called these religious songs "Spirituals."

The slaves knew that their songs were the spiritual guarantee of their personal oneness with life, even in a world that forbade them to live as human beings. What they did not know was that a people

who could not write their own names—in any language—were now
writing—for all time, one of the grandest pages in the history of
the whole world of music.

As time went by, musicians the world over became increasingly
aware that a musical miracle was taking place in the southern United
States of America. Gradually, through incessant, (though unconscious)
study, the slaves had succeeded in grafting onto their own native
musical gifts whatever they seemed to need from the western techniques to widen and extend their own creative efforts.

The slaves had brought from Africa:—

1. Fine, natural VOICES, developed by centuries of habitual singing out-of-doors.

2. An unerring sense of DRAMATIC VALUES—in words and music
—due to the wide variety of their functional songs.

3. A dazzling facility in IMPROVISATION and EMBELLISHMENT.

4. Above all, and underlying all, a supreme understanding of
the basic laws of RHYTHM—with all its implications and potentialities
as applied to music.

They discovered in the New World:—

1. A more serviceable MUSICAL SCALE—with longer range but
smaller intervals.

2. A wider view of musical structure by the use of the METRICAL
PHRASE.

3. The sensuous delights of rich HARMONY and exciting COUNTER-
POINT.

4. Lastly, the powerful, unifying psychological effects of GOOD
PART-SINGING.

The fusion of all these remarkable musical ingredients resulted in
far more than just *good* part-singing—with new songs and new singers. This amalgam bore golden fruits.

This musical alchemy soon began to attract the attention of the
professional musicians. Organized studies were set up for investiga-
tion; books were written; hundreds of melodies were transcribed; but
mere ink and paper could not record what was heard—and the phonograph was still to be invented. For the secret magic lay not so much
in the fresh wonder of the tunes and words themselves but in the
absolutely *new* musical *style* of *performance* by their creators. For
example:

1. The conscious and intentional *alterations* of *pitch* often made
in the accepted musical scale;

2. The unconscious, but amazing and bewildering *counterpoint*
produced by so many voices in *individual improvisation;*

3. The *absolute insistence* upon the pulsing, *overall rhythm* com-

bining many varying subordinate rhythms.

—to name only a very few effects which defy accurate notation but which are nevertheless essential to the character of the genuine old spirituals. Without these, many of the songs can sound quite trite, although never commonplace.

It must be kept in mind that the Negro Spiritual is essentially a group or choral form,—many people singing together. It reached its highest musical peak in the Negro Church during the early years succeeding the abolition of slavery—where large *crowds* sang *freely.* Gradually, with greater *individual* opportunities—economical and educational—the *group* impulse to sing and to make songs began to wane. For the newly emancipated slaves, singing was no longer the sole safety-valve of emotional activity. Freedom of choice brought variety of interest. The spiritual made room for the work-songs, love-songs and "blues". But the racial *singing-style* persisted—and persists to this day. Only the music itself has changed—according to the subject of the song. Still, such was the marvelous vitality inherent in the *old* songs themselves, that they are heard and loved all over the world—in whatever guise or disguise.

The Hall Johnson Negro Choir was organized on September 8, 1925. Its principal aim was not entertainment. We wanted to show how the American Negro slaves—in 250 years of constant practice, self-developed under pressure but equipped with their inborn sense of rhythm and drama (plus their *new religion*)—created, propagated and illuminated an art-form which was, and still is, *unique* in the world of music. The slaves named them "spirituals" to distinguish them from their worldly, "everyday" songs. Also, their musical style of performance was very special. It cannot be accurately notated but must be studied by imitation.

Even then, in 1925, I saw clearly that, with the changing times, in a few years any spirituals remaining would be found only in the libraries—and nobody would know how to sing them. I also knew that I was the only Negro musician born at the right time and in the right place ideally suited for years of study of the Negro musical idiom as expressed in the spirituals. I started right in. I had always been a composer and—here was virgin soil. I assembled a group of enthusiastic and devoted souls and we gave our first public concert on February 26, 1926.

Our earlier singers had no other broad outlet for their native talents—except in the churches. They soon united themselves into a sort of musical family, employing all of their spare time in daily rehearsals. Long years of success only deepened their relationship.

In forty years, the times have changed for Negro singers. Increased living expenses have decreased leisure time. Opportunities have opened up for *individual* Negro singers of talent. These are no longer "chorus-minded." All of these changes have gradually increased our rehearsal difficulties. No matter how fine the voice or how well trained, *every* singer must be in *every* rehearsal to study the old techniques together. In the meanwhile the impossibility of daily rehearsals has effectively put an end to the Hall Johnson Choir. Our last public concert was given in June of 1960.

The last six years have brought me many individual honors, guest-appearances, and citations. For many years, several leading publishers have been distributing my choral and solo arrangements of the old Negro folk-songs. Why not be satisfied to "rest on my laurels"—like an old worn-out prima donna? Why have this definite and desperate sense of having failed in my life-work? It is because the signs I saw forty years ago are coming true. In a few more years, nobody—not even the Negro singers—will know the words and melodies of a dozen spirituals and will be able to sing any one of the dozen properly. Because they will have never heard them. And there ARE NO RECORDINGS!

The Negro Spiritual reached its fullest flowering in the early years of the Emancipation when the ex-slaves gathered in great numbers to sing in their *own* churches—without let or hindrance. But alas! The recording-machine *had not yet been invented!*

In 1938 the RCA Victor Co. recorded a dozen or so songs of the Hall Johnson Choir. A few years later, during the Second World War, the priority on shellac necessitated drastic reductions in the output of the recording companies. The Hall Johnson Choir songs disappeared from the catalogue and have been unavailable ever since.

Of course, all the leading companies would say *their* catalogues are full of Negro songs, even spirituals, and they sincerely believe that. What they really have is a conglomeration of all sorts of modern derivatives sung by soloists or small groups in musical arrangements neither Negro nor spiritual. But they caught the public ear. It is good business and everybody's happy—but me. They don't know any better.

I have no quarrel with the multiple musical progeny of the spiritual: work-songs, game-songs, and later, chaingang-songs, love-songs, ballads, reels, "blues" and, much later, jazz and the "gospel-songs." They have had their uses and evidently will be around for a long time. Only, their musical progenitor has disappeared—the old Negro spiritual.

This amazing literature of folk-song that astonished the musical world came up and flourished under ideal artistic conditions—for two hundred and fifty *slave* years. A singing race, they had the same subject-matter—freedom; the same reason for making and singing their songs—mental release; and unlimited time for practice—even at work! And for crowning inspiration, [they had] an eloquent and unshakable faith in their new religion of *hope*. Why wouldn't they sing!

But after the abolition of slavery, with relative freedom came more individual problems and less spare time. In their own churches the spiritual still held sway. But, gradually, the fierce faith in "my" Jesus began to subside into the quiet trust in the less informal Jesus of the hymn-books. Time and the succeeding generations were closing in. Soon would arrive the various denominations—with vested choirs —and the good old spirituals would have a rest until the midsummer revival meetings—maybe.

So, the old Negro Spiritual is gone. Those who don't believe it never heard it in the first place. Most are too young; others were born in the wrong place. It is nobody's fault. Time ends all things. And because [a thing] is not missed, nobody thinks of making a record of it.

It is not difficult to understand that the spiritual began to wane with the conditions that had given it birth. It was no longer the only safety-valve, and yet the only cement, of the race. It is not indispensable even to the modern Negro. But it is simply irreplaceable in the world of musical history. Neither the Negro nor the United States of America can comprehend the immense value of the appreciation of the whole civilized world for this Negro folk-art, [although] they all agree that is the only authentic, indigenous creative art-form ever to come out of the New World.

It must be kept in mind that the authentic Negro Spiritual is a *choral* form, requiring many voices to color the lush harmonies and bring out the brilliant, syncopated counterpoint so characteristic in the genuine spiritual. No soloist nor small vocal ensemble can hope to produce the necessary effects. The singing of the Hall Johnson Choir in *The Green Pastures* and *Run, Little Chillun* was the only modern example. But, again, [there are] no recordings.

The Ethnic Records in the Library of Congress were collected by northern white researchers. These earnest people, armed with portable recording-machines, went into the rural districts of the South and picked up all kinds of sporadic dribble of Negro folk-singing. All of this is, of course, very interesting but has nothing to do with the grand old spirituals, either in composition or performance.

Of course, many books have been written about the Negro

Spiritual and many conscientious attempts made to transcribe the melodies and harmonies. But no printed word can ever describe the actual *sound* of music, and the written score of any song is but a dry skeleton until breathed upon by the living human voice. This is particularly true in the case of the spirituals done in the *true* Negro style. The racial tendency to improvise "between-notes" [and] the great variety of characteristic tone-color and rhythmic accent—all of these Negro techniques simply defy notation in any known system. They must be recorded from the living sound.

Now, I do not claim to be the only human being able to *recognize* the old Negro Spiritual. There is an always-lessening number of people old enough and musical enough to remember it. What I *am* asserting is its *importance* in world history. While the *slaves* were creating immortal melodies like "Swing low, sweet chariot," the *rest* of America had not yet reached its musical adolescence. American composers were still frantically grabbing at the musical apron-strings of Europe. American talent could not be recognized, even by Americans, until stamped and sealed by European approval. Naturally, under those conditions, the fairest flower might escape attention—in *its own* backyard. Significantly enough, the earliest books on the spirituals came from European-trained authors. The American composers came on board just in time to meet granddaughter Jazz. But, no matter the past periods of circumstances, America owes to itself and the rest of the world a definite, musical chronicle of this accidental but durable by-product of slavery-days.

There *must* be *musical recordings* of many of the finest of the old songs, *each* furnished with (1) an interesting program-note; (2) the plain folk-melody—unadorned; (3) then a development-section, along racial lines, showing future possibilities for composition. Such a record-library would not only rescue the grandest American art-form from oblivion, [but] would immeasurably heighten the artistic stature of the United States among the other civilized nations. Also, it would provide an authoritative model for American students. The school-choruses, especially in the West, are especially fond of the spirituals, which they learn as best they can from the sadly-inadequate printed arrangements. They *really need* records. They [i.e. the recordings] are the future *teachers*.

Now, I wish to prepare the record-library I have described. No one else has spent such a life-time of study, experience and dedication: Forty years ago, for my experience, I needed nothing but *people* and time—both *free*. But alas! Today I need money—to release both people and the time.

34. WILLIAM GRANT STILL

⇻ Best known of modern Negro composers, William Grant Still (b. 1895) earned a secure niche for himself in the history of American music while still in his thirties with his activity in the fields of composing, arranging, and conducting. After receiving his basic musical training at Wilberforce University and Oberlin Conservatory, Still later studied with Edgard Varèse and George Chadwick. In 1970, when music organizations all over the nation were celebrating Still's seventy-fifth birthday, the "Dean of Afro-American composers" could look back upon a career filled with honors and awards. His concert works—numbering more than a hundred, for symphony orchestra, band, ballet, opera, chorus, voice, ensembles, and solo instruments—had become favorites in the concert hall, particularly on college campuses and among the smaller symphony orchestras of the nation. In an earlier period, Still's orchestrations and arrangements had been used by leading radio and musical-show orchestras, popular singers, and performers of light concert music; his music had been heard as background for films and television programs.

Still did not let the birthday celebrations in 1970 interfere with his composing. Indeed, it was during such a celebration at Oberlin that one of his new symphonies, Symphony No. 5, was given a première performance on an all-Still concert. Critics found Still's music to be "pleasant, easy, graceful, completely traditional in approach," but they emphasized the originality expressed within the framework of the traditional. Still himself had firm convictions about the kind of music he wanted to write. Having passed through a stage in which he wrote experimental music, he had decided against continuing in that direction. He explained his creative philosophy again and again in lectures and in articles for periodicals and newspapers. He insisted, "We should function as individuals, musically and otherwise," and deplored the tendency of many musicians to compose according to the fashion of the times. ⇺

The Structure of Music [1950] †

Many people, attracted by the current frantic rush to discover new horizons in music, seem to think that musical form is a thing of

† Text: *Etude Music Magazine*, March, 1950, pp. 17, 61. Reprinted by permission of Theodore Presser Company.

the past. They believe that in order to compose, one need only find a few bizarre harmonies, string them together without thought of melody, form or sequence, and emerge with a "composition" that will bring them acclaim. Nothing could be further from the truth.

When a trained listener hears a new composition, he is inclined to listen analytically. To him, faulty form is immediately apparent. Perhaps it is his conscious mind that sounds a warning, noting that things do not follow each other in natural sequence, that there is too much or too little of this, that or the other, or that transitions are clumsy. Or perhaps it's the subconscious that detects the lack, after years of study and of developing an inner feeling for proportion and symmetry. This latter, in my belief, actually springs from our innate rhythmic sense.

Even an untrained listener will sense something wrong when he hears a composition faulty in form, though he himself may not realize exactly what it is. He will wonder why he has not been able to retain a coherent impression of what has been performed. He may even have no desire to hear the work again or to "learn to like it."

What is form, this powerful element which can make or break a piece of music, no matter in what era it is composed? Form is the basis, the *foundation,* the *structure.* On our physical plane we can't imagine anything that actually is formless. However, there is good form, where everything fits into its niche naturally, and faulty form, where things are weak, fragmentary or chaotic.

It has been of interest to me to note that some European critics are able to detect and analyze form on hearing new works, whereas our American critics often content themselves with a more or less literary description.

Every conscientious creator recognizes the importance of good form and in that, as in other respects, the arts are allied. My friend, the sculptor, Sargent Johnson, once remarked that he, too, is chiefly concerned with form, which, to him, means design and relationship: everything in its proper place. A layman with no feeling for form could construct an adequate shed, but a palace calls for an architect. A composer should be a musical architect.

In conversations with other contemporary composers, among them Howard Hanson, I've learned that most of them consider form the most difficult of all elements that go into composing. I can well understand this view, for I share it. In all my years of composing I have never stopped studying form, trying to learn more about it, and hoping that I will be able to master it ultimately.

Everyone who writes music, in my opinion, should learn what the established forms are, and should have a thorough grounding in

the forms developed by the classicists. Study and reference to textbooks can accomplish this. After that, a person with a creative mind
will make an effort to build on what he has learned, to add an individual touch.

For instance, the textbooks give examples of musical themes and
show how they were developed by the masters. But when a contemporary composer sets out to compose, he has his own thematic
material. Perhaps it is so different from the textbook examples that
he can't develop it along traditional lines. He will have to have,
therefore, a genuine instinct for form in order to know how to proceed. If he has this instinct and if he has fortified himself with study,
he will emerge with a well-formed composition even though he has
not adhered strictly to tradition.

Here, in my experience, is what is likely to happen during the
creation of a piece of music. First, a motif or germ is conceived.
This the composer would like to use in a large way, so he begins by
planning his form.

I have made it a habit to sit down and plan out the form of a
new work right after getting the thematic material. Then, perhaps I
devise variations. Perhaps I deliberately work away from the proposed
plan. No matter what I do, the finished product usually differs in
externals (since many things are changed during creation) but *basically* the planned form will remain.

Sometimes the peculiarities of the theme itself may lead to de-
viations from the original plan. Sometimes what has been planned as
a mere episode may assume such importance that it ceases to be an
episode. Transitions may be shortened, lengthened, or discarded altogether. A composer cannot anticipate everything, but he can
strengthen his craftsmanship so that his completed composition will
be satisfying from an architectural standpoint.

Of great importance to musical architecture is the development
of thematic material. Take, for instance, the process of extending a
motif into a phrase. This should be a spiritual rather than a mental
process. Composers who work only with the conscious mind have
difficulty in working out a melody.

Others, guided by inspiration, find it difficult to select from the
many that are suitable. One might say that the motif dictates its own
development, its own treatment and even its own form. Form follows
function, say the architects. That is as true of music as of the other
arts.

Actually, the *treatment* of a motif has very little to do with the
form. Mental gymnastics, such as adding unnecessary counterpoint,

or harmonizing melodies in an arbitrary fashion whether or not they are suited to that particular style of harmonization, are only attempts to delude the ear.

There is a lesson for all of us in the simple little ABA form. It was known to peasant musicians long before the classicists analyzed it and put it into the textbooks. The lesson it brings is that there must be a recurrence of thematic material in any musical composition before any listener, trained or untrained, can detect the form, or plan, that underlies the work. This recurrence of theme brings a well-defined unity—which, however, must not be made monotonous.

The classic masters believed that they had to hammer away at a theme in order to drive it into people's consciousness. I agree with them, except I do not believe in exact repetitions. (Here one might also make an analogy, for the great pianist, Harold Bauer, once told the pupils in one of his master classes that no matter how often a theme recurred in a composition, they must never play it the same way twice.) In composing I prefer to have shorter themes than the masters usually employed, so as not to tax the memory, and to repeat these shorter themes often, with alterations.

There exists today a school of contemporary composers, some in Europe and some in America, which apparently—at least on first hearing—disregards the laws of form. No recurring themes are evident. Indeed, it is hard to detect the actual themes, since the members of this school actually scorn what we know as melody. They have directed their efforts mainly toward exploring new harmonic effects because that is so much easier than constructing a well-proportioned composition. Their occasional consonant intervals are weak because of bad handling; their vaunted counterpoint is incorrect, disjointed and muddled. Because these composers scorn inspiration, I call them "cerebral" composers. Other people refer to them as "atonalists." They are certainly good reflections of the troubled world in which we live.

Under the general term of "contemporary" music, much of this work is being played now. My feeling is that a composer should be tested, not by the bizarre sounds he can produce, but by his ability to construct a simple, satisfying piece of music, harmonically, melodically, and architecturally.

35. THOMAS JEFFERSON ANDERSON

≫ In 1969 the Indiana University School of Music sponsored a five-day seminar on "Black Music in College and University Curricula" that attracted leaders in the field, both black and white, from all over the nation. Composers, performers, publishers, and educators discussed their common problems and how to solve them under the able leadership provided by the Black Music Committee of Indiana University—David Baker, Austin Caswell, and chairman Dominique-René de Lerma. The seventh session, a panel discussion, was titled "Black Composers and the Avant-Garde"; its participants were three well-known black composers: Thomas Jefferson Anderson, Hale Smith, and Olly Wilson. Anderson led off the discussion with impromptu remarks, which were followed by a statement from Wilson, then general discussion.

Like his two colleagues, panelist T. J. Anderson (b. 1928) had an established reputation among music critics, and his music was increasingly being performed in concert halls and on college campuses. He received his musical training at West Virginia State College, Pennsylvania State University, the Cincinnati Conservatory of Music, and the University of Iowa, where he received a Ph.D. in composition in 1958. Later he studied at the Aspen School of Music with Darius Milhaud. In 1969 Anderson left his chairmanship of the Music Department at Tennessee Agricultural and Industrial State University to assume the position of composer-in-residence to the Atlanta Symphony Orchestra, a notable first in the history of Afro-American music. ≪

From *Black Composers and the Avant-Garde* [1969] †

CASWELL: The purpose of this forum is to consider the avant-garde elements of composition as they relate to the Black cultural traditions. Too often we have associated the Black influence on music as stemming from past traditions only, from the spiritual, folk music, earlier jazz. This afternoon's discussion is to see what influ-

† Text: *Black Music in Our Culture*, edited by Dominique-René de Lerma (Kent, Ohio, 1970), pp. 63–67. Reprinted by permission of The Kent State University Press, copyright © 1970 by Dominique-René de Lerma.

ence the Black composer is having upon the more recent facets of composition.

ANDERSON: This is an attitude which is not only reflective of my opinion, but the opinion of many in the Black community. When one thinks of the avant-garde, one immediately thinks of revolutionary composers, those with a new musical language, those who are involved in experimentation, or anything outside of the establishment. If we take this as a definition, and since we can already assume that all Black composers have always been outside the establishment, one logically reaches the conclusion that all Black composers are avant-garde. Now on first thought, this may seem a bit facetious, but I can assure you that I say this in all seriousness. Those of you who laugh would immediately suggest the name of Ulysses Kay as being one that would be an exception. I grant you that Kay has made a tremendous impact in terms of the establishment in music. However, if you look at the Pan American Union's *Composers of the Americas*, where there is a bibliography of his works and publications, you can see that Ulysses Kay is very limited in terms of publications and recordings. Therefore, one has to conclude that Kay has only made an indentation on the visual establishment, but not the musical establishment at all. To say that Ulysses Kay is as good as any of his contemporaries is to miss the point, for he certainly is as good as any other composer writing today. However, Kay's activity within musical circles shows that he does not belong to the tradition of having-to-be-better, clearly a tradition which has prevailed throughout the society.

I was reading an article by Shirley Graham, the widow of W. E. B. DuBois, perhaps our most illustrious leader. It was titled "Spirituals to Symphonies" and appeared in *Etude* in 1936. In this particular article, she discussed the tremendous growth of potential in Black serious composers and the works of Florence B. Price, William Dawson, and Nathaniel Dett. What she actually came out with is a conclusion that we stood on the threshhold in 1936 of a renaissance period in which Black artists would move into the society and greatly enrich the cultural heritage of the country. It is ironic that some thirty-three years later we're still standing on that threshhold and, in fact, I think the case can be made that we have actually slipped back in terms of position. Instead of America's music being vitalized, in the last thirty-three years it has taken the road of imitation and is basically a poor imitation of European music lacking in rhythmic imagination, harmonic intensity, and also tends to be overly intellectualized.

Now, to develop further the point of all Black composers being avant-garde, one has to realize that the Black composer comes out of an aesthetic. Whether he is aware of it or not is not too important, for it's his duty to show the social and environmental relationships. Secondly, since Blacks feel the pressure of the system (political, economical and social), is it not therefore normal to assume that Blacks would be more sensitive in the art forms? Third, the total range of the avant-garde in America always finds Blacks to the left. If we had a convention of conservative composers, I would dare say that all of the conservative composers in this country would immediately place the Black composers who also attended such a convention to the left; for in considering intra-group variations of Whites, one has to assume that the intra-group variations are quite broad, while the intra-group variations of Blacks are quite small. And I would suggest that this variation is due to the fact that Blacks have been more responsive to social issues in their music. Fourth, composition does not reflect the feeling of the times, but is a response sociologically in terms of one's emotions in a particular time and a particular place. It's impossible to imagine a Sistine Chapel without a church with great finance. The affluent society can always produce pop and op art because it has money. Now what I'm saying here is that the study of music is not a history, but a social commentary on the human reaction to the environmental factors which relate to the individual. Therefore, the composer does not make a conscious choice, but selects unconsciously adaptations of things that exist in the society.

To define the Black avant-garde further, we would say these are the composers who have suffered the Negro experience in America. And the rate of this expression is therefore a quantitative measurement in terms of its relative relationship to Black people. My good friend, the late poet M. B. Tolson, put it another way in his book *The Harlem Gallery*. "Poor boy blue, the great White world and the Black bourgeois have shoved the Negro artists into a White and non-White dichotomy: the Afro-American dilemma in the arts, the dialectic of to be or not to be a Negro." This sense of being pulled from one pole to another is not only characteristic of the Black artist, but is characteristic of the society, for there should be a dichotomy in the existence of all White artists in the society. Can the White artist of today see the existence of Blacks in this country and not be affected by his own humanity?

When we look at the culture in which we are a part, we have to become overly concerned in the economic basis because that's where it's rooted, and one has to examine the sub-culture. Now I use the term "sub-culture" only to imply a small portion of a larger group, a sub-division. It has nothing to do with a value judgment. The economic basis of the Black community has been put out in governmental statistics and it's funny that in one way the government turned out to be a benefactor (that's in the publication of figures) and in another way turned out to be a supressor of human rights (I'm thinking in terms of the Justice Department's lack of prosecution of the laws in which relate to open housing and fair employment), and yet we still have to be aware that this dual role which is shared by the federal government has a great effect on us. By 1970 the percentage of Black families in poverty will be between 30.6 and 32.9 percent, compared to between 10.8 and 12 percent for White families. This figure is increasing. In 1966 Blacks had not achieved the employment status of Whites in 1940. Because we bear the brunt of the disproportionate processes in terms of jobs and money, we have been basically absorbed in our living. Thus, there is the same basis for Appalachian folk music and the blues of Harlem soul music, proportionately.

We live in a machine civilization, and all machine civilizations pride themselves in their efficiency. Webern represents the maximum in terms of time concept. African music, on the other hand, has no time consciousness. Webern's symphony, opus 21, would take approximately ten minutes to perform. Yet an African festival, in which the participants do the right thing at the right time, sometimes goes on for days. In the machine civilization it is inevitable that the artists tend to reflect other institutions and, therefore, they too are time oriented. What composer doesn't put on his score the amount of time this piece would take to be performed? What conductor doesn't look at this timing first to see how long his audience has to suffer through the contemporary work? Since the anatomy of the society is structured this way, we have become overly specialized. The arts have become compartmentalized and highly structured. Therefore, we have produced schools: impressionism, expressionism, and so forth. These are the results.

Before technology won over, art forms were most important because they relate to the whole fiber of the individual. And when we understand this, we understand truly what Black music is all about. Indians in America have no event without singing and dancing. African societies couldn't have a hunt without its being related to religion, singing and dancing. The statement of LeRoi Jones seems to sum up what I'm talking about: "Black music is total reality." By this we mean that the environmental understanding is related to the metaphysical torment which grows out of universal suffering and that the religious experience of the Black church is a classic example of dialectic theater.

Within the Black community there exist many points of fascination. In the area of instrumental music (marching bands, dance halls and clubs) one constantly sees experimentation. Musicians basically self-taught develop abilities on the basis of accident, or as a means of developing self expression. We see the development of new techniques to fit one's own personality or peculiar needs. Instrumental music is very much related to voice in that the music is sung and not played. And another term which I'd like to interject is "inspired intensity." I don't know if this exists in any other music, but this is a fusion of achieving the highest degree of expressive powers within a framework of limited technical facility or skill. I think we constantly see musicians who are limited in terms of background because of the lack of economic privileges, who are basically self-taught, or ill-taught in many cases, and who actually develop this means of communication through the development of expressive powers which transcend their limitation in terms of ability. In the area of vocal music, word inflections for dramatic intent can be seen. Tonal colors of the voice and the use of wide vibrato are constantly used for increasing emotional effect. These contributions have been made to the mainstream of the avant-garde movement in the country, and an examination of sources would clearly show these points: There are new methods of tone production which have been a part of the Black tradition for years. Tonal effects (mutes, distortion of tone, physical tricks) are quite common. The extended ranges of instruments, either by trick fingerings or mouthpiece pressures, are another by-product of the environment, and the greater use of the unestablished instruments (things like the tenor saxophone, the electric guitar) are quite common, of course again relating to playing the instruments that are available—this heterogeneous grouping of instruments.

In conclusion, the social and psychological infringements of the Black experience make the Negro composer unique. Whether he is a liberal or conservative is not important. His role in the society is only significant because his perspective is Black. These are the composers involved in the fundamental issues of existence.

WILSON: Art is experience consciously transformed. If an artist is honest with himself, transforming his experience is precisely what he does, consciously or not. Since his experience is a Black one, this is the only thing he can represent. Now the manifestations of this experience are going to vary even within the spectrum of Blackness, at different times, at different geographical positions, and at different levels of the sociological ladder. In spite of these variations, all Black people are united because of their Blackness. LeRoi Jones, in *Blues People*, talks about this very cogently, particularly regarding the various movements in jazz after 1940. The same kind of thing could be found by looking at Black musicians who have had experience in the jazz tradition and are involved at the same time in the mainstream of Western "art" music. And even here there would be differences in the reflection of this Black experience.

What is Black music? I don't think that's one of the basic things we're trying to grapple with. In order to do this, we would have to start with African music. This has already been done to a limited extent by A. M. Jones, the ethnomusicologist, in his book *Studies in African Music*. It's from this kind of study that the notion of time, which T. J. pointed out, became apparent. The Afro-American experience is different. The original African concept of art as life, and the concept of the musician as the bearer of truth and history—this philosophical heritage was broken down by forcefully moving people from one continent to another. At the same time, certain vestiges of African means of musical expression were maintained, and these are illustrated in Gunther Schuller's *Early Jazz*.

36. HALE SMITH

⇶ A native of Cleveland, Ohio, Hale Smith (b. 1925) earned the bachelor and master degrees in music from the Cleveland Institute of Music. He was one of a group of young black artists, writers, and painters nurtured at the celebrated Karamu House in Cleveland, where in an earlier decade poet Langston Hughes had found a receptive audience for his plays and poems. In 1959 Smith went to New York and began to win a name for himself as a composer. His best-known work, *Contours for Orchestra* (1962), was recorded by the Louisville Symphony Orchestra. Toward the end of the sixties, with white America's awakened interest in black culture and black artists, Smith was increasingly called upon as a representative of his profession to explain on the lecture stage, in the college classroom, and on social occasions the position of the black composer. The following manifesto, although especially written for the present collection of readings, contains the essence of the many lectures given by Smith over a period of several years. ⇷

Here I Stand [1971] †

I must admit to being largely unconvinced as far as the current emphasis on things black is concerned, because a major characteristic of American cultural life has always been the setting aside of the creative efforts of Afro-Americans in "race" categories where they have rarely been considered on the same bases as the works of Europeans and white Americans. I view the black syndrome as yet another means, of evading the issue—but this time with the best of ostensible motives, and with the enthusiastic aid and support of black artists, who probably feel that any way of being seen and heard is better than *no* way.

As one who has been frequently performed, I, perhaps, should let the others speak for themselves, but for years I have faced the question as to whether or not my work was worthy of appearing on

† Text: By permission of the author. Copyright, 1971.

programs of music by the recognized masters of my art. That *I* might think so is beside the point. That the work—in reality—might be worthy is also beside the point. That those who function as the arbiters of taste and judgement recognize its value is of great importance because it is through their recognition that large reputations grow. And from those reputations, economic stability may be acquired.

Unless the work of Afro-American artists (musical and otherwise) is allowed to succeed or fail by comparison—or in competition— with the works of the entire national and world cultures, we will have no valid standards of measurement by which they can be measured and judged on their own merits. And unless they are treated in this way, we will continue to have the patronizing "Black Arts Presentations" which, in reality, solve no problems and still allow white America to suspend its critical faculties by deferring to the supposedly higher question of giving the black artist his day in the sun.

But what is to be expected when, inevitably, the day of black awareness is past. What does the black artist (not to mention the black man in the street) do when the fad has lost its popularity? Are we to be expected to sit back while white America takes the fertile seeds of our imaginations and benefits from their fruition, again? What else is to be expected as long as our work can be seen, heard, and absorbed, while at the same time being considered too inferior to the work of our white contemporaries and forbears to stand in direct competition with them.

I'm sorry! We have been this way before. I'm even more sorry that so many Afro-Americans fail to see that, in reality, this is a false road leading to a repetition of what we have had so many times before. Starving for recognition; starving for identification; they fail to see that it isn't enough for us to be measured against each other because, as a group, we can be written off as of no consequence to the needs of the world at large.

American Negro poetry has been largely ignored by being isolated, yet it is, perhaps, the richest literary lode this country has produced. The creators of this literary tradition range from Phyllis Wheatley through Arna Bontemps, Langston Hughes, and Jean Toomer to such writers of today as LeRoi Jones and Eldridge Cleaver. Some of the most brilliant Afro-American writers are nearly unknown, such as Russell Atkins, whose writings have appeared for years in nearly every "little magazine", and in several anthologies of Negro poetry— both in the United States and abroad. Atkins' "Psychovisual" theory of music was an important influence on early avant-garde music through an article printed in a quarterly, partly controlled by him, *The Free Lance*, but he has received *no* credit, even though much of the language used was first coined by him. The case of Langston Hughes is well known. He was one of the world's most widely published authors, yet he lived his entire professional life without a single dollar from film-rights—or even a decent job offer from Hollywood, while his demonstratable inferiors have made fortunes there.

Musically, conditions have been no better, though perhaps more subtle. The names of Dett, Swanson, Still and Clarence Cameron White have appeared but rarely on programs of concert music in this country, and they are among the most important of Afro-American composers. Several younger composers have benefited, at least in the short run, from the present emphasis on "black", but with few exceptions (such as T. J. Anderson, Olly Wilson, and Arthur Cunningham) their appearances have been largely on black oriented programs. Certain reviews of the past five years indicate that critics are still unwilling to credit the black composer with having the skills necessary for that craft—while acknowledging black accomplishments in the areas of song and jazz. One review in my memory actually went so far as to suggest that perhaps we don't possess the intellectual capacity to master such a refined and complex skill as musical composition—an attitude supported by the recent "Jensen" report on Negro intellectual capacity.[1]

The evidence indicates that the same attitudes and conditions prevail in the areas of the dance, the sciences, and the crafts: the building trades being but one example.

We *must* be part of the mainstream in this country or all of the black programs are a sham. Place our music not on all-black programs. We can do that ourselves, for the benefit of our own people. Place our work on programs with Beethoven, Mozart, Schoenberg, Copland, and—if they can stand the heat—the current avant-gardists. We don't even have to be called black. When we stand for our bows, that fact will become clear when it should—*after* the work has made its own impact.

As for myself—I am interested in writing the music truest to myself that I can. I object to "critics" who misrepresent my work by half-listening, or through their bias that I must be imitative (how else to account for the things I do?). However, they are of no real moment, except as they influence the attitudes outlined earlier in

1. A reference to Arthur Robert Jensen, "How Much Can We Boost IQ and Scholastic Achievement," in *Harvard Educational Review*, 39, pp. 1–123, 449–83. The articles, which presented arguments for the innate inferiority of black people, created a sensation among both scholars and laymen and received massive attention in the world press. [*Editor*]

this statement. If I cannot satisfy myself, I have no need to write. So my output is small, but I feel that each piece represents some aspect of my creative ability in such a way that I need have no fears regarding its quality. My experience has been that if a work of mine is well played, it can, and usually does, manage to reach the serious listener, for whom it is intended.

37. CARMAN MOORE

>>> Music critic, writer, teacher, and composer, Carman Moore (b. 1936) earned a B.A. degree in music at Ohio State University and an M.A. at Juilliard Institute. His article, published in the *New York Times*, and the answers it elicited from a white musicologist and a black-arts critic typify the often heated discussions that took place during the 1960s concerning black music and the role of the black composer. Moore was well qualified to be a spokesman for the black musician. He was one of the founders of the Society of Black Composers at New York in 1968. Among his books is the successful *Somebody's Angel Child: The Story of Bessie Smith,* a biography of the "Empress of the Blues." <<<

Does a Black Mozart—or Stravinsky— Wait in the Wings? (Black Art Music) [1969] †

If it is Sunday morning and you live in Harlem and you have just walked over to your open window to see what's doing on the street below, you are probably hearing some music at this moment. If it is 11 A.M. or so, you are hearing a church choir, either singing tambourine gospel out of the storefront church below or singing an old Protestant hymn en masse from the big temple on the corner. You may be hearing both at once. You may even be hearing both choirs plus The Temptations on the neighbor's phonograph. If it is Monday and you're walking past the shops on the Avenues or on 125th Street, you're probably hearing soul music competitively blasted out by two or more adjacent business establishments. And as you walk along, you may be holding your transistor radio on your shoulder and be listening to jazz on WLIB.

Sheets of sound, the term used by the late tenor saxophone giant John Coltrane to describe one of his own approaches to music, are what engulf the citizen of the American black community per-

† Text: *The New York Times,* September 7 and November 2, 1969. © 1969 by The New York Times Company. Reprinted by permission.

haps every day of his life. He walks to music, sleeps to music, works to music if he can, and he probably goes to his grave with a hymn ringing around his at-last deafened ear. He is not necessarily born with music in his soul, but he is definitely born to music in his environment. Therefore, the black man often finds himself walking in a music-affirming gait, talking and gesturing in quasi-musical and and filling much of his conversation with discussions of music and musicians. Music—the black American trusts this art form above all, and well he might, because throughout his trials in white America music has been his escape valve, his code in time of danger, and his quickest route to fame and fortune. It has also been his only un-broken link to the culture of Africa. The fountainhead of black American style is music.

In recent years, as black Americans have come to view themselves as 100 per cent human individuals and as a unique corporate entity and not, as taught by the white America for three centuries, a cul-ture-poor rabble band born to servitude, many members of the black intelligentsia have sought to catalogue elements which are "all black," so as to cleave to them as patterns and wash "Whitey" out of their systems. Some among the more hasty hearts have allowed them-selves to criticze the dress, hair styles, or speech of their black broth-ers as being too white or not African enough.

In music, such a critic of negritude might decide that the true black thing calls for elements he himself has found most compelling in jazz, gospel, blues, and soul music. He would X out cantatas, symphonies, sonatas and operas automatically. He would rail against modern mixed-media, electronic, and complex dissonant concert pieces, much as a typical middle-class, small-town white listener might. He would require "basic" materials—a heavy and steady four-four or three-four beat, basic harmonies, lots of riffing repetition, plenty of free impovisation, and instant understanding by the audi-ence. "That's what black music is all about," he might say, but he would be only partially correct.

The blackest music possible, presumably, is African traditional music, yet it does not fit easily into our mythical critic's not-so-mythical criteria. The glories of African traditional music are many, but one inescapable aspect is its quality of deep complexity—both tonally and rhythmically (and in many cases, harmonically). This music usu-ally defies the four-bar phrasing and simple four-four three-four met-ers, which were acquired in America under slavery. This music does not rest harmonically on the basic three chords which underpin gospel, folk blues, and soul music and which were introduced most cogently to the black slave through Protestant church hymns with help from reconstituted British folk tunes and French band music.

African music hypnotizes often but its repetitions are seldom devoid of subtle changes and constant growth. This music is often mass performance mixed-media stuff, calls for immaculate discipline from each performer, and seldom allows any old random player or singer to wildly play "what he feels." The Master Drummer is the chef d'orchestre and is free to improvise but is also charged with the responsibility of guiding the others by means of drum signals into the depths of the piece. African traditional music does indeed clutch and connect with its listeners (and this value remains in typical Afro-American music), but African tribal listeners know what they are listening for and have an umbilical feel for their music in its proper cultural environment. This is unavailable to most Afro-Americans, cut off from the mother continent for so long.

The search, then, is not so much for a pure black thing as it is for a pure American black thing. The clue to this search for musical identity lies in Africa, but the treasure is buried in American soil. The key words are "community" and "improvisation"—elements known in West Africa but indispensable to a New World experience of slavery followed by segregation. Close community has been the life blood of "soul," and improvisation—scuffling, resourcefulness, creativity and making do—has been the heart of black American life.

Black music making, then, is the perfect metaphor for three centuries of black American endurance, and the black music maker has always been both priest and hero to his community. As such, the musician's speech becomes the hip code of his followers. His dress often is the fashion pace-setter. His musical developments lead the march of his people. He is free to improvise style. He is the master drummer to his community's riffs. His response to this trust has been to treat his music with high seriousness.

Today, with the communications media at an all-time high of outreach, the forms of black musical culture available to each listener are widely varied. One of the forms which has been in black communities since slavery and is now beginning slowly to grow in importance is plain old "classical" music. In spite of Jim Crow, black musicians have written and performed string quartets, concertos, symphonies, opera and concert band works all along. The first American composer of international stature, Louis Moreau Gottschalk, is thought to have been at least octoroon. Many composers who gained fame in popular music also wrote concert music. W. C. Handy, James P. Johnson and Duke Ellington are a few of those names. As a matter of fact, Duke Ellington's genius virtually singlehandedly turned jazz into authentic art music—i.e., music seriously approached that is created to last.

Ironically enough, contemporary so-called classical music comes naturally to the present-day black composer—far more so than, say, the music of the Romantic Age to 19th-century blacks. The predictable rhythms, harmonies, and timbres of the last century were too European in gesture and esthetic for the strange asymmetric Afro-American musical canon. Now, however, at mid-20th century, the wide palette of instrumental and vocal colors, the tendency toward structured improvisation, the rhythmic complexity, even the tendency to mix the media in modern music, square well with much of the African music esthetic and many of the more popular Afro-American tendencies. Suddenly the number of black American composers has become sizable, and, as testimony to this sudden blossoming (and certainly as an outgrowth of the Black Revolution) an organization called the Society of Black Composers was born in May, 1968.

The society was formed in order to promote serious black music of all kinds and to take part in the age-old black music function of community uplift. Composers presented by the society are typical of Afro-American culture in that they carry with them their own strong Africanisms while knowing the white thing intimately. The black composer, university-trained like his white colleague, knows his Bach, Stravinsky and Webern and can notate complexities, score for orchestra, manipulate tone series, and in many cases permute on electronic devices. But, unlike most of his white colleagues, he has probably heard gospel, jazz and blues from the cradle and walked the polythematic streets of black communities all his life. The result of this collateral stewardship is that he brings certain gestural and lingual tastes to his musical understanding, has a special understanding about the value of un-notatable sound, and cherishes the notion that making music is a religious act and needs to touch its audience. How well the individual black composer synthesizes his European-derived impulses and his African impulses will depend on that individual's psychic make-up and his conscious choices for the given work.

A Society of Black Composers concert might present a mixed-media piece, a Webernesque serial piece, a spiritual-haunted cantata, a tortuously complex new-thing jazz work, and a work which seems to combine everything in collage. This young group of composers ranges in musical attitude from those who feel that their music is black simply because a black man wrote it to those who view their works as mystic instruments of a political-cultural liberation struggle. All are deeply concerned with music, but all are as well involved with making a spiritual contribution to black cultural awareness.

The number of black art composers seems to grow with the number of black college graduates. Because of the lack of opportunities heretofore and the consequent lack of interest, the black American community has not yet produced a Mozart or a Stravinsky, but it will. With the promise evident in the Society of Black Composers, and with a new adventurous attitude toward sound arising in the jazz world (which once was almost synonymous with show business music), black composers of worldwide historical proportion are on their way.

Serious music, and music is a serious matter in black culture, is music made by creators who take their work seriously. The Society of Black Composers hopes to act as a meeting ground for their efforts, whether they are called jazz, folk art or classic, and to present them in full splendor for the black community. The society imagines the day when a Sunday riser will go to his window and hear the church music and the soul music joined by strange new sounds, perhaps written by a black composer of world prominence. All of that music will seem inspiring to him, all of it full of the black style, and all will be sounding out together.

Music Mailbag: Of Black Art Music [1969]

TO THE EDITOR:

Carman Moore's article on the black composer was in many respects a surprising disappointment. As a founder of the Society of Black Composers, as a working composer, and as a music critic with an important reviewing stand (The Village Voice), Mr. Moore could be expected to offer some valid insights into the music problems facing today's composer, specifically when he is black. Instead, we were served Black Revolution propaganda with the musical realities facing serious music composition reduced to Black and white, fact and logic being lost in the process.

The article's question—is there a black Mozart or Stravinsky? —is simply answered by Moore: Not yet, but there will be. Such naive confidence would be refreshing except for a pervasive sense of racial superiority throughout the article which culminates in his affirmative answer. Ask any white or black composer is there is a white Mozart or Stravinsky in the wings and he will assuredly answer: Not yet, and there probably won't be.

Mr. Moore's argument is that contemporary classical music is particularly congenial to black composers because "the wide palette of instrumental and vocal colors, the tendency toward structured improvisation, the rhythmic complexity, even the tendency to mix the media in modern music, square well with much of the African music esthetic." Likewise, the previous obscurity of black classical composers is explained by the fact that "the predictable rhythms, harmonies and timbres of the last century were simply too European in gesture and esthetic" for the black composer.

The fact is, the complexities and subtleties of native African music are no more complex or subtle than those found in the music of the mountain-dwellers of Bulgaria or the cattle-callers of Northern Norway. The superficial attributes of modern music cited by Mr. Moore, which "square with much of the African music esthetic," happen to also square with the music esthetic of all primitive (as that term is understood by scholars) people from Iceland to Australia.

While Mr. Moore seems to find the effect of much of today's music analogous to the effect of African music, it is unknowledgeable to propose this superficial similarity of effects as giving any advantage to the black composer, any more than the lullabies of the Eskimo gave an advantage to Sibelius. (We are not talking here of the conscious utilization of folk material as in the case of Bartók or Villa-Lobos.) By equating the "subtleties and complexities" of African music with contemporary music, Mr. Moore betrays a distressing innocence of both African music and contemporary classical music.

To a musicologist who has spent hundreds of hours listening to field recordings of the musical expression of native Africans, this music soon loses the initial feeling of complexity, though not of charm. The serious listener quickly realizes why such music is properly termed "primitive." The scale used is simplistic, the rhythmic patterns, which at first intrigue soon become utterly predictable, the melodic motifs less and less imaginative. The music soon can be heard for what it is: a musical expression technically and emotionally caught and fixed in the rigid traditions of a closed society in which the ideals of imagination play no part. Amusingly enough from the Westerner's viewpoint, those European rhythms and harmonies which Mr. Moore, from his 20th-century pinnacle, finds so "predictable" are incomprehensible and incredibly mysterious to the African native.

The music of more "sophisticated" societies also proceeds from tradition but, importantly, is open to various influences which create change, as in the whole structure of the society itself. Because of such changes, we have history, and the history books illustrate time and again that those attributes given by Mr. Moore to contemporary art music are only those attributes given to art music of all periods by contemporary commentators since the beginning of the Renaissance. In addition, music students are still discovering amazing "palettes of instrumental and vocal color" in Gabrieli, "structured improvisation" in Rossini, "rhythmic complexity" in Brahms (not to mention Haydn), and countless instances of mixed media from Baroque machine operas to Scriabin. The point is that today's serious composer, like each musical giant for the past 600 years, works toward a personal expression within the framework of his time by a careful manipulation of resources available to him. This conscious use of resources has nothing to do with the rigidity of musical technique employed by African natives.

Mr. Moore cites the advantages held by the university-trained black composer over his white colleagues, when the woeful fact is there is a mere handful of university-trained graduates of any color each year who "know their Bach, Stravinsky and Webern and can notate complexities, score for orchestra, manipulate tone series" with any degree of competence. That the all but nonexistent black in this handful has a head start on his white colleagues because he grew up surrounded by "sheets of sound" is a nonsupportable assertion—nor does it take into account that music deals as much in silence as it does in sound. I hope Mr. Moore's article was just his black hand pulling my white leg.

JAMES HOLMES

New York City

TO THE EDITOR:

I sincerely hope that a Black Mozart or Stravinsky does not wait in the wings as Carmen Moore suggests in his recent article. The very idea of a Black any-White-man is indeed an Amos 'n' Andy, Black Carmen, Porgy and Bess insult.

Black music, in addition to influencing Stravinsky, has also affected all the world's contemporary music. Are Jews hoping for a Jewish Mozart or Stravinsky?

Carman Moore's article in search of a white black man only confirms the fact that what the black arts require at this point are knowledgeable critic-interpreters. His piece could well have been on the outstanding composer Coleridge-Taylor Perkinson. If he had done his homework, he would have known that what this giant needs is exposure similar to that which Mozart, as a composer, never received until he died. Maybe during his lifetime they were waiting for an Italian Bach.

Our black artists must have critics who can write about their plights and their works, or they will waste away while the world is waiting for a Black Mozart.

Shame on you, New York Times. I thought you had come out of the racist woods.

WILLIAM MOORE

New York City

Carman Moore replies:

This decade is one of the harder ones in which to write words about music. There has never been an adequate notation system, let alone an adequate descriptive vocabulary available to the composer and/or critic who wishes to fix on paper the process, effect, and power of organized sound. But in the 1960's, especially in New York, all the world's music is suddenly down front—European art-music centuries old, backed by the basic vocabulary and Italian markings; styles rooted in the old European way but in revolt against the past, looking for new vocabulary; styles rooted in Africa with their own aesthetics but traditionally un-notated and, until recently, despised in the U. S.; pure ethnic music; and incredibly varied syntheses of all these styles.

In my article of Sept. 7 on black art music, it was not enough for me to approach in some way all of these categories; I had to also discuss them within the greater cultural setting of the American racial situation. As a result, the black arts critic Mr. William Moore and the musicologist Mr. James Holmes were lost somewhere along the way.

Though the emphasis of my piece was somewhat thrown out of kilter by The Times's title "Does a Black Mozart—Or Stravinsky—Wait in the Wings?" (my own caption "Black Art Music" would have been more dull yet more to the point), could there be (Mr. Wm. Moore's contention) much wrong with a black composer who writes in the notated traditions rivalling a Mozart or Stravinsky in power and control? And, contrary to the musicologist's contention, is there any reason to doubt (since we assume there always will be people in the world, and therefore at least a law of averages) that composers of Mozart-Stravinsky stature—both black and white—will emerge at historical points?

Whether such super-creators are, as The Times puts it, "in the wings" or, more predictably, out there in somebody's chromosomes is not for me to say. I simply state that, as the black man overcomes the historical American shackles, he becomes free to take the already-rich musical values resident in his culture into whatever stylistic area he chooses and gets the very best training in that style if he wants it.

He may choose to journey into the small and presently slighted, one-man conceived, complex world of modern art music and become heir or colleague to Mozart, Stravinsky, Coltrane, Berio, and Society of Black Composers members Ornette Coleman and C. T. Perkinson. Or he may aspire to become a great blues singer. Or he may choose to become an entertainer and play his version of somebody's else's songs at the Copa. For pre-death fame and fortune, the latter route is obviously better. Interestingly enough, both the black art critic and the musicologist were offended that my article was not a towel-and-fiddle session on the plight of the modern composer who is black, but I felt there was something more vital to discuss.

At any rate, let me dutifully check off some of the mistaken and colonial ideas of Mr. Holmes's letter, lest some reader think them reliable: 1) Even though "scholars" may use the term "primitive" in regard to certain large musical cultures, I usually reject it on the ground that every vigorous culture products an aesthetic which, at one time or another, is fulfilled on the level of "masterpiece" or perfect sophistication and imagination by gifted practitioners; 2) I infer from Mr. Holmes's African music statements about such as the [one] "simplistic" scale (pentatonic?), the "predictable" rhythmic patterns, the unimaginative melodic motifs and the generally charming but rigid African native tunes that he is not aware 3) that the African continent is almost three times the size of the U.S.; 4) that there are thousands of tribal styles, scales, and practices—not one; 5) that many African styles call for polymetric, polytonal and polyrhythmic counterpointings of more than eight simultaneous parts (hardly a Strauss waltz or an Eskimo lullaby); 6) and that the Brahms-style rhythmic hemiola, to choose an example, far from being "incomprehensible to the African native," is a daily commonplace in most African music. I must also infer that Mr. Holmes's hundreds of hours listening to African field recordings were spent on repeated hearings of Hoagy Carmichael singing "Bingo, Bango, Bongo, I don't want to leave the jungle."

The article objected to by Messrs. Moore and Holmes was written by someone who quite simply loves music—Monteverdi, Otis Redding, Wolpe, Strauss, Bessie Smith, La Lupe, Ewe traditional. It was neither about individual black musical superiority nor inferiority. But it does try to document the fact that black musical culture is exploding into many directions, and it does concern itself with the author's main interest, modern art music, an area once thought solely European and elitist. The article simply says that nobody should be surprised to some day find Afro-American giants making giant statements in new art music before large audiences composed of the people.

CARMAN MOORE

New York City

Index

Topical entries refer to the musical activities of black Americans unless indicated otherwise. Musical examples are listed under class titles—for example, African songs, Slave songs, etc. The names of black musicians (but not other black Americans) are entered in boldface.